SIMPLIFYING SUCCESS

A NO-NONSENSE GUIDE TO ACHIEVING YOUR GOALS

RAE A. STONEHOUSE

LIVE FOR EXCELLENCE PRODUCTIONS

INTRODUCTION

Hey there! Welcome to the world where we redefine success. It's not just about piling up trophies, cash, or fame. It's about cutting through the noise and finding what makes you tick.

Simplifying Success: It's More Than Just Winning

Think about success like this: it's not just about what you've got in your pocket or your trophy cabinet. It's about feeling good, balanced, and finding meaning in your life. It's about not letting the extras take over - trimming down to the essentials that make you happy and give your life purpose.

Less is More: The Beauty of Simplicity

Remember, less is often more. Tossing out the extra stuff, the too-many commitments, and the weighty responsibilities opens up room for the real good stuff in life. Simplifying success means choosing what brings you joy and purpose.

Holistic Wellbeing: The Full Picture

It's not just about climbing the career ladder or filling up your bank account. Simplifying success means looking after your body, mind, and heart. Regular workouts, staying mindful, reflecting on yourself, and keeping up with people who matter - that's the real deal.

Aligning Actions with Values: Stay True to Yourself

Here's the thing: know your values and live by them. Forget what everyone else thinks you should do. Stick to your guns and be yourself - that's what simplifying success is all about.

Learning from Setbacks: Bouncing Back Stronger

Life's going to throw punches. But guess what? Every knockdown's a chance to learn and grow. Embrace the tough times, learn from them, and come back stronger. That's how you simplify success - by finding the silver lining in every cloud.

Purpose Beyond Yourself: Making a Difference

True success? It's about more than just what you gain. It's about what you give back. By shifting your focus to helping others and doing good, you'll find a sense of fulfillment that no paycheck can match. Whether it's volunteering, mentoring, or supporting causes you believe in, making a positive impact simplifies success.

Wrapping It Up

I'll be sharing strategies for simplifying success and helping you achieve goals important to you in this book. It's an invitation to strip down to what's essential, find balance, and live a life true to you. It's about finding joy in the journey, not just the destination.

We'll explore these topics in depth, sometimes revisiting them to gain new perspectives. My advice? Read through the entire book once, then come back to specific chapters when you need some extra guidance or a fresh outlook.

Note: I have provided case studies throughout this book. Unless they are stated as being true, they are based on fictional stories for illustrative and inspirational purposes.

INTRODUCTION

So, that's the scoop on simplifying success. Let's embrace this simpler, more meaningful way of living, shall we?

Rae A. Stonehouse

Author

February 2024

$\sim$

ISBN:

Ebook: 978-1-998813-63-6

Paperback: 978-1-998813-64-3

Audiobook: 978-1-998813-65-0

～

PART ONE
THE PHILOSOPHY OF SIMPLIFYING SUCCESS

GOAL SETTING: STRIKING A BALANCE BETWEEN PERSONAL AMBITION AND PROFESSIONAL GROWTH

LET'S dive into the world of goal setting. Having clear goals can light up your path, whether we're talking about your life outside the office or your career. It's important to understand that personal and professional goals are distinct but interconnected. Let's unpack how they differ and how you can juggle them effectively.

Personal Goals:

- **Aim for Fulfillment**: These goals are all about you – what you want, what brings you happiness, and what contributes to your wellbeing.
- **Life Beyond Work**: This realm includes everything from nurturing relationships to pursuing hobbies and personal development.
- **Tailor-Made for You**: Your personal goals are uniquely yours, shaped by your dreams and circumstances, and less influenced by external factors.
- **Evolving with You**: As you grow and change, so do your personal goals. They're flexible, adapting to your evolving needs and desires.

Professional Goals:

- **Career-Focused**: These goals center on your professional life and aspirations for career advancement.
- **Specific Milestones**: They're concrete, like aiming for a promotion, achieving a particular salary, or acquiring new skills.
- **Shaped by the Outside World**: Factors like industry trends and organizational needs can influence your professional goals.
- **Keep on Learning**: They involve continuously acquiring new knowledge and skills, essential for growth in your career.

Balancing these two sets of goals is key. When aligned properly, they can complement each other, enhancing different areas of your life. For example, achieving personal goals can help prevent burnout, positively affecting your professional life.

Here's how you can keep your personal and professional goals in sync:

- **Set Your Priorities**: Determine what's most important, both personally and professionally. Rank these priorities and focus.
- **Find the Overlap**: Look for areas where your personal and professional goals support each other.
- **Plan, But Stay Flexible**: Draft a plan that accommodates both goal types but be willing to adjust as situations change.
- **Get Support**: Don't hesitate to seek advice from friends, family, or mentors. Their insights can be invaluable in managing your goals.

Understanding and aligning your personal and professional goals sets the stage for a balanced, fulfilling life. By appreciating the importance of both, you're well on your way to achieving a meaningful sense of success.

The Power of Action in Achieving Goals

Setting goals is important for personal and professional growth, providing direction and motivation. Yet, having goals is the starting point. The actionable steps toward these goals transform dreams into reality.

A clear action plan keeps you focused and organized, offering a roadmap to follow. It turns vague aspirations into achievable targets. Taking concrete steps empowers you, giving you control over your destiny and instilling confidence. Each step forward is a victory, pushing you closer to your ultimate goal.

Facing obstacles is part of the journey. A solid plan lets you navigate these challenges, finding alternative paths to success. It also holds you accountable, making it harder to procrastinate or stray from your path. By tracking your progress, you can celebrate small wins, adjust your course as needed, and stay motivated.

Setting goals is important, but taking practical steps brings those goals to life. So, dive into action, and watch your goals turn into accomplishments.

Personal and Professional Success Stories

- **Emily's Wellness Journey**: Emily, a graphic designer, felt overwhelmed by her busy lifestyle. She set personal goals focused on wellness and balance, like joining a yoga class and scheduling time with friends. As she progressed, her goals evolved to include mental wellness practices. Her journey underscores the importance of setting personal goals that resonate with your needs and adjusting them as you grow.

Key Points:

- **Aim for Fulfillment:** Emily realized her happiness was closely tied to her personal wellbeing, which had been neglected.

- **Life Beyond Work:** She focused on areas outside her career, such as fitness, hobbies, and spending quality time with loved ones.
- **Tailor-Made for Emily:** Understanding her unique needs, Emily crafted goals that resonated with her, like joining a yoga class, dedicating weekends to outdoor activities, and scheduling regular meetups with friends.
- **Evolving Goals:** As she progressed, Emily's goals adapted. At first focusing on physical health, she later incorporated mental wellness practices such as meditation and journaling.

Action Items:

- Set clear, personalized goals that contribute to overall wellness.
- Give time for activities outside of work that bring joy and relaxation.
- Regularly assess and adjust goals to ensure they continue to align with personal growth.

Case Study 2: Professional Goals - Alex's Career Advancement

Background: Alex, a software engineer, aimed to advance his career. He set specific milestones, like leading a project and enhancing his coding skills. Recognizing the tech industry's fast pace, he committed to continuous learning and sought mentorship. Alex's story highlights the need for clear professional goals, ongoing education, and seeking feedback for career growth.

Key Points:

- **Career-Focused:** Alex's primary goal was to secure a senior engineering position by proving his expertise and leadership.
- **Specific Milestones:** He identified concrete steps such as completing a leadership course, leading a major project, and contributing to open-source projects to enhance his portfolio.

- **Influenced by External Factors:** Recognizing the rapid evolution of the tech industry, Alex committed to staying abreast of the latest technologies through continuous learning.
- **Ongoing Learning:** He enrolled in advanced coding workshops and sought mentorship to refine his skills.

Action Items:

- Identify career goals and outline specific, achievable steps to reach them.
- Embrace lifelong learning to remain competitive and adaptable in your field.
- Seek feedback and mentorship to enhance professional growth.

Balancing Personal and Professional Goals:

Both Emily and Alex show the importance of balancing personal and professional goals. While Emily focused on enriching her personal life to achieve fulfillment, Alex concentrated on advancing his career. Their stories highlight the necessity of setting priorities, finding an overlap between personal and professional aspirations, and staying flexible as circumstances change. By following their examples, you can create a more balanced and meaningful path toward achieving both your personal and professional goals.

∽

NAVIGATING YOUR AMBITIONS: BLENDING PERSONAL AND PROFESSIONAL GOALS

LET's get into the heart of setting goals, shall we? It's all about figuring out what you want to achieve in both your personal life and your career. Understanding the distinct roles of personal and professional goals is important, but here's the kicker: finding a way to make them work together seamlessly can set you up for success.

Personal goals are your compass for happiness and fulfillment. They're all about what you're passionate about, from nurturing relationships to personal growth. On the flip side, professional goals are your career roadmap, focusing on advancement, skill acquisition, and adapting to industry shifts.

But here's where it gets interesting – taking practical steps transforms those goals from daydreams into your reality. It's not just about knowing where you want to go, but also about laying down the steps to get there. By doing so, you make sure your journey toward personal and professional success is not just a vision, but a plan in action.

Here's a quick guide on making it all happen:

- **Identify what matters most** to you in both spheres of your life. Knowing your priorities is half the battle.

- **Look for synergy** between your personal and professional goals. Sometimes, what you learn in one area can be a game-changer in another.
- **Craft a flexible plan** that accommodates both sets of goals. Life is unpredictable, and pivoting is key.
- **Build a support system** of people who get it Whether it's friends, family, or colleagues, having people to bounce ideas off can be a huge help.

By distinguishing between your personal and professional aspirations and taking deliberate steps toward them, you pave a clear path to success. This approach ensures you grow not just in your career but as a person, too. Keep your goals aligned, stay committed to your action plan, and watch as your aspirations turn into achievements.

∼

PART ONE WRAP-UP:

UNDERSTANDING YOUR GOALS: **Personal vs. Professional**

Key Points:

- Distinction between personal and professional goals.
- Personal goals focus on fulfillment, life beyond work, individual circumstances, and adaptability.
- Professional goals are career-focused, defined by specific milestones, influenced by external factors, and require continuous learning.

Action Items:

- **Identify Personal and Professional Goals:** Clearly define what you aim to achieve in both areas of your life.
- **Focus on Goals:** Determine which goals are most important and urgent, both personally and professionally.
- **Seek Synergy:** Look for ways in which your personal and professional goals can support and enhance each other.
- **Stay Adaptable:** Be ready to adjust your goals as your circumstances and desires evolve.

- **Build a Support Network:** Engage with friends, family, colleagues, or mentors for guidance and balance.

The Importance of Practical Steps in Goal Achievement

Key Points:

- The necessity of a clear plan of action for goal achievement.
- Practical steps provide a roadmap, empowerment, and a way to overcome obstacles.
- Accountability and regular evaluation are important for progress.

Action Items:

- **Create a Detailed Plan:** Break down your goals into manageable tasks with specific timelines.
- **Celebrate Progress:** Recognize each completed step as a victory toward your larger goal.
- **Overcome Challenges:** Use your plan to navigate and adapt to any obstacles encountered.
- **Hold Yourself Accountable:** Track your progress and adjust your plan as needed to stay on course.
- **Regularly Evaluate:** Assess your progress toward your goals, celebrating successes and identifying areas for improvement.

In Our Next Part...

In the upcoming Part, we're set to start a journey that revolves around sharpening your focus and amplifying your effort to turn what you dream about into your reality. It's about zeroing in on your true wants, meticulously setting your goals, and then pursuing them with all the vigor you have. Picture refining your goals to the point they're not mere wishes floating in your mind, but destinations you're moving toward. We'll dig into the art of prioritizing with intent, making sure every step you take contributes significantly to what's genuinely important to you. And it's not just about reaching that final goal; it's about valuing the journey. We'll discuss the importance of recognizing and celebrating each victory, no matter its size, because every bit of progress deserves its time in the limelight.

But this journey is more than just about goal setting; it's about setting the right goals. We're diving deep to uncover your true desires, cutting through the external noise and societal expectations that cloud them. This Part is dedicated to aligning your goals with your deepest passions and values, ensuring they reflect the core of who you are. We'll navigate the delicate balance between ambitious dreams and realistic achievements, making sure your goals challenge you while remaining attainable. By the end of this exploration, you won't have grand dreams; you'll have a concrete plan and the determination to make those dreams an achievable reality. Get ready to transform your aspirations into real accomplishments, with a clear direction and a resolve that's unbreakable.

∾

PART TWO
SETTING YOUR GOALS

SHARPENING YOUR FOCUS: TURNING ASPIRATIONS INTO ACHIEVEMENTS

ALL RIGHT LET'S zero in on what it takes to get things across the finish line: the craft of setting goals and maintaining unwavering focus. Without well-defined goals and the ability to keep focused, it's all too simple to wander off course, become distracted, and miss the target. Let's navigate through perfecting your goal setting skills, aligning your priorities, and keeping a steady gaze on your aspirations.

Painting Your Future Picture

First up, let's imagine the future you're aiming for. This includes everything from your personal ambitions to career aspirations and relationship goals. Dedicate some time to contemplate what you aim to achieve. This overarching vision will guide your path forward.

Defining Your Goals

With your grand vision in hand, let's get down to breaking it into smaller, tangible goals. Ensure these goals are quantifiable so you can track your advancement. For example, if launching a business is your dream, outline a specific savings target complete with a deadline.

Prioritizing With Precision

It's important to recognize that not all goals carry the same weight. Some are pressing and demand immediate action, while others can take a backseat. Identify the goals that align closely with your overarching vision. At first, concentrate on your top three to five goals.

Deconstructing Your Major Goals

Next, dissect those primary goals into smaller, manageable tasks. These should be straightforward steps you can tackle within a specific timeframe. This approach demystifies larger goals and propels you forward, one step at a time.

Timelines Are Your Allies

Timelines motivate and keep you progressing. Establish deadlines that are realistic yet push you to stretch your capabilities, all while balancing them with your other commitments.

Minimizing Distractions

Staying focused is important. In a world brimming with distractions, identify what pulls you away from your goals and minimize or eliminate these distractions. Organize your environment and daily routine to bolster your focus.

Routine Reviews and Adjustments

Consistently track your progress and reevaluate your goals. Be ready to modify your deadlines, fine-tune your approach, or even overhaul goals as needed. Adaptability is your friend on this journey.

Acknowledging Every Achievement

Never underestimate the power of celebrating every success, no matter its size. These moments of recognition fuel your motivation and enthusiasm to continue pressing forward.

Remember, setting goals, establishing priorities, and maintaining focus is an ongoing endeavor. It requires genuine commitment and discipline. Adhere to these guidelines, stay focused, and you're on a solid path to turning your dreams into reality.

MAXIMIZING EFFICIENCY: STREAMLINING EFFORTS FOR GREATER IMPACT

LET'S get straight to the point: if you're set on meeting your goals not just well, but with efficiency and impact, fine-tuning your approach is key. Let's dive into how you can sharpen your efforts to ensure they pack the most punch:

Clarify Your Goals: Start by zeroing in on exactly what you're after. What's your end game? Having well-defined goals acts as your roadmap, making sure every move you make aligns with your ultimate goals.

Rank Your Priorities: With your goals in hand, it's time to sort through your to-do list. Identify which tasks are critical and demand immediate attention. This helps you channel your energy into the tasks that move the needle.

Eliminate Non-Essentials: Give your to-do list a thorough audit. If there are tasks that don't advance you toward your goals, it's time to let them go or delegate them. This creates more room for you to focus on high-impact activities.

Smart Delegation: Pass along tasks that others can take on, especially those that don't fully use your unique skills. Effective delegation not only frees up your schedule for critical tasks but also leverages the collective strengths of your team.

Refine Your Processes: Look for bottlenecks or inefficiencies in your workflow and seek ways to streamline them. Whether it's simplifying steps or automating processes, small changes can lead to significant time savings.

Leverage Technology: The digital world offers a lot of tools designed to streamline your efforts. From task automation to project management, the right technology can significantly enhance your productivity.

Focus on Quality: Aim for excellence in what you do rather than trying to do it all. Impactful work often means doing fewer things well, rather than spreading yourself too thin.

Optimize Resources: Evaluate what resources you have—time, budget, manpower—and use them wisely. Efficiency is about maximizing what you have and reducing waste wherever possible.

Embrace Continuous Learning: Always be in a mode of evaluation and improvement. Seek feedback, learn from your experiences, and be willing to adjust your strategies to become more effective.

Maintain Your Focus: Lastly, keep your eye on the prize. Establish clear boundaries, manage your time effectively, and stay committed to your goals to maximize your impact.

By sharpening your focus and streamlining your efforts, you're setting the stage for more impactful results. Remember, it's about continuous evaluation and adaptation, ensuring your approach remains aligned with your goals and yields the outcomes you strive for.

～

UNCOVERING YOUR TRUE DESIRES: A ROADMAP TO SELF-DISCOVERY

LET'S dive into one of life's big questions: what do you really want? It seems straightforward, but with the buzz of society's expectations and the pressures from every direction, zeroing in on your genuine desires can feel like navigating a maze. But here's the good news: a little intro-spection on your values, passions, and dreams can illuminate your path. Let's break down the steps to uncover your true desires:

Reflect on Your Values: What's steering your life's direction? Consider the core principles that hold significance for you—be it personal growth, family, community involvement, or career success. Pinpointing your fundamental values acts as your compass, guiding you toward your heartfelt desires.

Dive into Your Passions: What activities make your heart race with excitement? Think about the hobbies or interests that bring you joy and satisfaction. Whether it's art, writing, volunteering, or adventure, these passions are potent indicators of what you want. Pay attention to what energizes you.

Visualize Your Ideal Future: Take a moment to dream about your life in the next decade or two. What does your ideal career look like? How about your personal life and relationships? Envisioning your future isn't mere daydreaming; it's a strategic exercise to clarify your aspirations.

Acknowledge Your Strengths and Skills: Understanding your talents can shed light on your desires. Reflect on what you excel at and how these abilities could translate into achieving your dreams. Your unique skills are your tools for crafting a fulfilling life.

Tune into Your Emotions: Your feelings serve as a guide to your true desires. Observe your emotional responses to different activities or potential life directions. Are you exhilarated and content, or do you feel disengaged and weary? Listening to your emotions can reveal your genuine interests.

Foster Curiosity: Stay open to new experiences. Experimenting with new activities or learning opportunities can lead you to discover previously unknown passions. Exploration is key to uncovering hidden parts of your desires.

Understanding what you truly want is a deeply personal journey that may take time. Be patient and kind to yourself as you navigate through your values, passions, and aspirations. Trust in your intuition and let your inner voice guide you. Through thoughtful reflection, exploration, and a touch of adventure, you'll gradually unveil what brings you genuine happiness and fulfillment.

∼

CRAFTING GOALS THAT PROPEL YOU FORWARD

So, you're on the quest for success? It's all about setting goals that not only point you in the right direction but are also within your reach. Having these goals offers you a roadmap, keeps you laser-focused, and injects that much-needed dose of motivation. Plus, it's always rewarding to look back and see just how far you've journeyed—and have a little celebration for each milestone achieved.

Pinpoint Your Ambitions: Kick things off by zeroing in on what you're aiming for. What's that big dream of yours? Dive deep into your values, what gets you fired up, and where you see yourself eventually. Once you've got a handle on your broader aspirations, break them down into smaller, more manageable goals. It's about making the climb seem less like scaling Everest and more like a series of challenging hikes.

Keep It Real: There's nothing more disheartening than setting your sights too high and missing the mark. That's why it's important to set goals that are genuinely achievable. Look closely at the resources, skills, and time you have at your disposal. Be brutally honest with yourself about what's attainable. Yes, push your limits, but also be aware of them.

Detail It Out: Vague goals get you nowhere. Rather than saying you want to "be healthier" or "advance in your career," why not specify losing 10 pounds in three months or snagging a leadership role within the year? This specificity lets you track your progress accurately and keeps the motivational fires burning.

Deadlines Are Your Allies: Setting deadlines is not just for your 9-to-5. They bring a sense of urgency and momentum to your personal goals as well. Ensure these deadlines are challenging yet reasonable, giving you enough wiggle room to progress at a steady pace.

Spread the Word: Share your goals with those around you—friends, family, colleagues. This not only keeps you accountable but also opens up a support network that can offer invaluable advice and encouragement. It's always helpful to have cheerleaders in your corner.

Stay Adaptable: The only constant in life is change, and this applies to your goals as well. Life's twists and turns might mean your goals need reevaluation and tweaking. Regular check-ins with yourself to assess progress and make changes as necessary are key to staying on track.

The art of setting clear and achievable goals is foundational to any success story. They should be precise, measurable, and within the realm of possibility. Embrace deadlines to drive action, share your goals for added support, and remain flexible in your approach. Armed with this strategy, you're not just dreaming big—you're making those dreams your reality.

~

UNLOCKING SUCCESS WITH SMART GOALS

LET'S break down what it means to set goals that are not just wishful thinking but actually achievable. We're talking about SMART goals—those that are Specific, Measurable, Achievable, Relevant, and Time-Bound. Here's how to apply this strategy to something like boosting your customer base:

- **Specific**: Let's say, by the year's end, you're aiming to grow your customer base by 20% through well-thought-out marketing tactics. This gives you a clear target to hit.
- **Measurable**: To gauge the impact of your marketing efforts, you'll keep an eye on the influx of new customers and compare those numbers with last year's. This way, you can actually see how far you've come.
- **Achievable**: You plan to reach this goal by mixing up your marketing game—think online ads, social media buzz, and partnering up with businesses that complement yours. It's about using a variety of tactics to cover more ground.
- **Relevant**: Boosting your customer base isn't just a random aim; it ties directly into the heart of your business—increasing sales

and profits. It's a goal that makes sense for your business's growth.

- **Time-Bound**: You're giving yourself a year to make this happen. This deadline sets a clear timeline for putting your marketing strategies into action and evaluating their success.

By framing your goal within the SMART criteria, you're setting up a roadmap that's clear, actionable, and geared toward concrete results. It's about making your ambitions realistic and giving yourself a structured timeline to follow through.

~

STRIKING THE RIGHT BALANCE: AMBITION MEETS REALISM

LET'S explore how to walk the tightrope between reaching for the stars and keeping your feet firmly on the ground. On one hand, we have ambition, our driving force that propels you to dream big, set lofty goals, and push through challenges. Ambition is the spark that lights the fire of progress, inspiring you to strive for excellence and navigate through obstacles with determination.

On the flip side, there's realism—a necessary grounding force. It's understanding your strengths, recognizing your limits, and setting practical goals. Without realism, ambition can lead you astray, setting you up for disappointment by aiming for unattainable heights.

So, how do you find harmony between these two? Here's a guide to keeping your ambitions bold and your strategy grounded:

- **Evaluate Your Capabilities**: Take a hard look at what you're capable of. Are your goals in sync with your abilities? If there's a gap, consider ways to bridge it, whether through skill development or seeking support.

- **Embrace SMART Goals**: Anchor your goals with Specific, Measurable, Attainable, Relevant, and Time-bound criteria. This ensures your goals are ambitious yet grounded in reality.
- **Stay Adaptable**: The only constant in life is change. Be ready to modify your goals as circumstances evolve, always keeping your overarching vision in sight.
- **Seek Insightful Feedback**: Engage with mentors and trusted peers. Their perspectives can offer valuable insights and help refine your ambitions with a dose of reality.
- **Celebrate Every Achievement**: Small victories are milestones on the path to greater success. Recognizing these wins fuels your motivation and confirms your efforts.

Real-Life Inspirations: Julia and Marcus Navigate Success

Julia's Health and Fitness Odyssey: Julia, a busy marketing professional, aimed to balance her demanding career with a commitment to better health. She envisioned a more energetic, fit version of herself and set specific, measurable goals to run a half-marathon and improve her diet. By focusing on her health, creating a detailed training and meal plan, and regularly reviewing her progress, Julia integrated wellness into her busy life.

Key Points:

- **Visualize Your Future:** Julia envisioned a healthier version of herself, which included running a half-marathon and feeling energetic throughout the workday.
- **Get Specific with Your Goals:** She set a clear and measurable goal to run a half-marathon in six months and to incorporate vegetables into every meal.
- **Sort Out What's Most Important:** Julia focused on her health as her top goal, understanding that a healthier lifestyle would improve her personal and professional life.

- **Break Down the Big Goals:** She created a weekly training schedule that gradually went up in intensity and planned her meals in advance to include more vegetables.
- **Set a Timeline:** Julia marked her half-marathon date on the calendar and set smaller weekly and monthly fitness milestones.
- **Keep Distractions at Bay:** She limited social media use to reduce procrastination and prepared her meals in advance to avoid unhealthy eating.
- **Regular Check-Ins and Tweaks:** Julia regularly reviewed her progress and adjusted her training and diet plan based on her body's response.

Action Items:

- **Visualize and specify your health and fitness goals.**
- **Focus on your goals and integrate them into your daily routine.**
- **Set realistic timelines and track your progress regularly.**

Professional Case Study: Marcus's Career Advancement in Tech

Background: Marcus, a software developer, eyed a senior position as his next career milestone. He set out to expand his technical skills and take on leadership roles. By clearly defining his learning goals, aligning his efforts with his career ambitions, and adjusting his plan based on feedback and progress, Marcus carved a path toward his professional growth.

Key Points:

- **Visualize Your Future:** Marcus envisioned himself as a senior developer, contributing innovative solutions and mentoring junior developers.
- **Get Specific with Your Goals:** He committed to learning two new programming languages and leading a software development project from start to finish.

- **Sort Out What's Most Important:** Advancing his career was Marcus's primary focus, alongside maintaining a work-life balance.
- **Break Down the Big Goals:** Marcus planned his learning schedule around his work commitments and sought a leadership role in an upcoming project.
- **Set a Timeline:** He set deadlines for mastering each programming language and for project milestones.
- **Keep Distractions at Bay:** Marcus reduced distractions by giving specific times for learning and project work.
- **Regular Check-Ins and Tweaks:** He regularly assessed his progress in learning new skills and adjusted his project management approach based on team feedback.

Action Items:

- **Identify and focus on professional development goals.**
- **Allocate focused time for skill development and leadership roles.**
- **Regularly evaluate progress and adjust plans as needed.**

Action Steps for You:

- **Envision and Define Your Goals**: Whether it's personal wellness or career advancement, clarity is key.
- **Prioritize Wisely**: Focus on what aligns with your overarching vision.
- **Chart Your Progress**: Set milestones and adjust your course as needed.

These stories and strategies underscore the power of balancing ambition with realism. By following these steps and keeping both eyes open —one on the dream and the other on the practical path—you pave the way for a fulfilling journey toward success.

∾

PART TWO WRAP-UP:

SETTING YOUR GOALS, Prioritizing, and Focus:

Key Points:

- Importance of visualizing your future to set a clear direction.
- Necessity of specifying measurable and attainable goals.
- Prioritizing goals based on importance and alignment with your vision.
- Breaking down goals into smaller, actionable tasks with set timelines.
- Maintaining focus by reducing distractions and regularly checking progress.
- Celebrating achievements to stay motivated.

Action Items:

- **Visualize and Define Your Goals:** Picture your ideal future and set specific goals aligned with this vision.
- **Prioritize Your Goals:** Identify and focus on goals that are most critical to your vision.

- **Break Down Goals:** Split larger goals into smaller tasks with clear deadlines.
- **Reduce Distractions:** Identify and reduce sources of distraction to improve focus.
- **Regular Progress Checks:** Schedule regular reviews of your goals and progress, making changes as needed.
- **Celebrate Achievements:** Acknowledge and celebrate every success along the way.

Streamlining Your Efforts for Maximum Impact:

Key Points:

- Setting clear goals to guide your efforts.
- Prioritizing tasks to focus on the most impactful activities.
- Eliminating non-essential tasks and delegating when possible.
- Using technology and optimizing resources for efficiency.
- Continuous improvement through feedback and learning.

Action Items:

- **Set Clear Objectives:** Clearly define what you aim to achieve.
- **Prioritize Effectively:** Focus on tasks that offer the most significant impact toward your goals.
- **Streamline and Delegate:** Identify tasks to eliminate or delegate to focus on high-value activities.
- **Leverage Technology:** Utilize tools and software to automate and streamline processes.
- **Seek Continuous Improvement:** Regularly review and adjust strategies to enhance efficiency and impact.

Identifying What You Really Want:

Key Points:

- Reflecting on personal values and passions to clarify true desires.

- Visualizing the ideal future to understand what matters most.
- Recognizing the importance of aligning goals with strengths and emotions.
- Embracing curiosity to explore new interests and possibilities.

Action Items:

- **Reflect on Values and Passions:** Take time to identify what matters to you.
- **Visualize Your Ideal Future:** Consider where you want to be in the long term in all parts of life.
- **Align Goals with Strengths:** Use your skills and interests as a guide to setting your goals.
- **Embrace Exploration:** Stay open to new experiences and hobbies to discover deeper desires.

Balancing Ambition and Realism:

Key Points:

- The importance of balancing high aspirations with practicality.
- Assessing abilities to set achievable goals.
- The role of SMART goals in maintaining a realistic approach to ambition.
- Adjusting goals as circumstances change and seeking feedback.

Action Items:

- **Assess and Align Goals:** Honestly evaluate your abilities and align your goals.
- **Set SMART Goals:** Ensure goals are Specific, Measurable, Achievable, Relevant, and Time-Bound.
- **Stay Flexible:** Be ready to adjust goals in response to new information or changes in circumstances.
- **Seek Feedback:** Engage with mentors or peers for insights and advice to refine your goals.

CRAFTING A BLUEPRINT
FOR ACHIEVABLE DREAMS

LET's break down a solid game plan for hitting your goals with precision and purpose. It's all about homing in on what you want, cutting through the noise, and taking calculated steps forward. This approach isn't just about ticking boxes; it's a comprehensive strategy for personal and professional triumph.

- **Clarity is Key**: Start by defining exactly what you're after. Ditch the vague ambitions for specific, tangible targets. This clarity not only points you in the right direction but also makes the journey measurable and more manageable.
- **Priority Matters**: Not all goals are created equal. Figure out which ones deserve your immediate attention, and which can simmer on the back burner. This ensures you're investing your energy where it counts the most.
- **Stay Sharp and Focused**: With your priorities set, it's important to maintain a laser focus. This means reducing distractions and staying committed to your path, even when the going gets tough.

- **Resource Wisdom**: Use what you have wisely—whether it's time, money, or energy. Efficient resource allocation is the secret sauce to progressing without burning out.
- **Dig Deep**: Understanding what drives you is foundational. Reflect on your values, passions, and the essence of what makes you tick. Aligning your goals with these core parts ensures they resonate on a deeper level.
- **Balance Dreams with Reality**: Dream big but keep grounded. By balancing ambition with a healthy dose of realism, you set yourself up for goals that are not just aspirational but also attainable.
- **Embrace Flexibility**: Life's only constant is change. Be ready to tweak your plans, adapt your goals, and pivot your strategies as needed. This adaptability keeps you resilient and responsive to whatever comes your way.
- **Celebrate Every Win**: Don't wait until the finish line to celebrate. Every milestone reached and every obstacle overcome is a victory. Acknowledging these moments fuels your drive and keeps the momentum going.

By weaving together these elements—specificity, prioritization, focus, efficient resource use, self-awareness, balanced ambition, adaptability, and celebration—you create a robust framework for meeting your goals. It's a dynamic process of pushing forward, reassessing, and celebrating the journey, making sure your path to success is not just effective but also fulfilling and sustainable.

In Our Next Part...

Next up, we're zooming in on the essentials of navigating the journey from where you are now to where you want to be. Imagine breaking down your grandest dreams into tangible, actionable steps, each carefully focused on to align with your ultimate vision. But, as we all know, setting goals is the beginning. Real magic happens when you harness every resource at your disposal, keep your focus sharp, and pivot with grace when faced with new challenges. We're about to guide you through making strategic moves that not only bring your goals within reach but also make the journey there as rewarding as the destination itself.

We'll dig into tactics that streamline your path, enhancing both the effectiveness and the efficiency of your efforts. Think of it as fine-tuning your approach to success: identifying your core strengths, seizing every opportunity, and weaving continuous growth and innovation into the fabric of your journey. This Part is all about embracing a holistic view of success—one that includes setting solid goals, building meaningful collaborations, and embracing a mindset of constant learning. Gear up for a ride that's about more than just ticking off boxes on your to-do list; it's about evolving, overcoming, and thriving every step of the way. Join us as we transform your aspirations into real outcomes, charting a course that reflects your true values and ambitions.

~

PART THREE
MASTERING THE JOURNEY: FROM DREAMING TO ACHIEVING

NAVIGATING BIG AMBITIONS: THE STEP-BY-STEP STRATEGY

DIVING into big ambitions can feel overwhelming, much like standing at the base of a mountain looking up. Yet, when you break it down into manageable steps, the journey upwards becomes less intimidating. Imagine tackling a giant puzzle - you start with the corners and edges, working your way in piece by piece. This method not only keeps you driven and organized but also offers a clear view of your advancing progress. Here's your game plan for making those grand aspirations achievable:

- **Pinpoint Your Main Objective**: First off, clarify your ultimate aim. Whether it's starting a new business venture, getting into shape, or completing an extensive project, clarity is key. Ensure it ticks all the boxes for being specific, measurable, achievable, relevant, and time-bound - yes, we're talking about the SMART criteria.
- **Break It Down to Milestones**: Segment your major goal into smaller, manageable milestones. Think of these as checkpoints or mini goals along your path to the final destination. If your dream is to launch a business, milestones might include

conducting market research, drafting a business plan, securing financing, or establishing an online presence.

- **Assign Deadlines**: Set a realistic deadline for each milestone. This adds a sense of urgency and direction, ensuring you're steadily marching toward your goal. Aim for deadlines that push you but remain within the realm of feasibility.
- **Detail Out Tasks for Each Milestone**: Dissect those milestones further into detailed, actionable tasks. For example, if market research is your milestone, tasks could involve identifying your target market, gathering consumer feedback, or analyzing competitor strategies.
- **Prioritize Your Action Items**: Sort your tasks based on priority, focusing on what needs immediate attention or has the most significant impact. This helps streamline your efforts and ensures you're concentrating on what matters.
- **Tackle Tasks Sequentially**: Approach your tasks one at a time, completing one before moving on to the next. This method prevents overwhelming and guarantees each task receives your undivided focus.
- **Monitor Your Journey**: Regularly review your progress against your milestones and overall goal. This evaluation lets you identify any hitches early on and celebrate the milestones you've achieved, boosting morale.
- **Be Prepared to Pivot**: Recognize that plans may need to evolve. If new information comes to light or circumstances change, be willing to adjust your milestones or tasks. Flexibility is essential for overcoming obstacles and staying on course.

Transforming your grand goals into actionable steps is akin to plotting a route on a map. It offers a clear direction, celebrates small wins, and maintains flexibility for detours. By adopting this structured approach, you're equipping yourself with a strategy not just for dreaming big, but for making those dreams a physical reality.

∼

FINE-TUNING FOCUS: HOW TO PRIORITIZE WHAT MATTERS MOST

DIVING into the world of goal setting, it's clear that not all goals are created equal. With the clock ticking and our energy finite, zeroing in on the goals that pack the biggest punch in enhancing our lives is key. Let's unwrap some savvy tactics to put your goals into perspective and prioritize like a pro:

- **Align Goals with Your Core Values**: Kick things off by reflecting on what sings to your soul. What values steer your ship? Identifying these cornerstones helps in sculpting goals that resonate with your true self, ensuring they carry meaning and drive.
- **Weigh the Impact**: Take a moment to ponder the ripple effect of achieving each goal. Ask yourself, "Will crossing this off my list significantly enrich my life or propel me toward my ideal future?" Elevate those goals to the top of your list that promise substantial positive shifts.
- **Deadline Dynamics**: Timing isn't just a tick-tock. It's about urgency and the natural rhythm of opportunities. If a goal is ticking toward a deadline or demands immediate attention,

bump it up your priority list. Deadlines can be the nudge you need to transition from planning to doing.

- **Chunk It Down**: Facing a behemoth goal? Slice it into digestible pieces. Targeting bite-sized tasks not only makes the journey less daunting but also clarifies which steps are pivotal for momentum. This way, you tackle your goals with precision, one manageable task at a time.
- **Resource Reality Check**: Cast a critical eye on what's in your arsenal—time, skills, finances, and support network. If a goal seems out of reach with your current toolkit, pivot toward those within your grasp. It's about smart allocation to make the most of what you have.
- **Harness External Insights**: Sometimes, we're too close to the canvas to see the big picture. Don't shy away from seeking insights from those you trust. A fresh pair of eyes can offer invaluable perspective, helping to refine your focus on what deserves your energy.
- **Maintain Focus, Flexibility is Key**: With your priorities set, channel your energy with intent. Sidestep distractions that don't serve your primary goals. Yet, remember the virtue of adaptability. Life's curveballs may call for a reshuffling of your priorities, and that's okay.

Prioritizing goals is deeply personal and varies from one individual to another. It's about marrying your ambitions with practicality, carving a path that's uniquely yours. By embracing these strategies, you set the stage for making informed decisions that resonate with your aspirations, steering you toward the milestones that matter most.

LEVERAGING YOUR ASSETS: MAKING EVERY RESOURCE COUNT

IN THE HUSTLE and bustle of today's world, where the pace is relentless and the competition stiff, the secret to success often lies in how well you leverage what's already at your fingertips. Whether you're on a personal quest for success or steering a business toward greater profitability, the knack for making the most of your existing resources is invaluable. Let's explore smart moves to maximize your assets effectively:

- **Spot and Rank Your Resources**: Kick off by taking stock of what's in your arsenal. This could range from financial assets and unique skills to your network and even the tech at your disposal. Figure out which assets pack the most punch in helping you reach your goals.
- **Clarify Your Aims**: Sharp, well-defined goals are your roadmap. Knowing precisely what you're aiming for lets you pinpoint the resources that will be most important in your journey and deploy them smartly.
- **Craft a Resource Deployment Blueprint**: With your targets set, map out a plan detailing how you'll allocate your resources. Balance is key here — divvy up your time, money,

and energy in ways that align with your priorities and the impact each goal has.

- **Play to Your Strengths**: Zero in on what you or your business does best. Pouring resources into your strong suits can amplify your effectiveness and give you an edge. It's about doing more of what makes you standout, thus maximizing returns on your efforts.
- **Build and Leverage Connections**: There's power in partnership. Keep an eye out for opportunities to team up with others whose strengths complement yours. Collaborations can unlock new avenues for success and amplify the impact of your resources.
- **Streamline for Success**: Efficiency isn't just a buzzword; it's a strategy. Look for ways to make your processes smoother, cut out waste, and boost productivity. Regular check-ins on how resources are being used keep you agile, allowing for tweaks and improvements.
- **Embrace Continuous Growth**: Staying static isn't an option. Cultivate a mindset of perpetual learning and innovation. Keeping abreast of new trends and technologies can make your resources work harder and smarter.
- **Track, Measure, and Adjust**: Keep a close eye on your progress with regular reviews and metrics. This visibility lets you fine-tune your approach, ensuring you're always moving efficiently toward your goals.
- **Stay Nimble**: Flexibility is your friend in a world that's constantly changing. Be ready to recalibrate your resource plan in response to new challenges and opportunities, embracing change as a catalyst for growth.
- **Value Feedback and Reflect**: Actively seek insights from those around you — customers, partners, mentors. Their perspectives can shine a light on how to optimize resource use. And don't forget to learn from every step of your journey, celebrating wins and gleaning lessons from setbacks.

Making the most of your resources is about smart strategy and adaptability. It's not just about what you have; it's about how well you use it. By focusing on strategic allocation, efficiency, and continuous improvement, you can unlock the full potential of what you have at your disposal and chart a course for success that's both ambitious and achievable.

~

CRAFTING YOUR BLUEPRINT FOR SUCCESS

YOU'VE ALREADY TAKEN a leap by setting your sights on a goal—kudos for that! Now, it's all about charting a path forward with a solid action plan. Think of this plan as your personal guidebook, detailing the route from where you are now to where you want to be. Let's walk through crafting a plan that not only outlines your journey but also keeps you energized and on track.

- **Clarify Your Destination**: Kick things off by pinpointing exactly what you're aiming for. Lean into the SMART framework to ensure your goal isn't just a wish but a well-defined target. For example, rather than a broad goal like "get fit," zero in on something tangible, such as "drop 10 pounds in three months by hitting the gym five days a week and eating right."
- **Map Out Milestones**: Break down your ultimate goal into smaller, digestible pieces. These milestones will act as progress markers, offering a boost of motivation each time you tick one off. If launching an online business is your aim, milestones might include getting your website live, rolling out a marketing plan, or making your first sale.

44

- **Detail the Steps**: With your milestones laid out, explore the specific actions needed to hit each one. These should be straightforward and manageable tasks that collectively move you closer to your goal. For getting that website up, actions could range from selecting a hosting service to designing your site and crafting compelling content.
- **Organize and Schedule**: Now, focus on your tasks, focusing first on what moves the needle most. Assign realistic deadlines to keep you accountable and inject a sense of urgency. This step is important for maintaining momentum and ensuring you're always moving forward.
- **Gather Your Toolkit**: Take stock of what you must cross each task off your list—be it time, money, know-how, or support. If you're missing anything, now's the time to figure out how to fill those gaps, whether that means learning a new skill or calling in reinforcements.
- **Keep Tabs on Your Journey**: Make it a habit to check in on your progress regularly. This could mean weekly reviews or a monthly sit-down to assess how you're doing against your plan. It's about celebrating the wins, identifying any roadblocks, and recalibrating as needed.
- **Embrace Flexibility**: Life's full of curveballs, so be ready to tweak your plan when necessary. Adaptability is key to overcoming challenges and seizing new opportunities that align with your overarching goal.
- **Fuel Your Fire**: Staying motivated is half the battle. Recognize your small victories, lean on your support network for a boost, and keep your eyes on the prize. Visualize the success awaiting you and remind yourself why you started this journey.

Starting this planning phase is the start—execution is where the magic happens. Commit to your plan, stay disciplined, and trust in your capacity to achieve what you've set out to do. Your action plan isn't just a document; it's your compass, steering you toward your dreams. Here's to your success!

MAPPING OUT YOUR JOURNEY: NAVIGATING THROUGH SHORT-TERM AND LONG-TERM GOALS

LET's talk about laying out a roadmap for your goals. Whether you're plotting to conquer the world or just looking to improve yourself bit by bit, understanding how to navigate through your short-term and long-term aspirations is key. It's about making your ambitions real, keeping you organized, and ensuring you're consistently making strides in the right direction. Here's a step-by-step guide to get you rolling:

- **Clarify Your Ambitions**: Kick things off by spelling out what you're aiming for in the short term (think a year or less) and the long haul (we're talking years down the line). Each set of goals serves its purpose, with short-term goals acting as steppingstones to your bigger picture.
- **Sort Your Priorities**: It's game time—decide which goals get top billing. Consider how pressing each goal is, the impact it'll have, and how doable it seems right now. This helps you figure out where to channel your energy first.
- **Chop It Up**: Break those bigger goals into bite-sized pieces. These milestones are your markers along the path, each with its own mini deadline, nudging you closer to the finish line.

- **Time It Right**: Assign each milestone a timeframe, being realistic about what you can achieve and when. It's all about balancing ambition with your actual bandwidth, so you're setting yourself up for wins, not frustration.
- **Visualize the Path**: Bring your timeline to life with a visual tool—a calendar, a spreadsheet, or even a wall chart. Color-code, use charts, or whatever helps you see your progress at a glance. Seeing it all laid out can be a huge motivator.
- **Keep Yourself on Track**: Deadlines are your friends. Set them. Then, sprinkle reminders like confetti. Whether it's alarms on your phone or notes stuck to your fridge, keep those deadlines front and center.
- **Stay Nimble**: Life loves a curveball. Check in on your progress regularly and be ready to tweak your plan as needed. Adjusting your timeline isn't admitting defeat; it's smart strategizing.
- **Celebrate the Wins**: Every milestone reached deserves a high-five. Celebrating these moments fuels your drive to keep pushing forward. It's about enjoying the journey as much as reaching the destination.

Crafting a timeline isn't just about ticking boxes; it's about creating a clear, actionable path to your dreams. With a little planning, some flexibility, and a whole lot of determination, you're not just dreaming; you're doing. Stay focused, adjust when necessary, and remember to revel in every success along the way.

Emma's Path to a Healthier Lifestyle: A Personal Journey

Let's dive into Emma's story, a 30-year-old graphic designer who decided it was time to step up her health and wellness game. She had a big vision: to boost her fitness levels, switch to a healthier diet, and find peace through meditation and yoga. Knowing well that this would not be an overnight transformation, Emma smartly broke her ambitious goal into more manageable chunks.

- **Setting the Scene**: At the heart of Emma's journey was a commitment to her physical and mental health.
- **Mapping Milestones**: She charted her course with clear milestones—completing a 5K run, embracing a plant-based diet, and weaving a daily meditation routine into her life.
- **Timing Is Everything**: Emma gave herself six months to prep for the 5K, three months to fully transition to plant-based eating, and a month to make meditation a daily habit.
- **Detailing the Steps**: To reach these milestones, Emma planned meticulously. For the 5K, she sketched out a weekly running schedule, joined a local running club, and picked out a race. Transitioning to a plant-based diet started with meal planning and gradually cutting out meat. Meditation kicked off with just five minutes a day, slowly extending to twenty.
- **Focusing on the Journey**: Emma started with what would immediately affect her the most—meditation for stress relief, followed by dietary tweaks, then ramping up her running regimen.
- **One Thing at a Time**: She tackled each task singularly, beginning with easy meditations and simple dietary swaps, then gradually increasing her running distance.
- **Keeping Tabs**: A journal became Emma's companion, capturing her dietary shifts, running progress, and meditation lengths.
- **Flexibility is Key**: Life, with its occasional curveballs, meant Emma had to sometimes recalibrate her plan, especially when balancing work pressures or dealing with injuries.

Actionable Steps for a Healthful Turnaround:

- Define your wellness goals with clarity and precision, ensuring they're tailored to you.
- Lay out a detailed blueprint of milestones and tasks to guide your progress.
- Stay on top of your progress with regular check-ins and be ready to tweak your strategy in response to life's ebb and flow.

Emma's narrative isn't just inspiring—it's a blueprint for anyone looking to make significant life changes. By breaking down a grand goal into smaller, achievable tasks and staying adaptable, Emma shows us that transforming your lifestyle for the better is within reach.

Liam's Path to Leadership: A Career Growth Blueprint

Dive into Liam's journey, a 35-year-old software engineer with his sights set on a leadership position within his company. Recognizing the challenge ahead, Liam crafted a step-by-step approach to develop his technical prowess, leadership skills, and project management know-how.

Setting the Goal: At the forefront was Liam's ambition to step into the role of a lead software engineer.

Mapping the Course: His roadmap featured key milestones: completing a leadership course, mastering a new programming language, and steering a project team.

Timing the Journey: With deadlines set, Liam aimed to wrap up the leadership course in three months, get comfortable with the new programming language in six, and take the helm of a project within the year.

Detailing the Steps: For the leadership course, Liam scheduled weekly study times and applied his learning through practical leadership tasks. To conquer the new language, he committed to daily coding sessions and joined coding bootcamps. And for project leadership, he planned to shadow an experienced leader and gradually take on more project responsibilities.

Setting Priorities: Learning the new programming language took precedence, an important step for managing technical projects. Leadership skills came next, with project management experience closely following.

Focusing on the Process: Liam carved out specific times for each task, maintaining a balanced push toward his milestones.

Monitoring Progress: A digital planner became Liam's tool of choice for tracking his advancements in learning, leadership, and project oversight.

Being Adaptable: As opportunities presented themselves, Liam flexibly shifted his focus, sometimes putting project leadership ahead of technical learning to soak in valuable real-world experience.

Steps to Elevate Your Career:

- Articulate your goals for career progression.
- Develop a comprehensive plan outlining milestones and detailed tasks.
- Keep a close eye on your progress, ready to tweak your plan in response to new opportunities and challenges.

Liam's story isn't just motivational—it's a practical guide for any professional eyeing an upward trajectory in their career. By methodically breaking down ambitious goals into actionable steps and staying nimble, Liam shows how focused effort and adaptability pave the way to achieving significant career milestones.

∼

PART THREE WRAP-UP:

KEY POINTS FOR PART THREE: **Planning Your Path**

1. **Breaking Down Big Goals**: Transform overarching goals into smaller, achievable milestones and tasks.
2. **Prioritizing Goals**: Align goals with personal values and assess their potential impact to prioritize effectively.
3. **Maximizing Resources**: Identify and prioritize available resources, focusing on strengths and fostering collaborations to enhance outcomes.
4. **Creating an Action Plan**: Develop a detailed plan with clear goals, milestones, and prioritized actions, including deadlines and resource allocation.
5. **Creating a Timeline**: Design a timeline that differentiates short-term and long-term goals, incorporating milestones and specific timeframes for each.

Action Items for Part Three: Planning Your Path

Breaking Down Big Goals into Smaller Steps

- Define a SMART big goal.

- Segment the goal into measurable milestones.
- Assign deadlines to each milestone.
- Detail actionable tasks for each milestone.
- Prioritize tasks based on impact and urgency.
- Focus on completing one task at a time.
- Regularly track progress against milestones.
- Adjust the plan as necessary based on feedback and changing circumstances.

Prioritizing Your Goals

- Reflect on personal values to align goals.
- Assess the impact of each goal on personal and professional growth.
- Prioritize goals based on urgency, deadlines, and potential benefits.
- Break down large goals into smaller, actionable tasks.
- Evaluate available resources and allocate them wisely.
- Seek external feedback to refine goal priorities.
- Maintain focus on prioritized goals, adjusting as situations evolve.

Maximizing Your Resources

- Identify key personal and professional resources.
- Set clear, objective-based goals to guide resource allocation.
- Develop a plan to distribute resources effectively.
- Capitalize on strengths and seek partnerships for resource enhancement.
- Embrace technology and innovations to streamline efforts.
- Continuously evaluate and adjust resource allocation to maximize efficiency.

Creating an Action Plan

- Define a specific, measurable, achievable, relevant, and time-bound (SMART) goal.
- Break the goal down into smaller milestones with key actions for each.
- Focus on actions and set realistic deadlines.
- Give necessary resources for each action step.
- Put a tracking system into practice to track progress.
- Stay adaptable to changes and be willing to revise the plan as needed.
- Celebrate achievements to maintain motivation throughout the process.

Creating a Timeline

- Define and prioritize short-term and long-term goals.
- Break goals down into milestones with specific timeframes.
- Use visual aids to create an easily understandable timeline.
- Set deadlines and reminders to keep on track.
- Regularly review and adjust the timeline based on progress and any new developments.
- Celebrate reaching milestones to acknowledge progress and maintain motivation.

In Our Next Part...

In our next part, we're diving deeper into the world of mastering our days and making every moment count towards reaching our goals. Imagine having a toolkit at your disposal, one that not only keeps you on track but also boosts your motivation and clarity. We're going to explore how to leverage the power of time management to transform your productivity from the ground up. From setting laser-focused goals to prioritizing tasks that make a real difference, we're unlocking the secrets to managing your time like a pro. You'll learn how to plan your day with intention, maximize your peak productivity periods, and say "no" to distractions that don't serve your ultimate objectives. It's about making smart choices that align with your path to success.

But let's be real, even the best of us get sidetracked. Distractions and procrastination are like those pesky hurdles that seem to pop up just when we're gaining momentum. So, what do you do? We've got you covered. Our discussion will include real-life strategies to tackle these challenges head-on, turning them from obstacles into opportunities for growth. You'll discover how to identify the root causes of procrastination, break down daunting tasks into manageable bites, and create an environment that's conducive to focus and creativity. Plus, we're sharing stories of individuals who've been right where you are and how they navigated their way to success. Get ready to arm yourself with the tools and mindset shifts needed to push through barriers and stay committed to your journey, no matter what comes your way.

～

PART FOUR
TOOLS AND TECHNIQUES FOR GOAL MANAGEMENT

ESSENTIAL TOOLS FOR TRACKING PROGRESS

GOAL SETTING APP OR SOFTWARE: This tool lets you set and track your goals in a clear and organized manner. It helps you stay focused and motivated by breaking down your goals into smaller, manageable tasks. Some examples of goal setting apps include Trello, Asana, and Todoist.

Progress tracker: This can be a simple spreadsheet or a dedicated progress tracking tool that lets you log and track your progress. It helps you visualize your achievements and identify areas where you may need to make changes. Tools like Google Sheets or Microsoft Excel are commonly used for this purpose.

Time management tool: An effective time management tool helps you track how you spend your time and identify any inefficiencies or distractions. It can be as simple as a timer or an app that helps you prioritize tasks and schedule your day effectively. Examples include Toggl, RescueTime, or Pomodoro Technique timers.

Note-taking tool: Taking notes is essential for tracking progress, as it lets you document insights, key lessons, and observations along the way. Whether it's a digital note-taking app like Evernote or a pen and paper journal, having a tool dedicated to recording your thoughts and reflections is important.

Data analysis tool: For more complex tracking projects, such as tracking sales or website analytics, using a data analysis tool becomes important. Tools like Google Analytics, Excel, or specialized data analysis software let you gather and analyze data to measure progress and identify trends or patterns.

Habit tracker: Tracking habits is an effective way to monitor progress in building new behaviors or breaking old ones. A habit tracking app, such as Habitify or Habitica, helps you set daily goals and track your consistency. The visual representation of your progress encourages accountability and motivates you to stay on track.

Accountability partner or group: Sometimes, having someone else to hold you accountable can greatly enhance progress tracking. Whether it's a friend, mentor, or a dedicated accountability group, they can provide support, encouragement, and help you stay focused on your goals.

Journal or reflection tool: Reflecting on your progress is an essential part of tracking. Having a dedicated tool, whether it's a journal or a digital reflection app, helps you evaluate your actions, emotions, and challenges, enabling you to make better decisions moving forward.

Visualization tool: Visualizing your progress can be incredibly motivating. Using a tool like a vision board, a visual progress tracker, or creating a graph/chart to represent your achievements can help you see how far you've come and provide a sense of accomplishment.

Project management software: For more complex projects or multiple goals, using a project management tool helps you keep track of tasks, resources, deadlines, and progress. Tools like Monday.com, Basecamp, or Trello offer features for collaboration, communication, and progress tracking within a team or individual projects.

Remember, the key to effective progress tracking is consistency and finding tools that work best for you. Experiment with different tools and find what helps you stay organized, motivated, and focused on meeting your goals.

~

TIME MANAGEMENT STRATEGIES FOR GOAL ACHIEVERS- MASTERING THE ART OF PRODUCTIVITY

TIME MANAGEMENT IS an important skill for goal achievers. With so many tasks and responsibilities vying for our attention, it is essential to focus on our time effectively to ensure maximum productivity. Here are some time management strategies to help master the art of productivity:

Set clear and specific goals: Start by defining your short-term and long-term goals. Knowing what you want to achieve will help you better allocate your time and prioritize your tasks.

Prioritize tasks: Divide your tasks into categories based on priority. Focus on high-priority tasks that align with your goals and have significant impact. This will help you stay focused and avoid wasting time on less important tasks.

Create a to-do list: Make a daily or weekly to-do list to keep track of your tasks. Be realistic about what you can accomplish in a given timeframe, and cross off tasks as you complete them. This will help you stay organized and motivated.

Plan your day in advance: Take a few minutes each evening to plan your schedule for the next day. Identify your most important tasks and determine when you will work on them. Having a plan in place will help you start your day with focus and intention.

Manage your energy levels: Be aware of your peak productivity periods and schedule your most important tasks during those times. Take regular breaks to recharge and avoid burnout. This will help you maintain high energy levels and work more efficiently.

Learn to say no: Don't be afraid to say no to tasks or commitments that don't align with your goals or that you don't have the capacity to handle. Protecting your time and energy is essential for maintaining productivity.

Eliminate distractions: Identify the common distractions that hinder your productivity and try to reduce or eliminate them. This may involve turning off notifications on your phone, blocking distracting websites, or finding a quiet workspace.

Delegate tasks: Recognize when it is appropriate to delegate tasks to others. If someone else can complete a task more efficiently or if it is not aligned with your core strengths, consider passing it on to someone else. This will free up your time to focus on more important responsibilities.

Break tasks into smaller steps: Large tasks can often feel overwhelming and lead to procrastination. Break them down into smaller, more manageable steps. This will make the task seem less intimidating and help you make progress consistently.

Reflect and review: Regularly reflect on your time management strategies and evaluate their effectiveness. Identify areas for improvement and make necessary changes. Learning from your experiences will help you continually refine your time management skills.

Mastering the art of productivity requires effective time management strategies. By setting clear goals, prioritizing tasks, planning ahead, managing energy levels, and eliminating distractions, you can make sure you use your time efficiently and effectively. With consistent practice and reflection, you can become a goal achiever who maximizes productivity and accomplishes great things.

DEALING WITH PROCRASTINATION AND DISTRACTIONS

PROCRASTINATION AND DISTRACTIONS can be major obstacles when completing tasks and achieving goals. Here are strategies to help you overcome and tackle these challenges:

Identify the underlying reasons: Take a moment to understand why you usually procrastinate or get easily distracted. Are you feeling overwhelmed, bored, or lacking motivation? Recognizing the root cause can help you develop strategies to combat these feelings.

Set specific goals and deadlines: Create clear and attainable goals for yourself and set realistic deadlines. Break down big tasks into smaller, more manageable steps. This will help you stay focused and provide a sense of accomplishment as you complete each milestone.

Prioritize and plan your tasks: Determine which tasks are most important and prioritize accordingly. Develop a plan or schedule to help you stay organized and allocate time for each task. Having a clear roadmap will reduce the chances of getting sidetracked.

Reduce distractions: Identify the most common distractions in your environment and try to reduce or eliminate them. Put your phone on silent mode, turn off notifications, or use website blockers to restrict access to distracting websites. Create a designated workspace where you can focus without interruptions.

Break tasks into smaller chunks: Instead of overwhelming yourself with the entire task, break it down into smaller, more manageable sub-tasks. This makes the task seem less daunting and helps maintain motivation as you complete each part.

Use productivity techniques: Experiment with productivity techniques such as the Pomodoro Technique, where you work for a set amount of time (e.g., 25 minutes) and then take a short break (e.g., 5 minutes). Structuring your work into timed intervals can help you stay focused and prevent burnout.

Find accountability and support: Share your goals and progress with a friend, colleague, or family member who can hold you accountable. This external support can help you stay motivated and on track. Consider joining study or work groups where you can collaborate and maintain discipline together.

Reward yourself: Celebrate your accomplishments by rewarding yourself after completing tasks or reaching milestones. This positive reinforcement can help maintain motivation and make the process more enjoyable.

Cultivate self-discipline: Practice self-discipline by avoiding unnecessary temptations and staying committed to your goals. Remind yourself of the long-term benefits and the negative consequences of procrastination.

Learn from setbacks: If you find yourself procrastinating or getting distracted, don't be too hard on yourself. Instead, reflect on what went wrong and figure out how to improve. Learn from your setbacks and adjust your strategies.

Remember, dealing with procrastination and distractions is an ongoing process. It requires self-awareness, commitment, and perseverance. By implementing these strategies and making them a part of your routine, you can gradually overcome these challenges and meet your goals.

Personal Case Study: Maria's Study Plan for Bar Exam

Background: Maria, a recent law school graduate, aimed to pass the Bar Exam on her first attempt. Understanding the volume of material and her tendency toward procrastination, she sought effective tools and techniques to manage her study goals.

Key Points:

- **Essential Tools for Tracking Progress:** Maria used Trello for setting and tracking her study goals, breaking down the vast syllabus into manageable topics. She used Pomodoro Technique timers to manage her study sessions, ensuring focused study times followed by short breaks.
- **Time Management Strategies:** Maria identified her peak productivity periods to schedule her most challenging study sessions. She created a detailed study plan that prioritized topics based on their importance and her familiarity with them.
- **Dealing with Procrastination and Distractions:** Recognizing her propensity to procrastinate, Maria set specific daily and weekly targets. She reduced distractions by studying in a designated, quiet space and used website blockers to avoid social media.

Action Items:

- **Develop a comprehensive study plan using a goal setting app.**
- **Adopt the Pomodoro Technique for effective time management.**
- **Set daily and weekly study targets to combat procrastination.**

Professional Case Study: Alex's Startup Launch

Background: Alex aimed to launch a tech startup within a year. Knowing the importance of goal management and productivity, he explored various tools and techniques to streamline his efforts and stay on track.

Key Points:

- **Essential Tools for Tracking Progress:** Alex used Asana to manage his startup's development milestones, Google Sheets for financial tracking, and Evernote for capturing ideas and meeting notes. He also implemented a CRM system for tracking customer engagement and feedback.
- **Time Management Strategies:** To maximize productivity, Alex prioritized tasks critical to the launch and delegated less critical tasks to team members. He used Toggl to track how he and his team spent their time, adjusting priorities as needed.
- **Dealing with Procrastination and Distractions:** Aware of the potential for distractions in a startup environment, Alex created clear workspace guidelines to reduce interruptions. He fostered a culture of accountability within his team, encouraging open discussions about challenges and progress.

Action Items:

- Use project management software for tracking development milestones.
- Implement time-tracking tools to ensure efficient use of time.
- Create a distraction-free workspace and promote a culture of accountability.

These case studies illustrate the practical application of tools and techniques for goal management in both personal and professional settings, showing how structured planning, disciplined time management, and strategic use of technology can significantly enhance productivity and goal achievement.

PART FOUR WRAP-UP:

Chapter Summary: **Tools and Techniques for Goal Management**

Key Points:

- **Essential Tools for Tracking Progress:** Incorporating goal setting apps, progress trackers, time management tools, note-taking apps, data analysis tools, habit trackers, accountability partners, journals, visualization tools, and project management software into your strategy can significantly enhance your ability to track and achieve goals.
- **Time Management Strategies for Goal Achievers:** Setting clear, specific goals, focusing on tasks, planning your day in advance, managing energy levels, learning to say no, reducing distractions, delegating tasks, breaking tasks into smaller steps, and reflecting and reviewing are critical for mastering productivity.
- **Dealing with Procrastination and Distractions:** Understanding the root causes of procrastination, setting specific goals and deadlines, focusing on and planning tasks, reducing distractions, breaking tasks into smaller chunks, using

productivity techniques, finding accountability, rewarding yourself, cultivating self-discipline, and learning from setbacks are important strategies to overcome these obstacles.

Action Items:

- **Implement Goal setting and Tracking Tools:** Select and use goal setting apps or software like Trello, Asana, or Todoist to set, track, and manage your goals. Use time management and progress tracking tools to track your advancement toward these goals.
- **Develop Time Management Plans:** Create detailed plans that allocate specific times for tasks, incorporating prioritization of activities based on their urgency and importance. Experiment with productivity techniques like the Pomodoro Technique to enhance focus and efficiency.
- **Create Strategies to Overcome Procrastination:** Identify the reasons behind procrastination tendencies and devise actionable plans to counter them. Schedule tasks according to priority and break them into manageable steps to help with completion. Seek accountability partners to maintain motivation and track progress.
- **Reduce Distractions and Delegate Appropriately:** Identify common distractions and put measures into practice to reduce their impact on your work. Learn to delegate tasks that can be better handled by others, freeing up your time for more critical activities.
- **Regularly Review and Adjust Your Approaches:** Continuously assess the effectiveness of your strategies and tools, making necessary changes to improve productivity and goal achievement. Be open to changing tactics as you learn what works best for your individual goals and needs.

By focusing on these key points and action items, individuals can optimize their approach to goal management, enhancing their ability to achieve both personal and professional goals with greater efficiency and success.

In Our Next Part...

As we venture forward, we're setting our sights on the power of resilience, an indispensable ally in the quest for success. Acknowledge that the road to achieving our dreams is seldom a straight line; it's woven with challenges and setbacks that test our resolve. But fear not, for we're about to unlock the secrets of transforming these hurdles into launchpads for growth. We'll dig into practical strategies for early challenge detection and equip you with the tools to face them head-on. Think of this as learning to surf the waves of adversity, where each wave strengthens your balance and propels you further toward your goals.

This upcoming exploration isn't just about weathering storms; it's about thriving amidst them while keeping your wellbeing in check. The hustle toward our ambitions often sidelines the critical aspects of self-care and stress management, yet these are the foundations that sustain our journey. We'll shine a light on the significance of mindfulness, the art of setting boundaries, and the joy found in celebrating each step, no matter how small. Gear up for a Part dedicated to building that inner fortitude that keeps you moving forward, ensuring that your path to achievement is as enriching as it is rewarding. Get ready to transform challenges into milestones and learn the art of thriving, not just surviving, on your journey to success.

$\sim$

PART FIVE
NAVIGATING THROUGH CHALLENGES WITH RESILIENCE

NAVIGATING SUCCESS: EMBRACING RESILIENCE TO OVERCOME CHALLENGES

THE JOURNEY toward our goals is rarely a clear, obstacle-free path. Instead, it's dotted with challenges that test our mettle, pushing us to learn the art of resilience. This resilience enables us to push past personal setbacks, professional hurdles, and the unexpected twists life throws our way. In this exploration, we delve into why resilience isn't just beneficial but necessary for success. We'll look at how to spot potential roadblocks and arm ourselves with strategies to leap over them.

Fostering Resilience: The Heart of Perseverance

- **Cultivating a resilient mindset** is about more than just surviving; it's about thriving through adversity. Successful folks aren't those who never face challenges; they're the ones who meet them head-on and keep going. Recognizing that obstacles aren't stop signs but steppingstones is your first step toward resilience.
- **Pinpointing challenges** involves a mix of introspection and reaching out. Reflect on where you're headed and the hurdles you might face, acknowledging your vulnerabilities and areas for growth. Don't hesitate to seek insights from mentors or

peers. Their external perspectives can shine a light on blind spots, helping you prep better.

- **Learning from setbacks** is important. Each stumble holds a lesson, offering us a chance to refine our approach. Embrace these learning moments, using them to forge a clearer, more informed path forward.

Strategies to Tackle Obstacles:

- **Adopt a solution-focused attitude.** Instead of dwelling on the hurdles, redirect your energy toward finding ways around them. This shift in perspective can turn daunting obstacles into manageable challenges.
- **Break your ultimate goal into bite-sized tasks.** This method not only makes your goal seem less intimidating but also allows for regular progress checks, keeping you motivated through the satisfaction of small victories.
- **Lean on your support network.** Facing challenges alone can be tough. Don't shy away from seeking advice or support from those who've been in your shoes. Their experiences can offer invaluable insights and encouragement.

The road to success is intertwined with challenges that require us to be resilient. By understanding the critical role of resilience, using strategies to identify obstacles, and mastering techniques to navigate through them, we equip ourselves for a successful journey. Challenges then transform from barriers to catalysts for growth, propelling us forward with a renewed sense of purpose and strength. Embrace the hurdles with a resilient spirit and watch as every obstacle becomes a milestone on your path to success.

$\sim$

TACKLING CHALLENGES HEAD-ON: A GUIDE TO PERSEVERANCE AND GROWTH

FACING challenges is an integral part of growth and success. The journey begins with recognizing and understanding the hurdle in front of you. It's about getting to the root of the issue and acknowledging its presence in your path. From there, the real work begins.

Laying the Groundwork for Success:

- **Clarify Your Goals:** Keep your eyes on the prize by setting clear, achievable goals. Break the big picture into smaller tasks to avoid feeling swamped.
- **Map Out Your Route:** With your goals in sight, sketch out a plan. Organize the steps you'll take, focusing on them to keep your journey smooth and on track.
- **Gather Your Support Crew:** Remember, going it alone is tougher. Lean on mentors, friends, or family for advice and encouragement. A little perspective from your support network can make a big difference.
- **Keep Spirits High:** Staying upbeat is key. Celebrate the small wins and use them as fuel to keep pushing forward. Immerse yourself in positivity, from uplifting stories to the company of go-getters.

- **Build Your Resilience:** Bouncing back from setbacks is all about resilience. Find healthy ways to cope, be it through mindfulness practices or talking things out with a professional.
- **Embrace Learning Opportunities:** Mistakes aren't the end; they're steppingstones. Each misstep is a chance to learn and refine your approach.
- **Stay Nimble:** Be ready to tweak your plan as you go. Flexibility can be your best ally when unforeseen challenges pop up.
- **Focus on Self-care:** Keeping your tank full is essential. Ensure you're well-rested, nourished, and taking time to recharge with activities that make you happy.
- **Celebrate Your Triumphs:** Crossing the finish line deserves recognition. Bask in your success, reflecting on the journey and the growth you've experienced.

Overcoming challenges is a multifaceted process that involves clear goal setting, strategic planning, and an unwavering belief in oneself. It's about being resilient, learning from the lows, and adapting as needed. By taking care of yourself and celebrating your victories, big or small, you reinforce your capability to navigate future hurdles. Let each challenge shape you into a more resilient, knowledgeable, and inspired individual, ready to take on the world.

~

TURNING SETBACKS INTO STEPPINGSTONES

Nobody sails through life without hitting a few bumps along the way. Whether it's a project that didn't pan out, a job opportunity that slipped through our fingers, or personal relationships that didn't go as planned, setbacks are a universal experience. But here's the thing - these moments aren't just hurdles; they're invaluable chances for growth.

Embracing the Lessons from Life's Letdowns:

- **Building Resilience:** Each setback is a lesson in bouncing back. It's about picking ourselves up, dusting off, and learning that resilience isn't just about enduring but also growing stronger with each challenge.
- **Self-Reflection:** Failures are like mirrors, reflecting our strengths and areas where we can improve. They invite us to take a deep dive into our choices and behaviors, helping us to understand ourselves better and craft a sharper strategy for the future.
- **Sparking Creativity:** Sometimes, a closed door forces us to look for a window. Failures can push us to think creatively,

leading to innovations and solutions we might never have considered otherwise.

- **Teaching Perseverance:** The journey to success is rarely a sprint; it's more of a marathon. Setbacks remind us that patience and persistence are key, teaching us to keep pushing forward, even when the finish line seems far away.
- **Cultivating Humility and Empathy:** Experiencing failure keeps us grounded. It teaches us empathy for others facing similar challenges and reminds us that we're all human, navigating the ups and downs of life.

While setbacks can sting, they're not the end of the story. They're actually hidden opportunities to learn, grow, and emerge more resilient and prepared. By viewing failures as lessons rather than losses, we equip ourselves with the wisdom to navigate future challenges more effectively. So next time you face a setback, remember it's setting the stage for your next big comeback.

～

BALANCING THE MIND: A GUIDE TO MENTAL WELLNESS AND STRESS RELIEF

IN THE WHIRLWIND of daily life, it's all too easy to let stress accumulate while we put our mental and emotional health on the back burner. Yet, caring for our minds is as critical as attending to our physical health or professional achievements. Let's dive into some actionable ways to manage stress and nurture your wellbeing, ensuring you're not just surviving, but thriving.

Navigating Stress with Care:

- **Spotting Stress Early:** Understand that stress signals can vary, from sleep disruptions and quick tempers to trouble focusing. Identifying these early signs lets you tackle stress head-on, preventing it from taking the wheel.
- **Self-Care is Key:** Self-care should be your steadfast rule, not an afterthought. Whether it's through regular exercise, ensuring quality sleep, nourishing your body with healthy foods, or indulging in hobbies that light you up, self-care fortifies both your body and mind.
- **Embrace Mindfulness:** Stepping into mindfulness, whether through meditation, breathing exercises, or yoga, can transform your relationship with stress. It's about grounding

yourself in the now, navigating your thoughts and feelings with grace.

- **Boundaries for Balance:** Learning to say no is a skill worth mastering. It's important for preventing burnout and managing stress effectively. Identify what matters to you and have the courage to set boundaries that honor your wellbeing.
- **Lean on Your Tribe:** Whether it's contacting friends, family, or professionals, remember that seeking support is a sign of strength. A supportive network can be a lifeline during challenging times.
- **Find What Soothes You:** Discover stress management activities that resonate with you, from physical workouts and writing down your thoughts to music or engaging in joyful activities. Tailor your stress relief to suit your unique needs.
- **Digital Detox:** In our hyper-connected world, sometimes unplugging from technology can bring much-needed peace. Carve out time daily to step away from screens and immerse yourself in the real world around you.
- **Mindful Reflection:** Keep an ear tuned to your inner voice. Challenge negative thoughts with kindness and affirmations. Cultivating a compassionate inner dialogue can significantly affect your stress levels and overall happiness.

Managing stress and nurturing mental health is a journey, not a destination. It demands continuous attention, practice, and patience. By embracing self-care, mindfulness, setting boundaries, and seeking support, you're paving the way for a fulfilling, balanced life. Remember, it's not just about coping with life's challenges but thriving amidst them.

Personal Case Study: Overcoming Professional Setbacks

Turning Setbacks into Steppingstones: Sarah's Journey

Meet Sarah, a marketing professional whose journey took an unexpected turn. Despite pouring her heart and soul into her job, hoping for a promotion, she was overlooked. This blow hit hard, stirring doubts about her career direction and self-worth.

Navigating Through Professional Turbulence:

- **Introspection:** Sarah didn't let disappointment define her. Instead, she looked inward, reassessing what she wanted from her career. This period of reflection helped her see beyond the setback, clarifying her aspirations.
- **Constructive Feedback:** She didn't shy away from seeking opinions about her work. Conversations with her mentor and peers shed light on her strengths and areas ripe for development, offering a blueprint for her growth.
- **Redefining Success:** With fresh insights, Sarah recalibrated her career goals. She homed in on digital marketing, aiming to master the craft and set a new standard for herself.
- **Building a Support Network:** Recognizing the power of community, Sarah engaged with a network of marketing professionals. This community became a source of inspiration, advice, and encouragement, reminding her she wasn't alone.

Sarah's story didn't end with that first setback. Through determination and strategic actions, she carved a new path, eventually securing a lead marketing position that aligned more closely with her passions and skills. Her journey underscores that sometimes, setbacks aren't just obstacles but opportunities for growth and realignment with our true goals.

Professional Case Study: Navigating Business Obstacles

Strategic Overcoming in the Tech Trenches: Jason's Startup Saga

Jason, at the helm of a burgeoning tech startup, found himself in choppy waters right from the get-go. His journey was fraught with the hurdles that make or break a business: technical glitches that threatened to derail product development, a bank balance hardly encouraging, and a market that was as crowded as it was competitive.

Plotting a Course Through Startup Storms:

- **Optimism as a Strategy:** Rather than viewing these hurdles as dead ends, Jason saw them as hidden doorways to innovation. This shift in perspective was his first step in transforming challenges into steppingstones.
- **Milestone Mapping:** Launching a product seemed daunting, so Jason broke it down into smaller victories—tackling one technical hiccup at a time, launching a crowdfunding campaign to beef up the budget, and crafting marketing moves that made noise in the right circles.
- **Community and Collaboration:** Understanding the power of collective wisdom, Jason leaned into his network. He sought guidance from tech veterans, found synergy in partnerships with fellow startups, and tuned into his target audience's feedback like never.

The fruits of Jason's labor were sweet. Creative solutions ironed out the technical kinks, the crowdfunding effort didn't just meet its mark—it soared beyond expectations, and his marketing maneuvers ensured the product launch was nothing short of a sensation. Jason's startup didn't just weather the storm; it emerged as a force to be reckoned with in the tech arena.

These narratives spotlight the essence of resilience and strategic agility in overcoming both personal and professional adversities. Through a blend of positivity, pragmatic goal setting, community engagement, and actionable strategies, Sarah and Jason show how perceived setbacks can be reimagined as platforms for growth and triumph.

∼

PART FIVE WRAP-UP:

KEY POINTS:

- Resilience is essential for overcoming obstacles and succeeding.
- Identifying obstacles involves self-reflection, seeking feedback, and embracing failure as a learning opportunity.
- Overcoming obstacles requires developing a positive mindset, setting realistic goals, and seeking support from others.
- Strategies for overcoming challenges include setting clear goals, developing a plan, seeking support, and staying positive.
- Learning from failures and setbacks is important for personal growth and resilience.
- Managing stress and self-care are important for maintaining mental and emotional wellbeing.

Action Items:

- **Identifying and Overcoming Obstacles:**
- Engage in self-reflection to understand personal strengths and weaknesses.
- Seek feedback from mentors or peers to identify unseen obstacles.
- View failures as opportunities for growth and learning.
- **Techniques for Overcoming Obstacles:**
- Cultivate a positive mindset toward challenges.
- Break down goals into smaller, manageable tasks and celebrate small wins.
- Reach out for support and guidance from experienced individuals.
- **Strategies for Overcoming Challenges:**
- Acknowledge challenges and understand their causes.
- Create a detailed plan of action for each goal.
- Build a support network and ask for help when needed.
- Maintain a positive outlook and celebrate achievements.
- **Learning from Failures:**
- Reflect on past failures to identify patterns and learning opportunities.
- Develop resilience by facing adversities with a constructive attitude.
- Embrace creativity and innovation as responses to setbacks.
- **Managing Stress and Self-Care:**
- Recognize signs of stress and take proactive steps to manage it.
- Incorporate self-care practices into daily routines.
- Use mindfulness and relaxation techniques to improve emotional wellbeing.
- Set healthy boundaries in personal and professional life to reduce stress.
- Disconnect from technology regularly to recharge.

By implementing these strategies and action items, individuals can better navigate the challenges on their path to success, turning obstacles into opportunities for growth and development.

• • •

In Our Next Part...

Next up, we're tackling the journey of keeping your drive in gear and making the most of your cheer squad. This is where the rubber meets the road: turning the "maybe laters" into "let's do this," aiming for the stars while keeping your goals within reach, and curating your circle with folks who spark that fire within you. We'll unwrap the secrets to breaking down those big, scary tasks into manageable nuggets, focusing on what counts, and sweeping aside distractions that muddy the waters. It's less about the grind and more about smart strides and savoring the strides you make toward what you're passionate about.

And let's get real about what fuels us—keeping that spark bright, even on the gloomiest days. We're talking about painting the picture of your victories in your mind, throwing a party for every win, no matter its size, because motivation is personal. It's about finding your "why," harnessing your inner grit when times get tough, and having a solid crew of supporters—be it family, pals, or mentors—to lift you up. We're setting off on a voyage to forge a network that not only supports but catapults you toward your goals, and learning to view every stumble as a step up. Buckle up for a ride brimming with tips and tricks that will arm you with the zest to keep moving forward and turn your dreams into reality.

~

PART SIX
KEEPING THE DRIVE ALIVE

BREAKING FREE FROM PROCRASTINATION: MASTERING THE ART OF GETTING THINGS DONE

WE'VE all been there putting off tasks for later, only to end up in a panic mode as deadlines loom. It's a cycle many of us know too well. But there's good news: you can break free from the procrastination trap. It's all about adopting the right strategies and changing how we think about our to-do list.

Here's how to kick procrastination to the curb and keep your motivation tank full:

- **Dig Deeper:** First up, let's figure out why you're procrastinating. Is it the dread of failure, the quest for perfection, or maybe just not feeling up to the task? Pinpointing the root cause can shine a light on the path forward.
- **Set Achievable Targets:** Big projects can intimidate. The trick is to slice them into bite-sized pieces. When tasks feel more manageable, they're less likely to be pushed aside.
- **Line Them Up:** Draft a list of everything you need to get done, then highlight the non-negotiables—the tasks that need your immediate attention. Knocking out the biggies first can prevent a last-minute scramble.

- **Cut Out the Noise:** Distractions are procrastination's best friends. Find your productivity sweet spot, whether that means going offline for or finding a quiet corner to work in.
- **Embrace the Clock:** Time management techniques, like the Pomodoro Technique, can transform your work rhythm. These short bursts of focused effort followed by brief breaks can keep the momentum going strong.
- **Small Steps for Big Wins:** Feeling overwhelmed? Break your tasks down even further. Every small step forward is progress, and it's way more satisfying than standing still.
- **Rally Your Cheer Squad:** Let someone in on your goals. Sometimes, just knowing someone else is rooting for you can give you that extra push to cross the finish line.
- **Treat Yourself:** Who says hard work can't be rewarded? Plan little treats for hitting milestones—it's a fun way to keep your spirits high and your focus sharp.
- **Keep Your Spirits Up:** Motivation can ebb and flow, and that's okay. Find what inspires you, whether it's visualizing the end game or drawing energy from role models who've walked this path.
- **Kindness Counts:** Be gentle with yourself. Mistakes and missteps are part of the journey. Each time you pick yourself back up, you're building resilience and getting one step closer to your goals.

Navigating the road to success means learning how to deal with procrastination head-on. It's about making peace with the process, embracing each step, and remembering that progress, no matter how small, is still progress. With these strategies in hand, you're well on your way to turning procrastination into productivity and keeping that drive alive.

~

STOKING THE FIRE WITHIN: MASTERING MOTIVATION

MOTIVATION IS the powerhouse behind our drive to reach our dreams, acting as a beacon through the rough patches and keeping us glued to our true purpose. The secret sauce helps us leap over hurdles, dust ourselves off after a tumble, and charge ahead with an unwavering spirit. Yet, it's no secret that maintaining this drive can sometimes feel like trying to keep a candle lit in a storm. That's where a toolkit of motivation strategies comes into play, ensuring we never lose sight of our north star. Let's dive into some tactics to keep that inner fire burning bright.

Crafting the Blueprint: Kick things off by laying out your aspirations with precision. Crafting SMART goals gives you a roadmap and a compelling reason to wake up and chase those dreams every day. If the mountain seems too steep, break it down into manageable base camps to celebrate along the ascent.

The Power of Visualization: Spend a moment daily to picture your victory—feel it, see it, live it in your mind's eye. This mental rehearsal not only boosts confidence but also keeps the fire of ambition burning.

Craft Your Inspiration Board: A visual feast of your dreams and desires can act as a daily nudge toward your goals. Whether it's a collage of images, powerful quotes, or symbols of your aspirations, let this board be a constant reminder of where you're headed.

Digging Deep for Your Why: Connecting with the core reason behind your goals infuses your journey with meaning. It's this emotional anchor that will hold you steady through storms.

Lean on Your Tribe: The journey is sweeter and less daunting when shared. Surround yourself with cheerleaders, mentors, and fellow dreamers who echo your enthusiasm and offer a shoulder or a word of advice when needed.

Celebrate the Milestones: Recognizing your progress is important. It's about acknowledging the sweat and tears shed along the way and using that to fuel your next leap forward.

Embrace the Lessons in Failure: Stumbles and falls are inevitable, but they're also rich with lessons. Rather than letting them snuff out your spark, let them be the lessons that guide your next steps.

Self-Care is Non-Negotiable: Remember, a well-oiled machine goes the distance. Nourishing your body, mind, and soul isn't just good practice; it's essential for keeping the motivation engine running smoothly.

In the grand tapestry of meeting our goals, motivation is both the thread and the color that brings the whole picture to life. It's not about a relentless grind but about finding joy in the journey, learning from every twist and turn, and keeping your eyes on the glittering prize at the end. With these strategies in your arsenal, you're more than equipped to keep the flames of motivation alive, no matter the weather.

~

CULTIVATING YOUR CIRCLE: LEVERAGING COMMUNITY FOR GROWTH

STARTING a journey toward personal or professional success isn't a solo expedition. Behind the scenes of every triumph, there's usually a chorus of voices offering wisdom, encouragement, and a helping hand. Establishing a strong support network isn't just a boon for your morale; it's a pivotal piece of the puzzle in reaching your aspirations. Let's walk through the steps to cultivate a circle of support that propels you toward your goals.

Identifying Your Tribe: Kick things off by pinpointing exactly what you're seeking. Is it a shoulder to lean on, a cheerleader for your victories, a sage for advice, or perhaps a connection to broader opportunities? Knowing what you need is the first step in drawing your circle closer. Scan your current landscape for individuals who resonate with your mission—think friends who light you up, family who believe in you, colleagues who challenge you, and mentors who guide you.

The Mentor Quest: Mentors are like lighthouses guiding you through murky waters. Look for those who've walked the path you aspire to tread. Please reach out, remembering the value of their time and insights. A mentor-mentee relationship is a two-way street; approach it with openness and a willingness to learn.

Plugging into Communities: Dive into pools where like-minded souls swim. Workshops, seminars, and professional groups are goldmines for connections that share your passion. Active participation can spark collaborations and friendships that enrich your journey.

The Art of Giving Back: Remember, a support system thrives on give-and-take. Be the support you seek. Share your skills, lend an ear, and celebrate others' wins as if they were your own. This not only cements your relationships but also builds a foundation of mutual respect and appreciation.

Heartfelt Communication: The glue that holds any relationship together is communication. Be open about your hurdles and victories. Seek and offer feedback with grace. This transparency fosters trust and deepens bonds within your support network.

Tending to Your Garden: Relationships are living, breathing entities that require care. Check in regularly, express your thanks, and be there for your circle just as they are for you. A well-nurtured network is a wellspring of continuous support and joy.

Creating a vibrant support system is an investment in your success. It's about surrounding yourself with a tapestry of individuals who offer diverse perspectives, unwavering support, and invaluable insights. As you lift each other up, you'll find that the path to achieving your dreams becomes a shared adventure, rich with collective victories and learning. Together, you're unstoppable.

~

NURTURING SUCCESS: THE PILLARS OF SUPPORT IN LIFE'S JOURNEY

IN THE GRAND tapestry of life, our journey toward personal and professional milestones is heavily influenced by the people we lean on. These pillars of support—family, friends, and mentors—each play a distinct, important role in guiding us, lifting us, and propelling us forward. Let's dig into how these key relationships shape our paths to success.

Starting with the bedrock of our support system, the family stands at the forefront. From the beginning, they're the cheerleaders who know us inside and out, offering a foundation of unconditional love and a safe space to voice our deepest aspirations and fears. Beyond just emotional backing, family members often steer us through life's major crossroads, providing both practical advice drawn from their own journeys and, when needed, financial support. Their influence is profound, helping to mold our values, decision-making, and ultimately, our sense of self.

Then there are friends—the chosen family whose bonds are forged on shared interests, mutual respect, and trust. Friends sprinkle our lives with different perspectives, brought about by diverse backgrounds and experiences. They're our confidants in times of turmoil, offering solace, understanding, and sometimes, a gentle push toward clarity and resolution. The companionship of friends is a beacon against isolation, playing a critical role in our mental and emotional equilibrium.

Mentors, on the other hand, are the guiding stars in our professional skies. With their wealth of knowledge and experience, mentors illuminate the paths we aspire to tread. They're the sounding boards for our ideas, the critics of our missteps, and often, the connectors to opportunities beyond our reach. Through their guidance, we learn not just to navigate our careers but to envision and stride toward broader horizons.

These three pillars—family, friends, and mentors—form a support system fundamental to navigating both life's storms and its triumphs. They enrich our journeys, teaching us about resilience, belonging, and growth. As we forge ahead, it's the wisdom, love, and encouragement from these relationships that often become our greatest source of strength and inspiration, charting the course toward our successes.

～

CELEBRATING MILESTONES

Milestones in life are moments worth celebrating,

To acknowledge the progress we've made and the goals we've been achieving.

Whether big or small, they deserve recognition,

A reminder of our resilience and determination.

Perhaps it's graduating from school or starting a new job,

Or maybe it's buying a house or becoming a parent, oh my!

These milestones mark the different chapters in our lives,

And they're worth cherishing as each arrives.

Celebrating milestones brings us a sense of pride,

For all the hard work that we've put in, side by side.

It's a chance to reflect on the challenges we've faced,

And to feel the joy that comes with knowing we've aced.

Sharing the joy with loved ones makes it even more special,

As they've been there for us through every high and every low.

They've offered support and encouragement along the way,

And now it's time to celebrate together, hip-hip-hooray!

It's not just about the destination, but also the journey,

The lessons we've learned and the personal growth we carry.

Each milestone marks a step toward our dreams,

And with every accomplishment, our confidence gleams.

So, let's raise our glasses and toast to the milestones we've achieved,

For they are reminders of all that we have believed.

Let's celebrate the highs and learn from the lows,

And keep striving and reaching for more, wherever life goes.

Milestones in life are worth acknowledging and celebrating,

A chance to reflect and appreciate the journey we've been creating.

So, let's gather together and rejoice in the achievements we've made,

For these milestones are memories that will forever be displayed.

Source: Unknown

~

PERSONAL CASE STUDY: OVERCOMING PROCRASTINATION
JOURNEY THROUGH TIME MANAGEMENT: JOYCE'S STORY

LET'S TALK ABOUT JOYCE, a university student whose battle with procrastination is a tale many of us can relate to. Picture this: deadlines looming, stress levels skyrocketing, and yet, the lure of "just one more video" keeps her from hitting the books. It's a cycle many students find themselves in, but Joyce decided it was time for a change. She was determined to conquer her procrastination, boost her grades, and dial down the anxiety that came with cramming sessions.

First things first, Joyce dove into some introspection. Why did she put off studying until the last minute? It boiled down to a cocktail of fear— fear of not being good enough—and a motivation tank running on empty. With this realization, she started to craft a game plan. She chopped up her mountain of study material into bite-sized tasks, complete with their own mini-deadlines. A to-do list became her roadmap, with tasks lined up like dominoes, ready to be ticked off one by one. Social media, her main nemesis, was put on a leash with the help of app blockers, freeing her from the clutches of endless scrolling.

The Pomodoro Technique became her new best friend, turning her study time into focused sprints, with the promise of a break at the finish line. And speaking of friends, she found a study buddy. This wasn't just any partner; this was her accountability ally, someone to share goals with, celebrate victories with, and sometimes, share a groan over the less thrilling parts of academic life.

The transformation? Remarkable. Joyce's grades started to climb, the cloud of stress began to lift, and she wielded a newfound confidence in her ability to manage her time. Her story is a beacon for anyone caught in the procrastination trap, a reminder that with reflection, strategy, and the right tools, turning the tide is well within reach.

~

PROFESSIONAL CASE STUDY: BUILDING A SUPPORT SYSTEM

NAVIGATING NEW WATERS: MARK'S LEADERSHIP JOURNEY

LET'S dive into Mark's story, a fresh-faced manager thrust into the whirlwind of leadership. Imagine stepping into a role with the weight of expectations on your shoulders, the challenge of guiding a team, and the daunting task of making strategic decisions. That was Mark's world, a sea of responsibilities where he felt like he was swimming against the current.

Mark's primary hurdle? Building a support network strong enough to help him steer through his leadership challenges and hit his professional milestones. So, what did he do? He started by pinpointing exactly what he needed: a crash course in leadership, team dynamics, and the art of strategic thinking.

Next up, Mark went mentor hunting within his company, seeking seasoned leaders who'd walked the path he was starting on. But why stop there? He expanded his horizon by diving into professional networking groups and leadership forums, a treasure trove of individuals navigating similar waters.

The game-changer for Mark was finding a mentor, a guiding light who offered personalized advice, helping mold Mark's leadership style and strategic approach. But Mark knew leadership wasn't a solo sport. He brought his team into the fold, championing open communication, which cultivated a space where support and collaboration flourished.

The result? Mark didn't just survive his new role; he thrived. His journey from overwhelmed newbie to a confident leader, steering his team toward their goals, underscores the transformative power of a solid support system. This tale of mentorship, community, and team synergy sheds light on the essential tools for any professional facing new challenges.

These case studies highlight the importance of overcoming procrastination and building a strong support system for personal and professional growth. By addressing the root causes of procrastination and leveraging the power of community and mentorship, both Joyce and Mark overcame obstacles and met their goals.

~

PART SIX WRAP-UP:

- **Understanding Procrastination**: Recognizing the reasons behind procrastination, such as fear of failure or lack of motivation, is important for overcoming it.
- **Goal Setting**: Clear and realistic goal setting helps in breaking down larger tasks into manageable steps, enhancing focus and motivation.
- **Prioritization and Time Management**: Prioritizing tasks based on urgency and importance and using time-management techniques like the Pomodoro Technique, are effective in combating procrastination.
- **Reducing Distractions**: Identifying and reducing distractions are key to maintaining productivity.
- **Building Support Systems**: Engaging with a supportive network of family, friends, and mentors can provide the motivation and accountability needed for success.
- **Motivation Techniques**: Utilizing techniques like visualization, setting SMART goals, and celebrating milestones can help in maintaining motivation over the long term.

- **Self-Care**: Practicing self-care and managing stress through mindfulness, relaxation techniques, and healthy boundaries is important for sustained effort and wellbeing.
- **Learning from Failure**: Embracing failure as a learning opportunity fosters resilience and adaptability, essential traits for overcoming challenges.

Action Items:

- **Reflect on Procrastination Causes**: Spend time understanding the root causes of your procrastination to effectively address them.
- **Set SMART Goals**: Define your goals using the SMART criteria (Specific, Measurable, Achievable, Relevant, Time-bound) to increase clarity and achievability.
- **Create a Prioritized To-Do List**: Organize your tasks by priority and tackle them in order, starting with the most critical ones.
- **Implement Time-Management Strategies**: Apply techniques like the Pomodoro Technique to enhance focus and productivity.
- **Identify and Reduce Distractions**: Take proactive steps to reduce distractions in your work environment.
- **Seek Accountability**: Share your goals with someone who can offer support and hold you accountable.
- **Celebrate Small Wins**: Reward yourself for completing tasks or reaching milestones to reinforce positive behavior.
- **Practice Mindfulness and Self-Care**: Incorporate mindfulness practices and prioritize self-care to manage stress and maintain wellbeing.
- **Analyze and Learn from Setbacks**: Reflect on any failures or setbacks to identify learning opportunities and adjust your approach.

- **Engage with Your Support System**: Actively seek guidance and encouragement from your support network to stay motivated and on track.

By addressing procrastination head-on, setting clear goals, and using a support system, you can enhance motivation and navigate toward success with resilience and determination. Remember, every step forward, no matter how small, is a step toward meeting your goals.

In Our Next Part...

Ready for a deep dive into mastering the art of adaptability in both our personal journeys and career paths? Life has a funny way of shaking up our best-laid plans, sending unexpected challenges our way, and sometimes, offering us opportunities we hadn't even dreamed of. This Part isn't about stubbornly sticking to the old blueprint; it's about recognizing when it's time to draw up a new one. We'll walk through recognizing the signals that suggest it's time to pivot—like feeling like you're running in place or stumbling upon paths that light a fire in your heart, aligning more closely with your true calling.

But navigating these shifts is more than just realizing it's time to mix things up. It involves arming yourself with the right tools and mindset for continuous adaptation and growth. We're talking about the building blocks of resilience, that unbeatable strength that helps you recover from setbacks and come back even stronger. Together, we'll explore how to fortify ourselves for the journey ahead, from weaving a tight-knit support web to committing to never stop learning and seeing every hurdle as just another step on the staircase to success. Let's start this enlightening path together, learning how to turn the winds of change into the currents that propel us forward, toward thriving in an ever-changing world.

~

PART SEVEN
EMBRACING CHANGE: NAVIGATING LIFE'S TWISTS AND TURNS

NAVIGATING SHIFTS: WHEN IT'S TIME TO REFRAME YOUR GOALS

REFRAMING your goals is an important step on the journey to personal and professional growth. As we sail through life's varying chapters, our priorities shift, life throws curveballs, and what we want out of life can evolve. Recognizing when it's time to tweak our goals ensures we stay in tune with our changing desires and keeps us on track toward success. Let's talk about a few telltale signs it might be time for a goal makeover:

- **Hitting a Wall**: Ever feel like you're giving it your all but not getting anywhere? That's a clear signal to reconsider your goals. They should stretch you but also be within reach. If progress feels like an uphill battle, consider recalibrating your aim or breaking it down into bite-sized, more achievable milestones.
- **Life's Curveballs**: When life changes, our goals need to keep pace. New job roles, significant life milestones, or any big change might mean it's time to adjust your sights. Being flexible and realistic with your goals in response to life's ebbs and flows is key.

- **The Joy Has Left the Building**: If your goals don't spark excitement or offer fulfillment like they used to, it might be a hint that they no longer align with what's important to you. Your goals should resonate with your passions and values; if they don't, it's time for some goal setting soul-searching.
- **Stress Overload**: Goals should motivate, not deteriorate, your mental and physical health. If chasing your goals leaves you more frazzled than fulfilled, consider this a red flag. Achieving personal growth should feel enriching, not draining.
- **New Doors Open**: Life can surprise us with unexpected opportunities that better match our interests or offer a clearer path to our dreams. When such opportunities knock, it might mean your goals need reshaping to embrace these new avenues.

Remember, revising your goals isn't admitting defeat—it's about being smart, flexible, and growth-oriented. Continually reassessing and fine-tuning your goals keeps your focus sharp and your motivation high. It's okay to change course; what matters is that you're moving in a direction that's right for you. Stay open to change, keep a positive outlook, and watch as you navigate your way to success.

∽

NAVIGATING LIFE'S TRANSITIONS: A GUIDE TO EMBRACING CHANGE

LIFE'S only constant is change, touching both our personal and professional spheres in forms like new career paths, relocating, shifts in relationships, or personal growth. While the prospect of change can seem intimidating, it presents a fertile ground for development, learning, and new prospects. Here's how to lean into change across all facets of life.

Acceptance is Key: Begin by acknowledging change is imminent and largely beyond our control. Fighting against the tide of change only breeds frustration. Instead, accepting change as a part of life lets us adapt and glean lessons from our experiences.

Stay Positive: Maintaining a positive outlook is important during times of change. Focus on the potential benefits and growth opportunities change brings, rather than the negatives. View each change as a chance to learn something new about yourself and the world around you.

Reflect on Your Experiences: Look back at how you've managed change before. What worked? What didn't? Learning from these experiences can bolster your confidence and provide a roadmap for navigating current changes.

Goal Setting and Planning: Facing change head-on with clear goals and a plan of action can demystify the unknown. Define what success looks like in this new chapter and chart a course to get there, breaking down the journey into manageable steps.

Build Your Support Network: Change is easier with a supportive crew by your side. Lean on friends, family, colleagues, or mentors for insight, encouragement, and a fresh perspective. A strong support system can turn the daunting into the doable.

Embrace Uncertainty: The unknown can be a playground for growth and opportunity. While uncertainty can be uncomfortable, it also opens doors to new paths and experiences. Let curiosity lead the way as you explore these uncharted territories.

Be Adaptable: Change is less intimidating with adaptability in your toolkit. Stay open to new ideas, be ready to pick up new skills, and welcome continuous learning with open arms. Flexibility is your ally in the face of change.

Prioritize Self-Care: Change can tax, making self-care more important than ever. Make sure you're sleeping well, eating right, staying active, and carving out time for things that make you happy. A strong foundation of physical and mental health can help you weather any storm.

Celebrate the Little Things: Every step forward, no matter how small, is progress. Celebrate these milestones to maintain motivation and remind yourself of how far you've come.

It's About the Journey: Ultimately, change is not a destination but a path we walk, complete with its highs and lows. Embracing change means embracing this journey, with all its lessons and challenges, as an opportunity to evolve.

Change, with its twists and turns, is an integral part of life's journey. By adopting these strategies, we can transform change from a source of anxiety into a catalyst for growth, unlocking new opportunities and experiences along the way.

∿

LIFELONG LEARNING: THE JOURNEY OF PERSONAL AND PROFESSIONAL EVOLUTION

LIFELONG LEARNING IS all about keeping the flame of curiosity alive and constantly seeking new knowledge, skills, and experiences. It's recognizing that the journey of learning doesn't wrap up the moment you step out of a classroom; it stretches far into the horizon, encompassing every day of our lives. Whether it's diving into the pages of a book, attending dynamic workshops, exploring online courses, or finding mentors who inspire us, the avenues for expanding our horizons are endless.

The beauty of lifelong learning lies in its embrace of challenges and setbacks not as dead ends, but as rich opportunities for growth. It encourages us to venture into the unknown, to experiment and perhaps falter, but to always emerge wiser and more resilient. This adventurous spirit propels us beyond the familiar limits of our comfort zones, urging us to reach for heights we once thought unattainable.

Goal setting plays a pivotal role in this ongoing journey. By defining what we aspire to achieve, we can tailor our learning endeavors to pave the most impactful path forward, whether those goals are nestled in the personal realm or the professional sphere. Keeping these goals fluid and responsive to the ever-changing landscape of our lives makes sure our learning journey remains relevant and invigorating.

Self-reflection and awareness are the compasses that guide us through the vast terrain of lifelong learning. Understanding our strengths and areas for growth helps us pinpoint exactly where we should direct our learning efforts. It also deepens our connection to our own values, interests, and passions, making each step on the learning path more engaging and meaningful.

Committing to lifelong learning is not a casual stroll but a marathon that demands discipline, dedication, and a hearty dose of perseverance. The rewards, however, are boundless—fueling personal and professional success, bolstering self-confidence, and enriching our lives with purpose and joy.

Lifelong learning is the heartbeat of personal and professional development. It's about nurturing a spirit of inquiry, daring to push past boundaries, and intentionally crafting a life that's as rich and varied as the lessons it comprises. By welcoming challenges, articulating our goals, diving into the depths of learning, and taking time to reflect on our journey, we unlock the door to endless possibilities and the best version of ourselves.

~

CULTIVATING A MINDSET FOR GROWTH: LEARNING THROUGH LIFE'S UPS AND DOWNS

HAVING a growth mindset is all about seeing the world as your classroom where every challenge and misstep is a lesson in disguise. It's understanding that your talents and smarts aren't just handed to you but are muscles you can build and strengthen with grit and grind. This perspective empowers you to roll with life's punches, turning setbacks into comebacks and challenges into chances to shine.

At the heart of a growth mindset is the courage to tackle challenges head-on. It's about swapping the "I can't" with "I can learn." When you're faced with something tough, instead of backing down, you lean in, excited about the opportunity to stretch your skills and push the boundaries of what you thought was possible. This doesn't just add new tools to your toolbox; it builds confidence and bravery to venture even further next time.

Failing isn't fun, but with a growth mindset, it doesn't spell the end—it's the beginning of understanding and evolving. It's about dissecting what went wrong, not to assign blame but to chart a smarter course forward. Every stumble is a step on the staircase to success, teaching resilience, grit, and the art of the pivot.

So, how do you start cultivating this powerhouse mindset? Begin by questioning and flipping those self-doubt scripts in your head. Embrace the awkwardness of stepping out of your comfort zone—yes, it might feel like showing up to a party where you know no one, but that's where the magic happens. Break down your big dreams into bite-sized goals that feel more like adventures than chores.

Remember, failure is your professor, not your nemesis. Analyze your flops with the curiosity of a scientist, extracting lessons and plotting your next move with enhanced intel. Create a circle of fellow growth-seekers—people who cheer on your efforts, offer constructive critiques, and share your appetite for personal evolution.

Lastly, be as kind to yourself as you would to a friend who's trying something new. Cut yourself some slack when things don't go as planned. Celebrate the small wins and know that growth often happens in the quiet moments when it feels like you're standing still.

In wrapping up, embracing a growth mindset is about seeing life as endless lessons and opportunities for enhancement. It's a commitment to perpetual learning, resilience, and self-improvement that not only propels you toward your goals but makes the journey there enriching. So, get ready to dive in, learn, adapt, and grow—it's a thrilling ride that never stops.

~

MOVING FORWARD: THE ART OF CONSISTENT AND STRATEGIC ACTION

Navigating the path to our goals with confidence is all about the blend of consistency and strategy. It starts with laying out our aspirations— getting crystal clear on what we're gunning for and the reasons it's close to our hearts. This clarity isn't just motivational; it's our north star, keeping us on track even when the going gets tough. So, jot down those goals, keep them in your sights, and let them be the push you need when obstacles pop up.

Developing a game plan is next on the list. Break those lofty goals into bite-sized pieces that feel doable. Map out the steps, think about the resources you'll need, and keep an eye out for potential roadblocks. Having a solid plan in place isn't just about having a checklist; it's about giving your journey structure and direction, so you can stride forward with purpose.

What's critical here is figuring out which tasks pack the biggest punch toward hitting your goals and dedicating your time and energy there. It's recognizing that not all actions weigh the same in the scale of progress. By homing in on what moves the needle, you ensure your efforts are laser-focused on what matters most.

Sticking to the plan is where consistency comes into play. Dive into your tasks with regularity, building momentum and habits that edge you closer to your goals. Whether it's chipping away at it daily or carving out specific times each week, consistency is the fuel that keeps the engine running.

But here's the kicker—consistency doesn't mean inflexibility. Life's full of curveballs and staying open to tweaking your plan when new info or opportunities arise is key. Regular check-ins on your progress, assessing what's working and what's not, and being ready to pivot will keep you nimble and on course.

And don't forget to give yourself a pat on the back for the milestones you hit along the way. Celebrating your progress, no matter the size, isn't just about giving yourself a well-deserved moment of pride. It's about fueling your drive to keep going, bolstering your confidence in your ability to make your dreams a reality.

In wrapping up, the journey to meeting our goals is paved with consistent, strategic action. Set those goals, chart your course, prioritize wisely, and stick to the rhythm. Keep flexible, celebrate your victories, and watch as you move forward with unwavering confidence, turning aspirations into achievements.

~

NAVIGATING LIFE'S STORMS: THE POWER OF RESILIENCE

LIFE'S A ROLLERCOASTER, filled with its fair share of highs and lows. We all face tough times, but it's how we bounce back from these moments that counts. That's where resilience comes into play—a kind of inner strength that helps us roll with the punches and keep pushing forward. Let's dive into what makes resilience so important and share tips on how you can build it up in your own life.

Resilience is all about adapting well to stress, adversity, or trauma—it's not something you're born with but something you develop. Those who are resilient have a toolkit of skills like emotional intelligence, a knack for staying positive, flexibility in the face of change, and solid problem-solving abilities.

Why is resilience so important, you ask? Well, it's the backbone of good mental health, helping us deal with stress, leap over hurdles, and keep a sunny outlook on life. It not only encourages personal growth but also strengthens our relationships and boosts our overall happiness and satisfaction.

So, how can you cultivate this superpower? Here are pointers:

- **Surround Yourself with Support:** Keep good company with folks who lift you up—friends, family, mentors. A solid support network is invaluable when the going gets tough.
- **Embrace Your Emotions:** Getting in tune with your feelings is key. Recognize what you're feeling, express those emotions healthily, and don't shy away from asking for help when you need it.
- **Stay Positive:** Try to see the glass as half full. Be thankful for the good stuff, celebrate your wins, no matter how small, and look at challenges as chances to grow.
- **Develop Healthy Habits:** Find stressbusters that work for you, whether that's hitting the gym, meditating, or pouring your thoughts into a journal. These can help clear your mind and boost your mood.
- **Take Care of You:** Don't forget to put yourself first sometimes. Good sleep, nutritious food, fun activities—these are all parts of a resilience-building lifestyle.
- **Learn from the Lows:** Instead of seeing failure as a setback, view it as a lesson. It's an opportunity to pick up new insights and refine your approach next time around.
- **Set Achievable Goals:** Break down your dreams into steps you can actually take. This helps keep you motivated, especially when you need to navigate around obstacles.

Building resilience is a journey, not a destination. It takes time, effort, and soul-searching. But by embracing your emotions, leaning on your support network, staying positive, and seeing every challenge as a chance to grow, you'll find yourself more equipped to handle whatever life throws your way. Remember, it's not about avoiding the storm—it's about learning to dance in the rain.

Personal Case Study: Adjusting Goals for Personal Growth

Pivoting for Progress: Barbara's Journey in Digital Marketing

Let's talk about Barbara, a go-getter in the marketing world who dove into the digital side of things. She set her sights on making this big career shift within a year and got herself enrolled in online courses to make it happen. But halfway through, Barbara hit a snag—juggling her job, studies, and personal life started to feel like a circus act she hadn't signed up for.

Realizing she was stuck in a rut, Barbara stepped back to see where things were going awry. It dawned on her that she might've been a tad optimistic about how much she could squeeze into her already packed schedule. So, she gave herself some breathing room, stretching her original one-year plan to eighteen months. This wasn't a step back; it was a strategic sidestep to keep her on track without burning out.

Barbara then took a hard look at her daily grind, focusing on tasks that would directly fuel her move into digital marketing. She started saying "not now" to things that didn't align with this goal, freeing up more time for her studies. Plus, she didn't go at it alone—she found a study group that became her brain trust, offering support, advice, and that gentle nudge when procrastination tempted her.

With this new game plan, Barbara found her stride. The extended timeline took the pressure off, and having a circle of peers on the same journey made all the difference. By reshuffling her priorities and leaning on others for support, she not only kept her career transition on track but did it with less stress and more success. Barbara's story isn't just about setting goals; it's a reminder that it's okay to adjust our sails when the wind changes direction.

Professional Case Study: Embracing Change in Career Path

Navigating Career Shifts: Mike's Leap into Renewable Energy

Let's dive into Mike's story, a seasoned engineer in the construction world who found himself at a crossroads due to a market downturn. With job security on shaky ground and growth opportunities becoming scarce, he knew it was time for a change.

Mike didn't just see this as a setback; he saw it as a chance to grow and diversify his skill set. He turned his gaze toward the renewable energy sector, a field not only booming but also close to his heart because of his passion for sustainability. It was time to set new goals.

He didn't jump in blindly, though. Mike meticulously mapped out his journey into this new territory, pinpointing the additional training he'd need and the people he should connect with. Recognizing the value of guidance in unfamiliar waters, he sought a mentor already thriving in the renewable energy sphere.

Fast forward, and Mike's strategic pivot paid off. He landed a position with a leading firm in the renewable energy sector, marking a significant stride in his career. By embracing change with a positive mindset, scouting new opportunities, and leaning on the expertise of a mentor, Mike didn't just navigate through uncertain times—he thrived, proving that with the right approach, career transitions can lead to exciting new chapters.

These case studies illustrate the importance of flexibility and adaptability in personal and professional development. Whether adjusting goals to manage stress and ensure progress, like Sarah, or embracing industry changes for career growth, like Mike, the ability to adapt and adjust is important for overcoming obstacles and succeeding.

~

PART SEVEN WRAP-UP:

KEY POINTS:

- **Adjusting Goals:** Recognizing when to adjust goals is important for personal growth, especially when faced with lack of progress, changed circumstances, lack of fulfillment, overwhelming stress, or new opportunities.
- **Embracing Change:** Accepting and adapting to change in personal and professional life is essential. Strategies include maintaining a positive mindset, learning from past changes, setting new goals, seeking support, and being adaptable.
- **Continuous Learning and Growth:** Committing to lifelong learning enhances personal and professional development. This involves seeking new knowledge, embracing challenges, setting goals, and self-reflection.
- **Developing a Growth Mindset:** Embracing challenges, learning from failure, and believing in the potential for personal development are key to a growth mindset. Strategies include challenging fixed beliefs, stepping outside comfort zones, and practicing self-compassion.

- **Taking Action:** Setting clear goals, prioritizing tasks, and taking consistent, strategic actions are necessary for progress. Flexibility and celebrating small wins are important for maintaining motivation.
- **Cultivating Resilience:** Building resilience involves developing emotional intelligence, a support network, optimism, coping skills, practicing self-care, learning from failure, and setting realistic goals.

Action Items:

- **Reassess Goals:** Regularly evaluate your goals and adjust them based on your current situation, achievements, and shifts in your interests or external circumstances.
- **Adopt a Positive Mindset:** Cultivate a positive outlook toward change and challenges to help with adaptation and growth.
- **Engage in Continuous Learning:** Actively seek opportunities for learning and development to enhance your skills and knowledge base.
- **Practice Growth Mindset:** Challenge yourself to step outside your comfort zone and view setbacks as learning opportunities.
- **Plan and Prioritize:** Develop a strategic plan for meeting your goals, prioritize your actions, and remain consistent in your efforts.
- **Build Your Support Network:** Identify and engage with individuals who can provide support, advice, and encouragement as you pursue your goals.
- **Enhance Resilience:** Work on building resilience by practicing emotional intelligence, self-care, and developing healthy coping mechanisms for dealing with stress and setbacks.

In Our Next Part...

Next up, we will peel back the layers on the incredible impact habits can have on our lives. Whether your goal is to shake up your daily routine, amp up your work productivity, or simply lead a life that's richer and more satisfying, we're here to walk you through it. We'll show you how to spot those not-so-great habits and swap them out for behaviors that serve you better, diving into the science behind habit formation to give you an edge, and highlighting how the right environment and your circle of friends can make or break your success.

Prepare to dive deep into how tiny tweaks in your day-to-day actions can create massive shifts in your life. We're talking about getting into the nitty-gritty of why we do what we do, the brainy stuff that makes habits stick, and the tools that'll keep you on track and resilient. We're here to arm you with all you need to turn your life around, one habit at a time. By joining forces, we'll uncover how to maintain those positive vibes and keep leveling up, ensuring your new habits not only bring you immediate wins but also set you up for a lifetime of accomplishments. Ready to make lasting changes? Let's get to it!

$$\sim$$

PART EIGHT
HARNESSING THE
POWER OF HABIT FOR
LIFE TRANSFORMATION

THE BLUEPRINT OF HABITS: SHAPING YOUR DESTINY

EVER THOUGHT about how your daily routines, those things you do without even thinking, actually shape your life? It's like we're on autopilot, guided by these habits that influence every choice we make, for better or worse. This Part is all about diving deep into the essence of habits and how they mold our existence.

A habit, put simply, is a behavior we repeat so often it becomes automatic, like your morning coffee ritual or, on the flip side, hitting snooze on your alarm clock five times. Habits are powerful because they cut down on the mental effort we need to get through our day. They're the brain's way of saving energy, allowing us to focus on more important decisions.

However, habits come in all shapes and sizes - some propel us forward, like regular exercise or eating well, while others hold us back, think smoking or spending hours on social media. Getting to grips with how habits work is the first step in reshaping them to work in our favor.

Habits follow a three-part cycle: the cue, the routine, and the reward. The cue triggers the behavior, the routine is the behavior itself, and the reward is what your brain gets out of it, which reinforces the habit loop. By dissecting this loop, we can start to untangle and remake our own habits. If stress triggers your junk food binges, finding new stress-busters can redirect that habit into something healthier.

Changing habits isn't a walk in the park. It demands willpower, dedication, and a good dose of persistence. But the payoff - transforming your life for the better - is immense. Whether it's enhancing your health, upping your productivity game, or just feeling better about yourself, the benefits of positive habits are endless.

Throughout this book, we're going to unpack the science behind habit formation and arm you with practical steps to shake off the bad habits and foster good ones. We'll explore "keystone habits" that create a domino effect of positive changes and tackle the hurdles that often trip people up in their quest for change.

At the heart of it, our habits are the architects of our destiny. They sculpt our behaviors, steer our choices, and, ultimately, plot the course of our lives. By mastering the art of habit transformation, we take the reins of our fate, steering ourselves toward the future we envision. Let's kickstart this journey together, unveiling the power of habits and their capacity to transform.

DECODING HABIT FORMATION: STEPHANIE'S JOURNEY TO MASTERY

STEPHANIE WAS on a mission to crack the code of habit formation, puzzled by why some habits stick like glue while others just slip away. Her quest led her to "The Power of Habit" by Charles Duhigg, a book that shed light on the habit loop—a fascinating three-step process involving a cue, a routine, and a reward. It was an eye-opener that promised to explain the mechanics behind the habits shaping her daily life.

Diving into her daily routines, Stephanie picked her morning ritual as the test subject. Every morning, like clockwork, she'd grab her phone immediately after her alarm went off, brew a cup of coffee, and settle down with the latest news. It was an automatic sequence that had seamlessly woven itself into the fabric of her mornings.

Stephanie meticulously dissected this routine through Duhigg's lens. The alarm's buzz was the cue, prompting her to check her phone, followed by the coffee-making routine. The reward? A sense of being in the loop and the comforting ritual of her morning coffee. This loop, she realized, was reinforced by the immediate satisfaction she derived from it.

Curious about the impact of varying cues and rewards, Stephanie experimented by switching her alarm sound to something more calming and replacing her screen time with a book or podcast. This tweak in the cue and routine gradually shifted her mornings from a blur of notifications to a more tranquil start, proving that even small changes could significantly alter her habit loop.

This experiment was transformative. Stephanie found herself more centered and ready to tackle the day, appreciating the clarity that came with reducing her digital intake first thing in the morning. It wasn't just about breaking an old habit; it was about consciously crafting a new, more fulfilling one.

The deeper Stephanie delved into the dynamics of the habit loop, the more empowered she felt. Understanding that habits were not just mindless routines, but a complex interplay of cues, routines, and rewards opened up a new world of possibilities. She was now equipped not only to dismantle habits that no longer served her but also to build new ones that aligned with the life she aspired to lead.

Stephanie's journey into the heart of habit formation was more than just personal growth; it was a blueprint for intentional living. With her newfound knowledge and experience, she was ready to take control of her habits, understanding that each loop was an opportunity to mold her life into something even more meaningful.

~

THE BRAIN'S BLUEPRINT FOR HABITS: UNLOCKING THE POWER OF NEURAL PATHWAYS

HAVE you ever wondered why some habits stick with us, almost like they're hardwired into our brains, while we struggle to maintain others? It turns out, the secret lies within the intricate neural pathways of our brain. Let's peel back the layers of how our brain shapes and sustains habits, taking a closer look at the machinery behind our daily routines.

The Inner Workings: The Habit Loop and Basal Ganglia

At the heart of habit formation is a fascinating structure in our brain called the basal ganglia. This cluster of neurons plays a pivotal role in developing and carrying out our habits. Think of it as the brain's autopilot mode, taking over when we engage in routine behaviors.

When we encounter a cue, it's the basal ganglia that kickstart the habit loop. They process the signal and, drawing from past experiences, prompt us to act in a certain way—our routine. And when that routine gives us a reward, dopamine, our brain's feel-good chemical, reinforces the connection, making the habit even more automatic.

Neural Plasticity: The Brain's Adaptability

What's truly remarkable is our brain's ability to change—its neural plasticity. This adaptability allows our brain to form new habits by strengthening the neural connections associated with repetitive actions. Each time we repeat a behavior, it's like the brain is reinforcing a path through a forest, making it easier to travel the next time.

Enter the Prefrontal Cortex

But it's not just the basal ganglia running the show. The prefrontal cortex, our brain's decision-making center, plays a crucial role, especially early in habit formation. It's the one weighing the pros and cons, helping us decide if we should proceed with the action. As a habit becomes more ingrained, the prefrontal cortex steps back, letting the routine run more automatically.

The Path to Changing Habits

Armed with this knowledge, we're not just bystanders to our brain's habit-making process. We can actively influence it. To break a habit, we need to consciously disrupt the habit loop, introduce new cues, or swap out the routine for something healthier. It requires effort and intention, as we're essentially rerouting the brain's automatic response.

Creating new habits, on the other hand, is about forging and reinforcing new neural pathways. Consistency is key here repeating the new behavior and rewarding ourselves for it strengthens these new connections, gradually making the behavior more automatic.

Wrapping Up

Our brains are incredibly powerful in shaping our habits, but they also give us the tools to change them. Understanding how habits are formed and sustained on a neural level offers us a roadmap for altering our behavior. By leveraging our brain's plasticity and the interplay between different regions, we can break old habits and forge new ones, steering our lives in the direction we choose. So, let's harness the power of our brain's habit-forming capabilities to create the life we want.

~

TACKLING TOUGH HABITS: A GUIDE TO TURNING OVER A NEW LEAF

LET'S FACE IT, we've all got those pesky habits that we're not proud of. Maybe it's hitting snooze one too many times, doomscrolling through social media, or reaching for that extra slice of cake. While shaking off these bad habits might seem like a Herculean task, it's definitely within reach with a bit of strategy and a shift in mindset. This chapter is all about arming you with the tools you need to kick those habits to the curb and embrace healthier ones.

Pinpoint Your Triggers: The first step to breaking a bad habit is figuring out what sparks it. Take a moment to think about the scenarios or feelings that drive you toward your habit. Is stress your trigger for binge-watching TV shows? Once you've got your triggers down, you're better equipped to tackle them head-on.

Goal Setting: Clarity is your friend when it comes to ditching unwanted habits. Spell out what you're aiming for and why it matters to you. Keep these goals where you can see them; they'll serve as your north star, guiding you back on track when you're tempted to stray.

Swap It Out: Instead of trying to quit cold turkey, how about swapping your bad habit for a better one? For example, if you're guilty of endless scrolling on your phone, how about diving into a good book or exploring a new hobby? This way, you're not just cutting out negative behavior but filling that space with something enriching.

Track Your Triumphs: Monitoring your progress can be incredibly motivating. Whether it's marking a calendar, keeping a journal, or using a habit-tracking app, find a way to visually chart your journey. And don't forget to celebrate those milestones, no matter how small—they're a big deal!

Gather Your Cheer Squad: Going solo can be tough, so why not enlist some support? Share your goals with friends or family who'll cheer you on and keep you accountable. If you're feeling adventurous, joining a group or finding a buddy with similar goals can amplify your efforts.

Embrace Mindfulness: Being mindful can transform your approach to habit change. By being present and aware of your thoughts and actions, you can catch yourself before falling into automatic behaviors. This conscious pause can be the difference between succumbing to a habit and making a healthier choice.

Stay Positive: Remember, Rome wasn't built in a day, and neither is breaking a bad habit. Keep a positive outlook, even when slip-ups happen. Each mistake is a lesson learned, a steppingstone toward your goal. Stay patient and persistent; progress is progress, no matter the pace.

In Summary:

Kicking bad habits is no small feat, but it's far from impossible. With a strategic approach—identifying triggers, setting clear goals, substituting with healthier behaviors, tracking progress, seeking support, practicing mindfulness, and keeping a positive mindset—you're setting yourself up for success. Remember, you're not just breaking habits; you're building a happier, healthier you. Let's embark on this transformative journey together, one step at a time.

～

CORE HABITS: THE CATALYSTS FOR PERSONAL TRANSFORMATION

UNLOCKING your full potential and sparking personal transformation starts with zeroing in on those core habits that act as catalysts for change—what we call keystone habits. These are the habits that, once established, set off a chain reaction, enhancing various aspects of our lives. This chapter is dedicated to guiding you through the process of identifying these transformative habits and seamlessly weaving them into the fabric of your daily life.

Discovering Keystone Habits:

- **Reflect on What Matters**: Kick things off by thinking deeply about your ultimate goals and what aspects of your life you're eager to elevate. Identifying the areas you value most will steer you toward the keystone habits that promise the most significant impact on your growth journey.
- **Examine Your Daily Life**: Dive into an analysis of your everyday routines. Pinpoint those habits that contribute positively to your life and those that seem to pull you backward. Focus on habits that ripple out, affecting other behaviors and routines, whether for better or worse.

- **Align With Your Values**: Ponder your core values and principles. Are there habits in your life that resonate with these values? Zeroing in on habits that align with what you hold dear lays a sturdy foundation for meaningful personal development.

Keystone Habit Highlights:

- **Regular Exercise**: A classic keystone habit, exercise doesn't just sculpt your physique—it sharpens your mind, boosts productivity, and can lead to healthier eating and sleeping habits.
- **Mindfulness Practice**: Embedding mindfulness into your routine can dramatically uplift your personal development. It fosters self-awareness, melts away stress, and enhances emotional intelligence, leading to smarter decisions and stronger relationships.
- **Daily Reading**: Incorporating reading into your daily regimen is a powerhouse move for growth. It broadens your knowledge, sharpens your thinking, and opens doors to new perspectives and skills, enhancing communication and enriching your life in myriad ways.

Making Keystone Habits Stick:

- **Start With Baby Steps**: Choose one keystone habit to focus on at a time. Trying to overhaul your life overnight can be overwhelming. Commit to integrating this one habit, building consistency and gradually expanding your repertoire.
- **Craft SMART Goals**: Break down your ambitions into Specific, Measurable, Achievable, Relevant, and Time-bound goals. This approach makes your progress tangible and keeps the motivation flowing.
- **Accountability Is Key**: Keep yourself in check. Whether it's through journaling, app tracking, or partnering up with a

mentor, find a method that resonates with you to stay committed and on course.

- **Stay Nimble**: Embrace the journey of integrating keystone habits with an open heart and mind. Be ready to tweak your approach based on what you learn from any hiccups along the way. Remember, personal growth is a marathon, not a sprint, and adaptability is your best companion.

Wrapping Up:

Identifying and embedding keystone habits into our daily rituals is a game-changer for personal development. By focusing on habits that generate positive cascades throughout our lives, setting actionable goals, maintaining accountability, and embracing adaptability, we lay down the groundwork for a life of growth and fulfillment. Let's embark on this journey with open minds and resilient spirits, ready to transform our lives one habit at a time.

~

HABIT STACKING: A GAME-CHANGER FOR GOAL ACHIEVEMENT

LET'S get into how our daily habits are the secret sauce to achieving our big goals. Ever heard of habit stacking? It's this nifty strategy that's been getting a lot of buzz for helping folks seamlessly introduce new habits into their life by piggybacking them onto things they're already doing. It's like getting a two-for-one deal on your routines, making it way easier to stick to new habits because they're tied to old ones.

Here's how you can get habit stacking to work for you:

- **Spot Your Solid Habits**: Kick things off by jotting down the stuff you do every single day without fail. This could be anything from brushing your teeth to grabbing your morning coffee.
- **Pick a New Habit**: Now, think about a new habit you're itching to get into your life. Make sure it's something that lights a fire in you and ties back to your bigger goals. Want to read more? That could be your new habit.
- **Link 'Em Up**: Find a cozy spot for your new habit right next to an old one. Let's say you want to start meditating and you never miss your morning coffee. Once you've got that cup in

hand, sit down, enjoy a mindful moment with your coffee, then transition into a few minutes of meditation.

- **Write It Down**: Get specific. Lay out your habit stack in detail. "After I pour my morning coffee, I'll sip it with all my senses engaged, and then I'll meditate for 5 minutes." Seeing it in black and white makes it real and doable.
- **Consistency is Key**: Stick with your habit stack every day. Even just a few minutes can make a difference. It's all about building up over time and making these actions second nature.
- **Reflect and Tweak**: Keep an eye on how things are going with your habit stack. Is it working out? Do you need to shake things up a bit? Be flexible and ready to adjust to keep your stack on point and effective.

Remember, habit stacking isn't just about piling on more stuff to do; it's about smartly integrating new habits into your life in a way that feels natural. By aligning these habits with your ultimate goals, you're setting the stage for real, tangible progress. So, let's leverage what we're already good at to master new skills and edge closer to our aspirations.

$\sim$

MASTERING SELF-CONTROL: THE KEY TO UNLOCKING NEW HABITS

ALRIGHT, let's dive into something that might feel a bit elusive at times —willpower. Ever notice how tough it can be to kick old habits to the curb and usher in new ones? Well, that's where willpower swings into the picture, acting like our personal superhero in the battle to form new habits.

The Lowdown on Willpower: Think of willpower as your inner strength to say "no" to temptations and stay on course with your long-term goals. It's all about keeping those impulsive desires in check. Interestingly, willpower isn't limitless—it's more like a battery that drains out through the day. So, getting smart about how we use that willpower can make all the difference in setting up new habits.

Flexing the Willpower Muscle: Yes, you can actually give your willpower a workout to make it stronger. It's like hitting the gym but for your self-control. Start small, like swapping out that candy bar for a healthier snack or sticking to a bedtime routine. These daily exercises in self-discipline can gradually boost your overall willpower.

Strategies to Amp Up Your Willpower:

- **Goal Setting with Clarity**: Nail down exactly what you're aiming for and why. Keeping your eyes on the prize helps fend off those sneaky temptations.
- **Plan for the Hurdles**: Imagine those tricky spots where you might stumble and plan your move in advance. It's about having a game plan for those moments when your willpower is tested.
- **Mindfulness and Meditation**: These aren't just buzzwords— they're tools that can sharpen your focus and reinforce your self-control. Just a few minutes a day can make a significant impact.
- **Keep Stress in Check**: Stress is like kryptonite to willpower. Find ways to manage stress, like exercise or breathing techniques, to keep your willpower tank full.
- **Craft a Supportive Space**: Hang out with people who cheer on your goals and tweak your environment to reduce temptations. Making it easier to stick to your new habits by having the right setup around you.

Wrapping It Up: Boosting your self-control and willpower is crucial for bringing new habits into your life. It's not just about resisting temptations; it's about empowering yourself to make choices that align with your goals. Remember, it's a marathon, not a sprint. Strengthening your willpower is a journey, but with persistence and the right strategies, you're setting the stage for lasting change and personal growth. Let's get those willpower muscles flexing and turn those new habits into a part of who we are.

∾

THE BRAIN'S POWER TO EVOLVE: TAPPING INTO NEUROPLASTICITY FOR HABIT TRANSFORMATION
CASE STUDY:

STEPHANIE'S JOURNEY into the world of habit change took an exciting turn when she stumbled upon a concept that blew her mind—neuroplasticity. Until then, she'd thought of the brain as somewhat of a static entity, pretty much set in its ways after a certain age. But neuroplasticity threw that old idea out the window, introducing her to the brain's incredible ability to adapt and rewire itself throughout life.

As Stephanie dug deeper, she became fascinated by how our habits actually sculpt our brain's wiring. Every habit, she learned, strengthens certain neural pathways, making it easier to repeat that behavior without much thought. It was a double-edged sword, though. This meant her bad habits were well-entrenched, but on the flip side, it also meant she had the power to forge new, healthier pathways.

Armed with this knowledge, Stephanie felt a surge of hope. She understood that changing her habits was akin to blazing new trails in her brain. Although the old paths were deeply etched from repeated use, she could create new ones with persistence and the right strategies.

Mindfulness and meditation became her allies in this quest. These practices helped her observe her thought patterns and behaviors from a distance, giving her crucial insights into her habitual responses.

Moreover, she learned that challenging her brain with new activities—like solving puzzles or picking up a musical instrument—could spark neuroplasticity, laying down fresh neural connections.

Embracing the slow, steady process of change, Stephanie began to focus on modifying one small habit component at a time. This approach made the daunting task of habit transformation more manageable and less overwhelming. She also prepared herself for the inevitable setbacks, choosing to see them not as failures but as valuable learning moments.

Stephanie's deep dive into neuroplasticity empowered her in ways she hadn't imagined. Realizing she had the ability to rewire her brain for the better was a revelation. This knowledge fueled her determination to overhaul her habits, infusing her journey with a sense of purpose and excitement.

Now, with a clear understanding of her brain's dynamic nature, Stephanie felt ready to tackle her habit changes head-on. She knew the road ahead would be challenging, but armed with the secrets of neuroplasticity, she was more committed than ever to shaping her brain—and her life—into something truly remarkable.

~

CRAFTING HABIT-FRIENDLY ENVIRONMENTS: LEVERAGING ENVIRONMENTAL CUES FOR POSITIVE CHANGE

EVERY DAY, we navigate through a sea of choices that mold our habits, either propelling us toward growth or pulling us back. It turns out, the spaces where we spend our time wield a mighty influence over these habits. In this Part, we're diving into how environmental cues shape our behaviors and offering hands-on tips to tailor your spaces in ways that naturally encourage good habits.

The Power of Environmental Cues: Environmental cues are the subtle signals in our surroundings that affect our actions and choices without us even realizing it. These can range from what we see and hear to the scents that waft through the air. By tapping into these cues, we can cleverly nudge ourselves and others toward healthier, more productive habits.

Harnessing Visual Cues for Positive Habits:

- **Elevate the Good Stuff:** Keep healthier options visible and within easy reach, be it food or any other choice.
- **Color Your World:** Utilize color to influence mood and behavior. Think of serene blues for calm or vibrant greens to spark vitality.

- **Clear Signage:** Use labels and signs to guide behaviors, like pointing the way to recycling or demarcating a quiet reading corner.

Tuning into Auditory Cues:

- **Set the Tone with Music:** Background tunes can drastically shape the ambiance, from calming to energizing.
- **Positive Sounds:** Integrate sounds that celebrate achievements or signal completion, reinforcing good actions.

Smells That Shape Habits:

- **Aromatic Ambiance:** Use scents to craft the desired atmosphere, from energizing citrus to relaxing lavender.
- **Scent as Identity:** For places with a distinct purpose, like a gym, matching scents can amplify the experience and connection.

Design and Layout That Directs Behavior:

- **Purposeful Spaces:** Designate areas for specific activities, making it easier for people to engage in the desired behavior.
- **Accessible Essentials:** Keep tools for healthy habits visible and within arm's reach, encouraging their use.
- **Bring Nature In:** Incorporate elements like plants or natural light, known to boost mood and encourage wellbeing.

Encouraging Consistency and Reinforcement:

- **Immediate Feedback:** Utilize cues for instant feedback on behaviors, like showing how much energy you've saved by taking the stairs.
- **Foster Accountability:** Use communal spaces to display goals or progress, creating a shared environment of encouragement and motivation.

Wrapping It Up: Our environment is a silent partner in the dance of habit formation, constantly influencing our steps. By smartly deploying visual, auditory, and olfactory cues, along with thoughtfully arranged spaces, we can turn our surroundings into allies in the quest for better habits. This approach doesn't just nudge us toward positive change—it envelops us in a space where good habits can flourish naturally. Designing with intention means we can all enjoy spaces that not only look good but actually encourage us to live better.

～

HARNESSING EMOTIONAL SMARTS TO TACKLE HABIT TRIGGERS AND CRAVINGS

LET'S talk about something that's a game-changer in the world of habits: emotional intelligence. This isn't just about being in tune with our feelings; it's about using that understanding to navigate the mine-field of triggers and cravings that can throw us off course when we're trying to build better habits.

So, what's the deal with triggers and cravings? Essentially, they're the signals and desires that can lead us down the path of old, often unhelpful habits. But here's where our emotional smarts come into play. By getting better at recognizing and managing our emotions, we can take control of these triggers and cravings, rather than letting them control us.

First off, self-awareness is key. It's about tuning into our emotions and recognizing what's behind our cravings. Let's say stress is your trigger for binge-watching TV. Acknowledging that stress is the real culprit can help you find healthier ways to cope, maybe by choosing a walk or some yoga instead.

Once we've pinpointed our triggers, it's time to talk strategy. Finding healthier alternatives is one approach. If stress tempts you to dive into a bag of chips, why not try a stress-busting activity instead? It's all about replacing the knee-jerk reaction with a choice that serves you better.

Now, self-regulation is where the magic happens. This is our ability to keep our impulses in check. Feeling an overwhelming urge to indulge in a bad habit? This is where techniques like deep breathing or a quick mindfulness session can help you pause and choose a different response.

Empathy, especially toward ourselves, is another powerful tool. Messed up and fell back into an old habit? Instead of beating yourself up, treat yourself with the same kindness you'd offer a friend. This compassion can turn a slip-up into a learning moment and a step toward growth.

Lastly, don't underestimate the power of your tribe. Social awareness and a strong support network can make all the difference. Surrounding yourself with people who cheer on your progress and understand your struggles can keep you motivated and resilient in the face of those tough triggers and cravings.

In wrapping up, leveraging emotional intelligence in our fight against triggers and cravings is like having a superpower. It equips us with the awareness, strategies, and support we need to make lasting changes. By honing our emotional smarts, we're not just better equipped to tackle the challenges of habit formation; we're setting ourselves up for a richer, more balanced life.

~

MASTERING HABITS: TRACKING AND MEASURING YOUR WAY TO SUCCESS

GETTING a handle on our habits is a big deal if we're serious about personal growth. It's all about shining a light on our daily routines to see what's helping us thrive and what's holding us back. In this chapter, we will walk through the why and how of keeping tabs on our habits, using tools and strategies that can kick our self-awareness and progress into high gear.

Why Bother Tracking and Measuring Habits?

So, why take the time to track and measure our habits? For starters, it gives us a clear picture of where we stand - which habits are our allies and which ones are the villains. This clarity is the first step toward making intentional changes. Plus, keeping an eye on our progress helps us see how far we've come, shining a spotlight on our wins and areas for improvement. And let's not forget, tracking our habits keeps us honest and motivated to stick with the positive changes we're trying to make.

How to Track Your Habits:

Let's dive into some practical ways to keep track of our habits:

- **Old-School Paper Tracking:** There's something about the physical act of writing that makes things stick. Grab a notebook and jot down your daily habits. You can get as creative as you want, turning this into a mini project that's both helpful and fun.
- **Tech-Savvy Apps:** For those who prefer a digital approach, there's no shortage of apps designed to make habit tracking a breeze. These tools come packed with features like reminders, charts, and even community support to keep you on track.
- **Bullet Journaling:** If you're looking for a method that's both structured and flexible, bullet journaling could be your best bet. It's a neat way to combine goal setting, habit tracking, and reflecting all in one place, with the bonus of letting your creativity flow.

Measuring Your Progress:

Tracking is just one part of the equation. To get the most out of this process, we need to measure our progress. Here's how:

- **Quantitative Methods:** Nothing speaks louder than cold, hard numbers. By measuring your progress, you can see just how much you've improved. Whether it's tallying up workouts or counting the pages you've read, these metrics make your progress real.
- **Qualitative Insights:** Sometimes, the most significant changes are the ones we feel rather than see. Reflect on how new habits are affecting your mood, stress levels, or overall happiness. This can be as revealing as any number.
- **Reflective Practices:** Never underestimate the power of a good reflection session. Writing down your thoughts, challenges, and victories gives you invaluable insights into your habit journey, helping you fine-tune your approach as you go.

Wrapping It Up:

Keeping track of our habits is more than just a to-do; it's a pathway to deeper self-understanding and lasting change. By using these tracking and measuring tactics, we can steer our habits in a direction that aligns with our goals, paving the way for personal and professional triumphs. Let's embrace these tools and take charge of our habits, one day at a time.

～

THE RIPPLE EFFECT: HOW OUR CIRCLE INFLUENCES OUR HABITS

DIVING into the world of habits, we've seen how they're the architects of our daily life, sculpting our routines and, ultimately, our destiny. We've unpacked the mechanics behind habit formation—the cues, routines, rewards—and shared tactics for ditching the bad and championing the good. Now, let's pivot to a fascinating angle: the social dynamics of habits. Here's where we examine the sway our circle—friends, family, colleagues—holds over our habit landscape, for better or worse.

It's no secret we're social beings, wired to sync with the tribe around us. Our habits often mirror those in our immediate circle. Surrounded by junk food aficionados? You might find it tougher to munch on that kale salad. But, flip the scenario—your inner circle is all about that healthy living—and suddenly, you're jogging at dawn and sipping green smoothies.

Peer influence is a bit of a Jekyll and Hyde story regarding habit formation. It has the potential to catapult us toward positive change, creating an echo chamber of good vibes and healthy habits. Imagine the momentum when one person's commitment to wellness inspires the whole group! Yet, there's the flip side where negative influences can derail our goals, especially when those habits are woven into our social fabric. Breaking away from these habits might mean reevaluating our social connections to align more closely with our aspirations.

Tackling peer influence head-on calls for a hefty dose of self-awareness and a dash of boldness. It's about taking a hard look at how our current habits are shaped by those around us and deciding what we genuinely want to keep, toss, or adopt. Clear intentions pave the way for open conversations with our peeps about where we're headed and the support we need to get there.

And speaking of support, it's the secret sauce in this whole habit-changing endeavor. A cheerleading squad can make all the difference in sticking to new habits. It's about more than just encouragement; it's about accountability and shared journeys toward change. Sometimes, this means widening our support net beyond our immediate circle to include communities or online groups where like-minded souls gather.

Remember, support can come from the most unexpected places—online forums, virtual mentors, or a fitness group where no one knows your last name, but everyone shares your goals. These connections can offer fresh perspectives and invaluable guidance drawn from their own battles and victories.

In wrapping up, the influence our social circle wields over our habits is undeniable. Yet, armed with awareness, intentionality, and the right support system, we can navigate this complex terrain. It's about leveraging the positive, mitigating the negative, and sometimes, being the change agent in our circle. Habit formation is a collective dance—a blend of individual effort and communal rhythm.

∼

TRANSFORMING WELLBEING THROUGH HABITS: JILL'S JOURNEY TO A HEALTHIER SELF

A couple of years back, Jill found herself caught in a cycle of stress, lack of motivation, and unhealthy lifestyle choices. The demands of her job had her constantly on edge, and she struggled to find the energy or willpower to focus on her health.

Everything started to change when Jill picked up a book that shed light on the transformative power of habits and routines. The idea that small, consistent actions could significantly affect her health and happiness was a revelation. She learned about the habit loop—cue, routine, reward—and realized that to improve her wellbeing, she needed to dissect and rebuild her daily habits.

Jill's first step was to take a hard look at her routines, especially her evening ritual of unwinding with TV and junk food. Recognizing the cue (finishing work) and the routine (snacking while binge-watching), she set out to craft a healthier pattern. She swapped her couch sessions for evening walks, a change that not only changed her cue but also introduced a refreshing new routine. To tackle her snacking habit, she stocked up on healthy alternatives, gradually reducing her cravings for processed foods.

But Jill didn't stop there. She integrated regular exercise into her daily life, making it as non-negotiable as her work meetings. Whether it was a brisk morning run, a midday yoga session, or an evening strength workout, she moved her body daily. This consistent effort slowly became a cornerstone of her routine.

On top of physical habits, Jill turned her attention to cultivating a positive mindset. She began each day with a moment of gratitude and positive affirmations, grounding herself in positivity and mindfulness. This simple yet profound practice helped reduce her stress levels and keep her centered, reinforcing the mental part of her health transformation.

Jill's journey taught her an invaluable lesson: habits are powerful forces that shape our health and happiness. By strategically changing her cues, routines, and rewards, she not only broke free from harmful patterns but also established a lifestyle that nurtured her physical and mental wellbeing. Today, Jill stands as a testament to the fact that with determination, insight, and strategy, transforming our lives for the better is well within reach.

~

BOOSTING YOUR WORKDAY: THE HABIT ADVANTAGE

IN THE HUSTLE of today's work world, being on your A-game isn't just nice—it's necessary. So, how do we hit the mark on productivity and stand out? It boils down to the habits we curate. This chapter is your guide to weaving habits that not only boost your productivity but also your performance, ensuring you're not just busy, but impactful.

Harnessing Habit Power: Our daily routines are a mesh of habits, each steering our path toward or away from productivity. Recognizing this gives us a chance to tweak our autopilot settings. We can swap out those time-suckers—hello, endless social media scrolling—for practices that align with our career aspirations.

Spotting Productivity Pitfalls: First up, let's shine a light on what's holding us back. Whether it's the allure of "just one more episode" or the trap of trying to juggle a dozen tasks at once, identifying these pitfalls is step one toward transforming our workday.

Morning Routines That Energize: How you start your day can make or break your productivity. Picture this: a morning that kicks off with a run, some mindfulness, a rundown of your top priorities, and a nutritious breakfast. You're not just ready for the day; you're set to conquer it.

Mastering Your Time: The key to doing more isn't working more hours—it's working smarter. Techniques like the Pomodoro, time blocking, or even a simple to-do list app can turn your day from chaotic to streamlined.

Embrace Growth Every Day: Adopting a mindset that thrives on challenges and feedback fuels not just growth, but resilience. It's about seeing every hiccup not as a roadblock, but as a steppingstone.

Designing Your Space for Success: Never underestimate the power of a workspace that invites focus and sparks creativity. A tidy desk, some personal touches, and perhaps a plant or two can make all the difference in how you tackle your tasks.

Goal setting and Milestone Celebrations: Clear goals act like your career's GPS, guiding you through the day-to-day to reach your bigger picture. And tracking these goals? It's the nudge you need to keep pushing forward, celebrating the small wins on the way to the big ones.

Fostering a Supportive Work Circle: The people you surround yourself with at work can lift you up or weigh you down. Building relationships with colleagues and mentors who share your drive can turn the workplace into a powerhouse of mutual motivation.

Never Stop Learning: In a world that's always changing, staying sharp means staying ahead. Whether it's an online course after hours or a seminar that speaks to your soul, investing in your skills is investing in your career's future.

Wrapping Up: Crafting productive habits isn't just about doing more—it's about being more. From the rituals that start your day to the continuous quest for knowledge, these patterns pave the way to professional excellence. With the right habits in your toolkit, you're not just working smarter; you're building a career that thrives.

$\sim$

BUILDING FOUNDATIONS FOR LASTING SUCCESS: THE POWER OF HABIT

After diving deep into strategies for kickstarting positive transformations, it's clear that the real challenge lies in keeping the momentum going. This chapter isn't just another pep talk—it's about anchoring those initial wins into your daily life for the long haul. By embedding a set of core habits into our routine, we don't just enjoy fleeting successes; we set the stage for enduring progress in both our personal and professional spheres.

Reflection as a Routine: A cornerstone habit for anyone eyeing long-term success is regular reflection. Carving out moments to look inward and assess our journey not only sharpens our self-awareness but also highlights areas ripe for improvement. It's like having a personal audit session that keeps us aligned with our true north.

Strategic Goal Setting: No ship sails without a compass, and in our quest for sustained success, our compass is goal setting. Crafting clear, actionable goals keeps us tethered to our aspirations, turning the abstract into concrete steps forward. Adjust and recalibrate as life unfolds, but keep the goals in sight and the steps deliberate.

Embracing Accountability: Walking the path alone can be daunting, so why not bring an accountability partner into the mix? Sharing your roadmap with someone—a mentor, a buddy, or a colleague—can transform the journey. It's about having someone in your corner to remind you of the bigger picture when the details bog you down.

A Lifelong Learning Curve: The world doesn't stand still, and neither should we. Adopting a mindset that sees every setback as a setup for a comeback, and thirsting for new knowledge, keeps us agile and forward-thinking. Continuous learning isn't just about staying relevant; it's about constantly elevating ourselves.

Flex and Bounce Back: Resilience and adaptability aren't just buzzwords; they're survival tools. The ability to take life's curveballs and swing back with grace and strategy is what separates the enduring from the ephemeral. It's about cultivating an inner resilience that turns challenges into steppingstones.

Focus on You: Last but by no means least, self-care is the bedrock of sustained achievement. Ignoring your wellbeing while chasing goals is like running a marathon on an empty tank—it just doesn't work. A well-tended mind and body are your greatest assets; nurture them.

Wrapping It Up: To embed the positive changes, we seek into the fabric of our lives, a disciplined approach to cultivating supportive habits is non-negotiable. From introspection to learning, from resilience to self-care, these practices aren't just tasks on a checklist. They're the pillars that uphold the lasting success we all strive for. Stick to these principles, and watch as they transform not just your actions, but your outcomes.

∼

PART EIGHT WRAP-UP:

KEY POINTS:

- **The Role of Habits:** Our lives are significantly shaped by our habits, which influence our daily actions and long-term success.
- **Habit Formation:** Habits are created through a three-step loop: cue, routine, and reward. Understanding this loop is important for changing habits.
- **Positive vs. Negative Habits:** It's important to distinguish between habits that benefit us and those that are harmful.
- **Changing Habits:** Modifying habits requires identifying triggers, replacing negative routines with positive ones, and perseverance.
- **Keystone Habits:** These are habits with a ripple effect, positively affecting various areas of our lives.
- **The Science of Habits:** Our brain's structure, including the basal ganglia and prefrontal cortex, plays a significant role in habit formation and change.
- **Neuroplasticity:** The brain's ability to rewire itself, helping with the change of habits through consistent practice and

mindfulness.

- **Environment and Habits:** Our surroundings influence our habits, suggesting that designing supportive spaces can promote positive habits.
- **Emotional Intelligence:** Managing emotions and triggers is key in forming and sustaining healthy habits.
- **Habit Tracking:** Tools and methods for tracking progress can enhance self-awareness and motivate continued improvement.
- **Social Influence:** Peers can significantly affect our habit formation, making a supportive network essential for change.
- **Workplace Habits:** Developing productivity-enhancing habits is important for professional success.
- **Sustaining Change:** Long-term success depends on continuous self-improvement, resilience, and adaptability.

Action Items:

- **Assess Your Habits:** Regularly evaluate your habits to identify which ones serve you well and which ones need changing.
- **Understand Your Habit Loops:** Pinpoint the cues, routines, and rewards in your habit loops to better manage and change your behaviors.
- **Set Specific Goals:** Define clear, achievable goals for replacing negative habits with positive ones.
- **Implement Keystone Habits:** Focus on establishing keystone habits that can positively influence multiple parts of your life.
- **Practice Mindfulness:** Use mindfulness to learn of your habits and the choices you make daily.
- **Design Your Environment:** Arrange your living and working spaces to support the habits you want to cultivate.
- **Seek Support:** Build a network of friends, family, or colleagues who support your journey to change habits.
- **Track Your Progress:** Use a journal, app, or another method to track your habits and celebrate your successes.

- **Learn Continuously:** Stay open to new information and strategies for habit change and personal growth.
- **Practice Resilience:** Develop resilience by viewing challenges as opportunities for growth and learning from setbacks.
- **Focus on Self-Care:** Ensure regular self-care to maintain the energy and wellbeing needed to sustain positive habits.
- **Reflect Regularly:** Set aside time for self-reflection to assess your progress and adjust your goals and strategies as needed.

By focusing on these key points and action items, you can harness the power of habits to transform your life, improve your health and productivity, and achieve long-term success.

In Our Next Part...

As we venture further into our exploration of personal growth and development, prepare to dig into advanced strategies that build on the essential practices of mindfulness and emotional intelligence you've come to know. Imagine elevating your self-awareness to unparalleled levels, honing your emotional regulation skills to a fine art, and handling interpersonal relationships with a newfound depth of empathy and ease. We're about to unlock the secrets to turning life's hurdles into steppingstones for growth, aligning every facet of your existence with your core values and highest aspirations.

Get set for a transformative journey that not only polishes the skills you've nurtured but also introduces you to groundbreaking practices and perspectives poised to significantly uplift your life's quality. From enriching your meditation rituals, harnessing emotional intelligence in more intricate scenarios, to innovative applications of mindfulness, this upcoming Part is crafted to inspire, energize, and arm you with the tools essential for flourishing in all areas of your life. Together, we'll tap into the boundless capabilities of the human spirit and intellect, paving the path toward a future brimming with peace, satisfaction, and achievement.

PART NINE
ELEVATING YOUR JOURNEY: MASTERING ADVANCED PERSONAL GROWTH TECHNIQUES

MASTERING MINDFULNESS AND EMOTIONAL INTELLIGENCE: KEYS TO PERSONAL GROWTH

LET's break down two game-changing concepts vital for personal growth and success: mindfulness and emotional intelligence. They're not just buzzwords but powerful tools that can significantly affect how we navigate our lives.

Mindfulness Simplified: Think of mindfulness as being in the "here and now." It's about tuning into your current experience—thoughts, feelings, bodily sensations, and everything happening around you—without passing judgment. It's like watching a movie of your own life as it unfolds, observing without critiquing or trying to change the plot.

Emotional Intelligence Demystified: Emotional intelligence, on the other hand, is all about understanding and managing your own emotions and recognizing others' emotions. It's like being fluent in the language of emotions. This skill set includes being self-aware, controlling impulses, staying motivated, understanding social cues, and managing relationships effectively. It's what enables us to navigate social complexities with grace and make decisions that balance emotion and logic.

Why They Matter:

- **Self-Awareness:** Both mindfulness and emotional intelligence start with self-awareness. Mindfulness shines a spotlight on our internal states, while emotional intelligence requires us to understand our emotions. This awareness is the first step toward personal transformation, helping us identify what we need to work on.
- **Emotional Regulation:** These practices teach us to handle our emotions with finesse. Mindfulness offers a pause button, helping us respond to situations rather than react impulsively. Emotional intelligence provides strategies to manage our emotions, essential for resilience and a balanced life.
- **Building Better Relationships:** Here's where the magic happens in our interactions with others. Mindfulness encourages empathy and active listening, enhancing our connections. Emotional intelligence gives us the tools for smooth communication, conflict resolution, and collaboration, laying the foundation for meaningful relationships.
- **Smarter Decision-Making:** Both skills contribute to making informed, thoughtful decisions. Mindfulness keeps us from being swept away by emotions, allowing for clearer thinking. Emotional intelligence ensures we consider both our feelings and those of others, leading to decisions that are not only smart but also socially sensitive.

Mastering mindfulness and emotional intelligence is like acquiring a superpower for personal growth and success. They help us understand ourselves, navigate our emotions, connect deeply with others, and make decisions that propel us toward our goals. By dedicating ourselves to these practices, we unlock the potential for significant personal development, fruitful relationships, and a successful, fulfilling life.

～

THE SYNERGY OF MINDFULNESS AND EMOTIONAL INTELLIGENCE: ELEVATING PERSONAL AWARENESS AND CONNECTION

MINDFULNESS and emotional intelligence are like two peas in a pod; they go hand in hand, enhancing and enriching each other in ways that are deeply intertwined. Both concepts are centered on a keen awareness of our emotions and the emotions of those around us. Let's break down how these two are not just interconnected but also how they boost each other, paving the way for a more aware and connected existence.

Mindfulness: The Art of Presence Imagine mindfulness as the art of being immersed in the now, where every thought, emotion, and sensation is acknowledged with no judgment. It's about tuning in to the present moment with full attention, letting us observe our inner world without getting swept away. This practice is a gateway to self-awareness, offering us a clear window into our thoughts and feelings, making us more adept at handling life's curveballs with grace rather than impulsiveness.

Emotional Intelligence: The Power of Understanding Emotions Emotional intelligence, on the flip side, is all about mastering the realm of emotions—ours and those of others. It's a blend of recognizing, understanding, and managing our emotions, coupled with the empathy to sense and appreciate the emotional landscapes of others. This skill set is invaluable for steering through emotional undercurrents, fostering strong relationships, resolving conflicts, and making decisions that are not only smart but also emotionally attuned.

The Beautiful Interplay The magic happens in how mindfulness and emotional intelligence feed into and expand each other. Practicing mindfulness hones our self-awareness, making us more conscious of our emotions as they ebb and flow. This heightened awareness is the cornerstone of emotional intelligence, enabling us to better understand and navigate our emotional reactions and interactions with others.

Emotional intelligence enriches our mindfulness practice by deepening our understanding of our emotional states, which makes our mindfulness practice more nuanced and empathetic. It's a virtuous cycle; the more emotionally intelligent we become, the more mindful we are in our interactions and vice versa. Empathy, a key part of emotional intelligence, invites us to be more present and attentive to others' feelings, fostering a sense of connection and compassion—key elements in mindfulness.

Mutual Benefits for Stress Management and Wellbeing Both mindfulness and emotional intelligence are allies in our journey toward managing stress and improving our overall wellbeing. Through mindfulness, we learn to meet life's stresses with equanimity, responding thoughtfully rather than reacting on autopilot. Emotional intelligence complements this by equipping us with tools to manage our emotions effectively, thus reducing stress and enhancing our life satisfaction.

Wrapping Up In essence, the relationship between mindfulness and emotional intelligence is synergistic, each amplifying the benefits of the other. By weaving mindfulness into our daily lives, we lay the groundwork for greater emotional intelligence, and as we become more emotionally intelligent, our capacity for mindfulness deepens. This dynamic duo empowers us to navigate life with greater awareness, resilience, and empathy, enriching our personal connections and decision-making, and ultimately leading to a more fulfilled and balanced life.

ENHANCING LIFE WITH MINDFULNESS AND EMOTIONAL INTELLIGENCE

EMBRACING mindfulness and emotional intelligence in our day-to-day lives can be a game-changer for both our mental wellbeing and personal growth. These practices not only deepen our understanding of ourselves but also improve how we connect with others, offering a wellspring of empathy and compassion. Let's dive into how mindfulness and emotional intelligence can make a significant positive difference in our lives.

Mindfulness: The Art of Being Present Mindfulness means being engaged with the here and now, observing our thoughts, emotions, and sensations without passing judgment. It's about hitting the pause button, letting us respond thoughtfully to life's moments rather than reacting. This practice is key to managing stress, anxiety, and negative feelings more gracefully, promoting a sense of emotional balance and self-control.

By integrating mindfulness into our daily routines—through meditation, mindful breathing, or simply being present during routine tasks—we sharpen our focus and improve our engagement with the world. It's an antidote to the distraction-filled environment we navigate daily, boosting our productivity and attention in both personal and work-related activities.

Emotional Intelligence: The Heart of Connection Emotional intelligence is our ability to understand and manage our emotions and to empathize with the emotions of others. It's about being attuned to our emotional landscape and using that awareness to foster stronger, more meaningful relationships. Through emotional intelligence, we can communicate sharing our feelings with authenticity and consideration for the feelings of others.

Daily life offers countless opportunities to practice and benefit from emotional intelligence. It enhances essential interpersonal skills like active listening, resolving disagreements amicably, and appreciating the diverse perspectives of those around us. It equips us to handle feedback constructively, approach challenges with poise, and forge deeper connections with friends, family, and colleagues.

A Synergistic Impact Uniting mindfulness and emotional intelligence in our lives creates a powerful synergy. Together, they guide us toward more mindful decisions, enriching our lives with a sense of satisfaction and contentment. They bolster our resilience against life's challenges, clear our minds for better focus, and enhance our capacity for empathy and connection.

Why It Matters Incorporating mindfulness and emotional intelligence into our routines offers vast benefits: from heightened self-awareness and stress management to improved focus and stronger relationships. They are pillars of personal development, equipping us to navigate life with resilience, clarity, and a deepened sense of empathy.

Mindfulness and emotional intelligence are not just practices but pathways to a more fulfilled, balanced, and connected life. They empower us to cultivate a harmonious inner world and meaningful relationships, laying the foundation for continuous personal growth and well-being. So, why not make them a part of your daily journey and experience the transformation they bring?

~

BOOSTING SELF-INSIGHT AND CONTROL: THE IMPACT OF MINDFULNESS AND EMOTIONAL INTELLIGENCE

MINDFULNESS and emotional intelligence are like secret superpowers that can dramatically boost our understanding and management of ourselves. These approaches teach us to tune in to our inner dialogues and emotional landscapes, offering a richer, more nuanced understanding of who we are and how we interact with the world. Here's a closer look at how diving into these practices can level up our self-awareness and self-regulation skills:

Mindfulness Meditation: Imagine taking a moment each day to be. Through regular mindfulness meditation, we can cultivate a space where thoughts and feelings are seen without judgment. It's like becoming a mindful observer of our own minds. Say you get heated in certain situations; mindfulness lets you notice this pattern without getting tangled in it, opening up a pathway to understand and address the root cause more effectively.

Emotional Self-Awareness: This part of emotional intelligence is all about getting clear on what we're feeling and why. It's the difference between a vague sense of unease and pinpointing, "Hey, I'm actually feeling quite anxious or frustrated right now." This clarity empowers us to respond to our emotions in a way that serves us better, rather than being at the mercy of unexamined feelings.

Self-Regulation Through Mindfulness: Mindfulness teaches us not to be swept away by our emotions but to acknowledge them with a gentle, non-reactive curiosity. This creates a moment of choice—instead of spiraling into stress or anxiety, we can recognize these feelings and decide how we want to respond. It's a game-changer for managing stress and choosing actions that align with our values.

Empathy and Social Awareness: Being emotionally intelligent also means tuning into the feelings of those around us. When we practice empathy, we get better at sensing what others are going through, which can transform our interactions. Recognizing a colleague's stress, for example, lets us respond with kindness and support, building stronger, more empathetic connections.

Improved Conflict Resolution: Both mindfulness and emotional intelligence shine in conflict resolution. By understanding our triggers and emotional responses, we can approach disagreements with a cooler head and a clearer perspective. This doesn't just lead to more constructive conversations; it helps us find solutions that everyone can get behind.

Mindfulness and emotional intelligence equip us with the insight and flexibility needed to understand ourselves deeply and manage our reactions. They teach us to navigate our internal world with grace and interact with others in more meaningful, empathetic ways. By practicing these skills, we open up new possibilities for personal growth, better relationships, and more thoughtful decision-making. It's about moving through life with a greater sense of awareness and control, ready to meet its challenges with confidence and composure.

~

MASTERING INNER BALANCE: THE POWER OF MINDFULNESS AND EMOTIONAL INTELLIGENCE

MINDFULNESS and emotional intelligence are the powerhouse combo for anyone keen on personal growth. They're about getting a crystal clear picture of our inner emotional landscape and learning the art of steering through life's waves with grace. Let's dive into how these practices can transform our understanding of ourselves and improve our ability to manage our reactions.

Mindfulness Meditation: Imagine taking a moment to be with your thoughts and feelings, observing them without passing judgment. This practice gives us the insight to spot when we're starting to feel ticked off and to understand why, instead of reacting in the heat of the moment. It's like having a mental map that helps us navigate our emotions more skillfully.

Emotional Self-Awareness: Fine-tuning our emotional intelligence is like sharpening our emotional detective skills. It helps us break down that cloud of "I'm just not feeling right" into identifiable emotions, such as frustration or worry. This clarity is a game-changer, letting us tackle our feelings head-on and make smarter choices.

Self-Regulation Through Mindfulness: Mindfulness acts as a gentle reminder we need not be at the mercy of our emotions. Feeling stressed? Mindfulness offers a way to acknowledge this stress without letting it take the wheel. This important pause is what lets us choose how we want to respond, leading to more constructive outcomes.

Empathy and Social Awareness: Emotional intelligence isn't just about understanding ourselves; it's also about tuning into others' emotions. Spotting a friend or colleague in distress lets us offer a shoulder or an ear, transforming the way we connect. It's about nurturing relationships with empathy and understanding, enriching our social interactions.

Improved Conflict Resolution: When smoothing over disagreements, mindfulness and emotional intelligence are your best allies. Being aware of our role in a conflict and understanding what pushes our buttons helps us approach these situations with a level head. The result? Solutions that everyone can get behind, fostering a more harmonious environment.

Briefly, mindfulness and emotional intelligence don't just help us navigate our emotions with ease; they also pave the way for stronger, more supportive connections. By weaving these practices into the fabric of our daily lives, we step closer to achieving a state of balance and harmony, both within ourselves and in our interactions with others. They're essential tools for anyone looking to evolve personally and professionally, guiding us to live more authentically and in tune with our core values.

$$\sim$$

UNLOCKING PERSONAL AND PROFESSIONAL GROWTH THROUGH MINDFUL STRATEGIES

EMBRACE MINDFUL MOMENTS: Start by tuning into your inner world. Carve out time daily to sit quietly and breathe deeply. Let your thoughts flow freely, observing them without getting tangled up in their narrative. This simple act of mindfulness sharpens your emotional understanding, paving the way for a more refined emotional intelligence.

Master the Art of Listening: True connection begins with listening. When someone shares with you, give them your full attention—no interruptions, no preconceptions. This practice not only enriches your relationships but deepens your empathy, a cornerstone of emotional intelligence.

Reflect to Connect: Dedicate moments for self-reflection. Writing in a journal can be a powerful tool, letting you unpack your thoughts and feelings. Dive into your daily experiences, seeking the lessons they hold. This journey inward boosts your self-awareness, enhancing your emotional intelligence.

Mindful Meals, Mindful Life: Bring mindfulness to the dining table. Notice the colors and textures of your food, savor each bite, and appreciate the flavors. This practice extends beyond the plate, encouraging mindfulness in all facets of life.

Empathy Expansion: Walk a mile in another's shoes. Explore different stories and perspectives through literature, film, and open dialogue. Surround yourself with diverse voices and experiences. Strengthening your empathy enriches your emotional intelligence and nurtures meaningful connections.

Stress Management with Mindfulness: Don't let stress cloud your potential. Integrate mindful practices to keep stress at bay—deep breathing, physical activity, or any personal relaxation technique. A serene mind lays the foundation for both personal growth and emotional intelligence.

Live Without Judgment: Practice seeing the world without labels. Embrace the complexity of experiences and viewpoints without hastily categorizing them. This openness fosters emotional intelligence by promoting understanding and acceptance.

Cultivate Gratitude: Make gratitude a daily ritual. Reflect on the positives in your life, acknowledging them with a thankful heart. This practice roots you in the present, boosts positivity, and enhances emotional wellbeing.

Welcome Constructive Feedback: Seek perspectives on your blind spots. Embrace constructive criticism as a growth opportunity. Inviting feedback reflects humility and a genuine commitment to emotional and personal development.

Mindful Conversations: Communicate with intention. Before you speak, align your words with your true feelings and intentions. Mindful communication builds stronger, more empathetic relationships, contributing significantly to your personal growth and emotional intelligence.

Incorporating these mindful strategies into your daily routine can significantly enhance both your personal growth and decision-making skills. Cultivating mindfulness and emotional intelligence is a journey, requiring patience and persistence. Commit to these practices, and watch as they transform your approach to challenges, enrich your relationships, and steer you toward lasting success.

❧

EMBRACING MINDFULNESS: FINDING PEACE IN THE PRESENT

IN THE WHIRLWIND of our modern lives, finding a moment's peace can feel like searching for a needle in a haystack. Enter mindfulness, a beacon of calm with roots deep in ancient Buddhist practice, offering a way to navigate the chaos with grace. It teaches us to anchor ourselves in the now, opening a treasure chest of benefits that enhance our wellbeing.

Mindfulness is all about being in the moment—intentionally, without letting judgments cloud the experience. Our minds, often caught in the ebb and flow of past regrets and future anxieties, crave this return to the present. It's a practice that quiets the noise, letting us savor life as it unfolds, moment by moment.

The gifts of weaving mindfulness into our daily routine are profound. For starters, it's a proven stressbuster. By centering our focus on the here and now, we escape the relentless treadmill of worry, ushering in a sense of calm and resilience that buffers us against life's curveballs.

Beyond calming the storm, mindfulness sharpens our engagement with the world. It enhances focus and productivity, turning routine tasks into opportunities for deep satisfaction. Whether we're tackling a project, conversing with a friend, or enjoying a simple meal, mindfulness deepens our appreciation and enjoyment of these moments.

But there's more. Mindfulness is a catalyst for emotional intelligence. It encourages us to observe our thoughts and feelings with compassion, paving the way for improved self-understanding and empathy. This emotional clarity enriches our interactions, making for healthier communication and more fulfilling relationships.

The physical health perks are just as compelling. Mindfulness can lower blood pressure, boost the immune system, and alleviate chronic pain. It's a testament to the powerful connection between mind and body, emphasizing that our mental state can have real effects on our physical health.

Mindfulness transcends being merely a concept or trend. It's a transformative practice that equips us to live more fully in each moment. By embracing mindfulness, we invite peace, enhance our daily experiences, nurture our relationships, and promote physical and mental wellbeing. It's about living in the present, discovering joy and contentment in the simplicity of now.

~

MASTERING THE BREATH: THE KEY TO SELF-AWARENESS AND EMOTIONAL BALANCE

MINDFUL BREATHING STANDS as a cornerstone of mindfulness, a simple yet profound technique that tunes us into the rhythm of our breath, grounding us in the present. Its roots stretch back through centuries, embraced across meditation traditions for its power to forge a deeper connection to our inner selves and manage the ebb and flow of our emotions.

Here's how you can start this transformative practice: First, find a quiet spot where you won't be disturbed. Sit comfortably, keeping your back straight yet relaxed, and either close your eyes or soften your gaze. The journey begins by directing your attention to your breath, feeling its path as it flows in and out, without aiming to change it.

As you inhale and exhale, focus on the sensation of the air moving through your nostrils, or the gentle rise and fall of your chest or abdomen. Embrace each breath with open-hearted attention, letting go of judgments or distractions. Should your mind wander—and it likely will—kindly guide it back to the sensation of breathing. This moment-to-moment awareness is the heart of mindful breathing.

The impact of this practice on self-awareness is profound. It anchors us in the now, illuminating our physical sensations, thoughts, and emotions with the light of our full attention. This connection to the present moment helps us recognize and accept our feelings and bodily sensations with compassion and understanding.

Regarding emotional regulation, mindful breathing is a game-changer. Stressful moments often send our breath into shallow, hurried patterns. By consciously slowing our breath, we tap into the body's natural ability to relax, dialing down the volume on stress, anxiety, and irritation. This shift gives us the space to think clearly, decide from a place of calm, and choose our responses rather than being swept away by the tide of our emotions.

As we practice mindful breathing, we learn to observe our thoughts and feelings with detachment. This ability to see without getting entangled lets us experience our emotions without being defined by them, offering a clearer perspective and enabling us to face life's challenges with grace and wisdom.

Mindful breathing is not just a practice but a journey into the heart of our being, fostering a profound sense of self-awareness and emotional equilibrium. It teaches us to navigate our inner world with insight and compassion, transforming our relationship with ourselves and the world.

~

A GENTLE JOURNEY: THE ART OF BODY SCAN MEDITATION FOR MINDFUL AWARENESS

HERE'S A SIMPLE, step-by-step guide to practicing body scan meditation, a technique designed to enhance mindfulness by tuning into your body and the present moment:

1. **Find Your Peaceful Corner:** Choose a quiet spot where you can lie down or sit comfortably without interruptions. Ensure your posture is relaxed yet attentive.
2. **Ease Into Stillness:** Close your eyes, breathe deeply a few times, and allow yourself to arrive in this moment. Let any stress or tension melt away with each breath.
3. **Start with Your Feet:** Focus your attention on your feet. Observe sensations like warmth, coolness, or tingling. If your thoughts drift, kindly escort them back to the sensations in your feet.
4. **Legs and Upward Journey:** Move your awareness up to your legs. Notice any feeling or discomfort, letting your breath flow naturally, easing tension with each exhale.
5. **Explore Your Core:** Progressively scan through your pelvis, abdomen, torso, chest, and back. Be present with each

sensation, breathing into any tight spots and releasing them gently.

6. **Hands to Shoulders:** Shift focus to your hands, arms, and shoulders. Welcome any sensations here and use your breath to soften any areas of tightness or tension.

7. **Neck and Face:** Allow your neck to release any strain. Then, observe your face - the jaw, cheeks, eyes, forehead. Breathe into any tension, inviting relaxation.

8. **Crown of Awareness:** Bring your attention to the top of your head, embracing your body's full presence. Reflect on the sensation of unity and wholeness in your being.

9. **Return to Breath:** Gently refocus on your breathing. Feel the rise and fall of your chest or the air moving through your nostrils. Take deep, grounding breaths.

10. **Emerging Refreshed:** When you're ready, slowly open your eyes. Notice any shifts in your body or mind, carrying the calmness and awareness forward.

Remember, body scan meditation is a practice of patience and consistency. Starting with shorter durations and gradually extending your practice time can help you integrate this mindful exercise into your daily routine. Whether it's a brief 5-minute session or a longer dive into bodily awareness, each practice deepens your connection to the present and nurtures a serene mindfulness that benefits both body and mind.

～

MINDFUL MUNCHING: CULTIVATING AWARENESS AND EMOTIONAL BALANCE AT THE DINNER TABLE

MINDFUL EATING IS like putting a spotlight on the full experience of enjoying a meal. It's about being completely in the moment, noticing every bite, every flavor, and every sensation your food offers. But it's not just about enhancing the joy of eating; it's also about tuning into ourselves on a deeper level, understanding our body's cues, and navigating our emotions around food in a more conscious way.

When we talk about self-awareness when eating, we're looking into how well we understand our body's hunger signals, our satiety levels, and our unique emotional ties with food. Mindful eating throws us into this exploration, encouraging us to listen more closely to what our bodies are telling us.

This approach to eating can be a real game-changer. By focusing on our food—the taste, the aroma, the texture—we start to notice when we're hungry and when we've had enough. This attention can steer us away from eating just because we're bored, stressed, or because the clock says it's mealtime. We begin to eat in response to our body's actual needs.

Mindful eating also opens a window into our emotional connections with food. Let's be honest, food isn't just fuel; it's also comfort, celebration, and sometimes even a source of guilt. By eating mindfully, we give ourselves the chance to observe these feelings without getting caught up in them. Realizing why we eat the way we do can help us address our emotional needs in healthier ways, rather than automatically reaching for a snack every time we're anxious or down.

Consider someone who snacks when stressed. Through mindful eating, they might catch onto this pattern. Recognizing it's stress, not hunger driving their snacking, they can look for other ways to cope— maybe a quick walk, some deep breathing, or a few moments of meditation. This newfound awareness can gradually transform how they relate to food and emotions.

Mindful eating doesn't just help us get in touch with our hunger and emotions; it also reshapes our entire relationship with food. By savoring each mouthful, we find pleasure and satisfaction in the quality of our meals rather than the quantity. This can lead us to a more intuitive, balanced way of eating that's in harmony with our body's natural rhythms.

To sum it up, mindful eating is more than just a way to enjoy our food. It's a journey to self-awareness, a tool for emotional regulation, and a path to a healthier, more connected relationship with what we eat. It shows us that every meal is an opportunity to nourish not just our bodies, but our minds and souls too.

~

BRINGING MINDFULNESS INTO EVERY STEP AND WORD: WALKING AND LISTENING WITH AWARENESS

INCORPORATING mindfulness into our everyday lives need not be complicated. It's all about tapping into the present moment, whether we're on the move or lending an ear. Let's dive into two simple yet profound activities: mindful walking and mindful listening, which can significantly enhance our daily mindfulness practice.

Mindful Walking: Your Path to Presence

Mindful walking is a fantastic way to infuse mindfulness into your day, especially for those of us who find sitting still a challenge. It's about walking with awareness, feeling each step, noticing the sensation of your feet touching the ground, and being present with your surroundings. Here's how to get started:

Choose Your Path: It doesn't matter where you are; a hallway, a city street, or a park path can all be perfect settings.

Start with Intention: Before you begin, take a moment to acknowledge your intention to walk mindfully.

Focus on Your Feet: Pay attention to the feel of the ground beneath your feet. Notice the lift, the move, and placing each foot.

Engage Your Senses: Notice the sights, sounds, and smells around you. Feel the air on your skin. Each step is an opportunity to connect with the environment.

Embrace Slow Movement: There's no rush. Let your walking pace be slower than usual, letting you fully savor each step.

Return When Distracted: Your mind will wander, and that's okay. Gently bring your focus back to the sensations of walking whenever you notice you've drifted.

Mindful Listening: Connecting Deeply

Mindful listening opens the door to deeper connections and understanding in our conversations. It's about hearing the other person, beyond the words they're saying. Here's how you can practice mindful listening:

Be Fully Present: As the other person speaks, give them your undivided attention. Let go of the urge to think about your response while they're talking.

Observe Non-Verbal Cues: Pay attention to their body language, tone of voice, and facial expressions. Often, these non-verbal signals convey more than words.

Listen Without Judgment: Approach the conversation with openness and curiosity, rather than judgment or preconceived notions.

Reflect and Clarify: Show that you're listening by paraphrasing their words or asking clarifying questions.

Embrace Silence: Don't rush to fill pauses with words. Sometimes, silence can give both of you space to understand and process the conversation deeper.

Let Go of the Agenda: Enter the conversation without a fixed outcome in mind. Let the discussion flow naturally.

Whether you're mindfully pacing through a garden or intently listening to a friend's story, each moment is a chance to practice mindfulness. These practices aren't just exercises; they're pathways to a more present, connected, and fulfilling life. By walking and listening with awareness, we can cultivate a deeper sense of peace and under-standing in our daily lives.

∾

THE TRANSFORMATIVE POWER OF MINDFULNESS IN DAILY LIFE
BEV'S JOURNEY TO MINDFUL MASTERY

"I'VE BEEN on this mindfulness journey for a few good years now, and wow, the changes it's brought into my life are just incredible. Let me tell you, before mindfulness became a part of my every day, I was pretty much a leaf in the wind when it came to my thoughts and emotions. Negative spirals, impulsive reactions to stress—you name it, I was living it.

But then, mindfulness entered the scene. Sitting down to meditate, sinking into the now, and observing my thoughts and feelings without getting all judgmental about it—it's been a game-changer. It's like I've developed this superpower of noticing when I'm about to get hijacked by my emotions. Now, when those old triggers show up, instead of letting them run the show, I hit pause. I take that important breath and choose how I want to respond, not just react.

The coolest part? I've discovered this peace inside me I never knew I had. It's like being in the eye of the storm—things might swirl around me, but I can stay calm and centered. My emotions don't boss me around anymore; I see them, I hear them, but I get to decide what happens next.

Mindfulness hasn't just been about managing stress or keeping my cool; it's deepened my connections with others, too. Being present, listening, and responding from a place of understanding and compassion—it's changed the way I relate to everyone around me.

To anyone thinking about giving mindfulness a try, I say go for it. It's more than just practice; it's a pathway to finding your calm, getting to know the real you, and living life with a little more ease and a lot more heart." - Bev L.

Bev's story is a powerful testament to the transformative effects of mindfulness on self-awareness and emotional regulation. By embracing mindfulness, we too can navigate life's challenges with more grace and build stronger, more meaningful relationships.

Testimonial Two:

John's Transformation: Mastering Mindfulness Amidst the Hustle

"Let me share a bit of my story. Being knee-deep in the corporate world, I was no stranger to the constant buzz and high stakes. It was a cycle of stress and mental burnout that seemed never-ending. Emotional balance during crunch times? More like a distant dream. But then, I decided to give mindfulness a shot, and boy, did it turn things around for me.

Mindfulness, for me, has been like finding a secret passage out of the chaos. It's become this daily ritual where I tune in to what's happening inside my head and heart. Those little check-ins throughout the day? Game changers. They've helped dial down the stress and brought a sense of calm to the storm. Now, when those familiar waves of overwhelm or anxiety start creeping in, I can spot them early and steer myself back to calmer waters.

But it's not just about dodging stress. Mindfulness has opened up a whole new level of compassion and patience for me—toward others and toward myself. Diving into meditation and mindful breathing exercises has deepened my empathy and made me a kinder, more understanding person.

Wrapping it up, diving into mindfulness has been one of the best decisions of my professional life. It's not just about coping better; it's about living better. The shift in my self-awareness and emotional regulation has been profound. To anyone feeling the weight of their world, I can't recommend mindfulness enough. It's not just a practice; it's a transformation." - John M.

John's journey is a powerful reminder of how mindfulness can illuminate the path to personal growth and emotional balance, especially in the high-speed lanes of professional life.

~

THE PATH TO EQUILIBRIUM: EMBRACING MINDFULNESS FOR A FULFILLING LIFE

WRAPPING UP, it's clear that making mindfulness a regular part of our routine is like unlocking a door to a life filled with balance and serenity. This practice, centered on being in the here and now and embracing each moment without judgment, deepens our connection to ourselves and the vibrant world we're part of. With every mindful moment, we fine-tune our awareness of our inner thoughts, feelings, and bodily sensations, steering ourselves toward more deliberate and thoughtful responses to life's ups and downs.

What stands out about mindfulness is its power to pull us back into the present, away from the autopilot mode that often dominates our lives. In our busy, distraction-laden world, losing touch with our core selves is all too easy. Mindfulness acts as a grounding force, keeping us anchored amidst life's tumultuous waves.

A steady mindfulness habit enriches us, helping us to not just observe life's tapestry without judgment but to engage with it compassionately. This inner shift transforms how we interact with the world: we become more receptive to others, more compassionate, and present in every encounter. Our communication becomes more genuine, fostering deeper and more meaningful connections.

But the benefits of mindfulness go beyond personal and interpersonal enhancements. Studies underscore its positive impacts on reducing stress, anxiety, and depression while boosting focus, memory, and adaptability. It encourages us to recognize and adjust our habitual thoughts and actions, aligning them more closely with our deepest values and goals.

Perhaps the most profound gift of regular mindfulness practice is the inner peace and contentment it nurtures. Observing our mental and emotional landscapes with curiosity and detachment reveals that our inner wellbeing need not be at the mercy of external factors. We uncover a sanctuary within, a calm, accepting space that withstands life's storms.

In our fast-paced, achievement-oriented society, mindfulness invites us to pause, breathe, and connect with the essence of life. It encourages us to cherish each moment, find joy in the simple things, and live with intention and meaning. Committing to mindfulness paves the way for a life that's not just balanced and peaceful but also richly rewarding for ourselves and everyone we touch.

～

PART NINE WRAP-UP:

- **Mindfulness and Emotional Intelligence:** Defined as the practices of being present and understanding one's emotions and those of others. Essential for personal growth and success.
- **Self-Awareness and Emotional Regulation:** Both practices enhance self-awareness and help regulate emotions, leading to better decision-making and interpersonal relationships.
- **Interconnectedness:** Mindfulness and emotional intelligence support and enhance each other, contributing to improved wellbeing and interpersonal skills.
- **Benefits in Daily Life:** Incorporating these practices leads to reduced stress, improved focus, better relationships, and physical health benefits.
- **Impact on Relationships and Communication:** They foster empathy, effective communication, and conflict resolution.
- **Decision-Making and Problem-Solving:** Mindfulness and emotional intelligence contribute to clearer, more balanced decision-making and creative problem-solving.

- **Cultivation Strategies:** Includes mindful awareness, active listening, self-reflection, and managing stress mindfully.

Action Items:

- **Practice Mindful Awareness:** Dedicate time each day for mindfulness practices like meditation or mindful walking to enhance self-awareness.
- **Engage in Active Listening:** Focus on the speaker during conversations to improve understanding and empathy.
- **Reflect Regularly:** Use journaling or quiet reflection to deepen self-knowledge and recognize emotional patterns.
- **Incorporate Mindful Eating:** Pay attention to the experience of eating to improve your relationship with food and regulate emotions related to eating.
- **Develop Empathy:** Make an effort to understand others' perspectives and feelings to strengthen relationships and emotional intelligence.
- **Manage Stress Mindfully:** Utilize mindfulness techniques to deal with stress in a healthy way, promoting emotional regulation.
- **Practice Non-Judgment:** Approach your thoughts and emotions with a non-judgmental attitude to foster acceptance and reduce bias.
- **Foster Gratitude:** Cultivate a daily gratitude practice to enhance mindfulness and emotional intelligence, leading to a more positive outlook.
- **Seek Feedback:** Openly ask for and accept feedback from others to identify areas for growth and improve emotional intelligence.
- **Engage in Mindful Communication:** Communicate thoughtfully and intentionally, paying attention to your words, tone, and body language to improve relationships and understanding.

By focusing on these key points and action items, individuals can harness the transformative power of mindfulness and emotional intelligence, leading to enhanced personal growth, better relationships, and greater success in various parts of life.

In Our Next Part...

As we venture further, we're about to tap into the profound impact mindfulness and emotional intelligence have across all facets of our lives. This journey is more than just hitting milestones; it's about choosing goals that echo our core values and desires. We'll dive into how mindfulness not only sharpens our focus but also aids us in navigating through distractions and maintaining our cool in challenging times. This exploration is not only about the path we tread or the goals we reach; it's about savoring each step, learning from every moment, and crafting our lives with deliberate intent.

Gear up to uncover actionable strategies that promise not only to enhance your efficiency in both personal and professional realms but also to enrich your life with a deeper sense of satisfaction and joy. From journaling to unravel your thoughts, fostering empathy to connect on a deeper level with others, to mastering resilience in the face of adversity, we're here to steer you through. Embark with us as we reveal how to lead a life marked by intentionality, connection, and joy. This is your moment to reshape not only the way you pursue your goals but how you set them, starting a mindful journey toward a life that's not just lived but richly experienced.

~

PART TEN
NAVIGATING LIFE WITH MINDFULNESS AND EMOTIONAL INTELLIGENCE

EMBRACING EMOTIONAL INTELLIGENCE: THE KEY TO THRIVING PERSONALLY AND PROFESSIONALLY

EMOTIONAL INTELLIGENCE, or EI, is essentially our knack for recognizing, understanding, and managing not just our own emotions, but those of people around us too. It's about being clued into feelings —our own and others'—and using this awareness to guide our thoughts and actions smoothly. EI comprises a few core skills: knowing what we're feeling (self-awareness), managing those feelings (self-regulation), understanding others' feelings (empathy), and being awesome at communicating and getting along with folks (social skills).

Lately, EI has been spotlighted as a big deal for doing well in life and at work. It's not just about being smart in the bookish sense; it's about being smart with feelings. Getting a handle on emotions can make a huge difference in making smart choices, solving problems without freaking out, and being effective when dealing with people.

On the personal front, EI is like the secret sauce for building solid relationships. Being self-aware helps us catch our own emotional waves before they crash, making us more chill and capable of dealing with stress. Empathy lets us get where others are coming from, paving the way for smoother interactions and fewer arguments. And those social skills? They're all about communicating well, making friends, and working well with others.

At work, EI is golden. Bosses who get EI are usually the ones everyone likes working for. They know how to motivate their team, keep the peace, and steer the ship through stormy weather without losing their cool. These are the leaders who make workplaces more like a "we're in this together" kind of place, which can lead to everyone doing their best work, being creative, and actually liking their jobs.

Teams that gel well together often have a good dose of EI running through them. It makes the office a nicer place to be, where people feel heard, respected, and valued. This vibe leads to better teamwork, more out-of-the-box thinking, and employees who feel good about where they work.

The cool thing about EI is that it's not set in stone. Anyone can improve at it with some introspection, effort, and learning from life's ups and downs. Working on EI is an ongoing journey, but the payoff—in deeper connections, smoother sailing through life's challenges, and genuine success—is huge.

~

NAVIGATING EMOTIONAL INTELLIGENCE: UNDERSTANDING ITS CORE PILLARS

EMOTIONAL INTELLIGENCE, or EI, is like having a roadmap for navigating the complex world of emotions—ours and those of the people around us. It's about tuning into feelings with clarity and grace, and it's built on four pillars: Self-Awareness, Self-Management, Social Awareness, and Relationship Management. Let's break these down:

1. **Self-Awareness**: This is all about getting to know your emotional landscape. It's like being an emotion detective for yourself, figuring out what you're feeling, why you're feeling it, and how these emotions are messing with your thoughts and actions. Self-aware folks can incredibly pinpoint their emotions and understand the influence these feelings have on the world around them.
2. **Self-Management**: If self-awareness is about recognizing your emotions, self-management is about being the boss of them. It's having the reins in your hands and deciding how you react to different situations. Whether it's cooling down when you're angry or not jumping the gun under stress, about making choices align with your values, not just your immediate feelings.

3. **Social Awareness**: Imagine having a superpower that lets you tune into the feelings and moods of everyone in the room. That's social awareness. It's about picking up on those subtle cues that tell you what someone else is going through, understanding their viewpoint, and empathizing with their situation. It's a game-changer for connecting with people on a deeper level.

4. **Relationship Management**: The final piece of the EI puzzle is about how you use your understanding of emotions to play well with others. It's using everything you've learned from the first three parts to communicate effectively, resolve conflicts smoothly, and strengthen your bonds with others. It's about being a positive force in your relationships, whether at work or in your personal life.

These four parts of Emotional Intelligence are your toolkit for dealing with the emotional parts of life wisely and effectively. By mastering these areas, you can improve your interactions, make smarter decisions, and build a life rich in meaningful connections and personal fulfillment.

~

THE POWER OF EMOTIONAL AWARENESS: SHAPING BEHAVIOR AND BUILDING CONNECTIONS

GRASPING the essence of our emotions and recognizing their profound influence on our actions is a cornerstone for not just surviving but thriving. This deep dive into our emotional world, often dubbed emotional intelligence, is more than just a fancy term—it's an important skill for navigating the ups and downs of life with grace and insight.

Why It Matters: First off, getting to grips with our emotions is like having a roadmap for our behavior. Ever noticed how a bad mood can lead to a day where everything seems to go wrong? That's emotions steering the ship. By identifying and understanding these feelings, we can choose responses more in tune with how we genuinely want to act, rather than letting fleeting emotions call the shots. It's about catching ourselves before we snap in anger or retreat in fear, and instead, finding constructive ways to express what we're feeling.

Know Thyself: Beyond keeping our impulses in check, recognizing our emotions clues us in on what matters to us. It shines a light on our core values and motivations, guiding our decisions and propelling us toward goals that genuinely resonate with us. When we understand what fires us up or brings us down, we can pursue paths that fulfill us, leading to a more authentic and satisfying life.

Walking in Someone Else's Shoes: This emotional savvy doesn't just benefit us; it enhances our interactions with others, too. By tuning into our own emotions, we become better equipped to read and respond to those around us. Whether it's offering a shoulder to lean on or navigating a tricky conversation, understanding emotions can bridge gaps and forge stronger connections.

A Foundation for Wellbeing: Lastly, being in touch with our emotions is a form of self-care. Our emotions often signal our needs—whether it's time to step back and rest or to seek help. By listening to these emotional cues, we can try to maintain our mental health, whether that means indulging in activities that bring us joy, reaching out for support, or simply taking a moment to breathe and be present.

Delving into the world of emotions and their impact on our behavior isn't just beneficial—it's essential for leading a balanced, connected, and fulfilling life. It's about making conscious choices, fostering empathy, and caring for our mental wellbeing. As we grow in emotional intelligence, we not only navigate life's challenges more effectively but also enrich our relationships and enhance our personal growth. Let's embrace this journey of emotional discovery, one mindful step at a time.

~

ENHANCING SELF-AWARENESS: A GUIDE TO UNDERSTANDING YOURSELF BETTER

BOOSTING self-awareness is like turning the lights on in a dimly lit room—it helps you see who you are, where you're going, and what changes you might want to make along the way. Let's dive into some hands-on strategies for shining a light on your inner self.

Daily Journaling: Think of journaling as having a chat with yourself. Carve out a little time each day to jot down what's been happening, how you feel about it, and recurring thoughts that pop up. This isn't just about recording events—it's about reflecting on your reactions to them, which can reveal a lot about your personal values and areas for growth.

Self-Reflection Exercises: Grab a cup of tea and settle in for some self-discovery. Pose yourself thought-provoking questions: "What lights me up inside?", "What lessons have my mistakes taught me?", or "How do I react under stress?" Writing down your answers can lead to surprising insights about your true self.

Mindfulness Practices: Mindfulness is about being here, now engaged with whatever you're doing. Try spending a few minutes each day in meditation, focusing only on your breath and the sensations in your body, or perhaps take a mindful walk, noticing the sights, sounds, and smells around you. This practice can help you learn your thoughts and feelings in the moment.

Feedback Loops: Sometimes, we're too close to ourselves to see the picture clearly. Contact people you trust—friends, family, mentors—and ask them for their honest feedback about you. It can be tough to hear sometimes, but it's golden for uncovering blind spots and getting to know yourself from another perspective.

Emotional Intelligence Tools: Consider taking a formal assessment to gauge your emotional intelligence. These tools can offer a structured way to look at how you understand and manage emotions (yours and others') and point out specific areas where you can grow.

Regular Self-Check-ins: Make it a habit to sometimes pause and ask yourself, "How am I feeling right now?" This simple act can help you become more in tune with your emotional state and better equipped to handle whatever life throws your way.

Explore Personal Development Resources: There's a wealth of knowledge out there in books, podcasts, and workshops focused on self-awareness and personal growth. Diving into these can introduce new techniques and perspectives to help you understand yourself better.

Cultivating self-awareness is a journey, not a destination. It requires patience, curiosity, and a willingness to look within. By integrating these practices into your daily life, you're setting the stage for a deeper connection with yourself and, ultimately, a more fulfilling life.

～

NAVIGATING EMOTIONS AND IMPULSES: PRACTICAL STRATEGIES FOR EMOTIONAL MASTERY

MASTERING our emotions and impulses is key to living a balanced life and making wise decisions. Here's a rundown of strategies that can help us steer through our emotional waves and impulsive urges with grace:

Boost Self-Awareness: Tune into your feelings and actions. Notice what sets off your emotional responses or impulsive acts. Keeping a journal or a mood diary can shine a light on patterns and triggers, offering clues on what might need attention.

Embrace Mindfulness: Practice grounding techniques like deep breathing, meditation, or body scans. These mindfulness exercises help you pause and choose your reactions, rather than letting automatic responses take the wheel.

Challenge Negative Thoughts: Learn to spot and question unhelpful or exaggerated thoughts that fuel emotional intensity or impulsive actions. Swap out those thoughts for more balanced and constructive ones. Techniques from cognitive behavioral therapy (CBT) can be

useful here.

Get Moving: Regular exercise isn't just good for your body—it's a mood lifter and stress reducer that can help smooth out emotional spikes and tame impulses. Whether it's a brisk walk, a swim, or a yoga session, find an activity that gets you moving and stick with it.

Find Your Coping Toolbox: Identify activities that help you deal with stress and emotions constructively. This could be anything from diving into a hobby, chatting with a friend, losing yourself in music, or trying relaxation techniques. These are your go-to actions when you need to channel emotions or resist impulsive urges.

Lean on Your Support Circle: Surround yourself with people who get you. Having a network of supportive friends or family members to turn to can offer new perspectives, comfort, and guidance when emotions run high.

Cultivate Empathy and Patience: Understanding others' viewpoints can help in managing your own emotional responses. Techniques like taking deep breaths or counting to ten can give you the pause needed to respond thoughtfully in heated moments.

Seek Professional Insights: If you find your emotions or impulses regularly challenging to manage, it might be time to talk to a therapist or counselor. They can offer tailored advice, teach coping strategies, and help you work through underlying issues.

Focus on Self-Care: Don't underestimate the power of a good night's sleep, a nutritious diet, and effective stress management. When you're physically well-taken-care-of, handling emotions and impulses becomes more manageable.

Remember, taming our emotions and impulses is an ongoing journey that demands patience and practice. Treat yourself with kindness, celebrate the progress, and view any setbacks as opportunities to learn and grow.

∿

MASTERING LIFE SKILLS: GOAL SETTING, STRESS BUSTING, AND CULTIVATING GROWTH

CRAFTING AND CONQUERING GOALS:

- **Get Specific**: Kick things off by defining clear and attainable goals. Break those big dreams down into bite-sized tasks you can tackle without feeling overwhelmed.
- **Pen It Down**: Writing your goals can act like a compass, guiding you through the fog. Keep them somewhere visible to keep the fire of motivation burning.
- **Organize and Prioritize**: Lay out your goals with a plan of action. Setting deadlines and assessing what needs your immediate attention can keep you on track.
- **Celebrate Your Wins**: No victory is too small. Celebrating your progress keeps the journey exciting and fuels your drive to push further.
- **Stay Flexible**: Life throws curveballs, and your goals might need adjusting. Regularly revisit and tweak your goals to keep them in line with your evolving priorities.

Navigating Through Stress:

- **Know Your Nemesis**: Understanding what stresses you out is half the battle. Once you know, you can strategize your counterattack.
- **Time Management Mastery**: Sorting out your priorities and deadlines can declutter your mind and schedule, giving stress less room to breathe.
- **Healthy Habits**: Whether it's hitting the gym, meditating, or diving into your favorite book, find what calms your storm and make it a staple in your routine.
- **Self-Care Rituals**: Don't skimp on sleep, eat well, and cherish your connections. Nurturing your body and soul is your shield against stress.
- **Reach Out**: When the going gets tough, remember you're not alone. Talking things through with someone can shine a light on solutions you might not have seen.

Fostering a Growth Mindset:

- **Challenge Equals Opportunity**: Instead of dodging challenges, see them as your ladder to climb higher. Every stumble is a lesson in disguise.
- **Stay Positive**: Keep your eyes on the prize of learning and growing, not just on winning the race.
- **Feedback is Your Friend**: Openly seek and embrace feedback. It's the roadmap showing where you can grow and shine even brighter.
- **Choose Your Circle Wisely**: Surround yourself with cheerleaders and mentors who push you toward your best self.
- **Never Stop Learning**: Be a lifelong learner. New skills, experiences, and viewpoints keep your growth mindset thriving.

These aren't just strategies; they're steps toward a richer, more fulfilling life. Embedding them into your daily grind can transform the ordinary into extraordinary, turning challenges into victories, stress into peace, and aspirations into achievements.

EMPATHY: THE HEART OF CONNECTION AND UNDERSTANDING

EMPATHY ISN'T JUST about feeling for others; it's about stepping into their shoes, seeing the world through their eyes, and connecting with their emotional experiences. It's a superpower in our social toolkit, enhancing our relationships, supporting mental wellbeing, and knitting the fabric of a compassionate society.

- **Deepening Connections**: Empathy is the cornerstone of any strong relationship. It's about more than just understanding what someone is going through; it's about feeling with them, creating a bridge of trust and mutual respect. When we're empathetic, we're not just listening; we're connecting on a deeper level, making our friends and loved ones feel seen, heard, and valued.
- **Bolstering Mental Wellbeing**: Being there for someone in their hour of need doesn't just help them; it enriches us, too. Empathy lets us offer the support and encouragement that can be a lifeline during tough times. It's a two-way street that not only helps others feel less alone but also enhances our own emotional resilience.

- **Creating Inclusive Communities**: In our diverse world, empathy is key to building inclusive, understanding communities. It encourages us to look beyond our own experiences and appreciate the rich tapestry of human emotions and backgrounds. This understanding can dissolve barriers, challenge stereotypes, and foster a sense of belonging and unity.
- **Driving Social Change**: When we understand the struggles of others, we're moved to act. Empathy can be a powerful force for social justice, pushing us to stand up against inequality and advocate for a fairer world. It's about recognizing injustice, feeling compelled by others' experiences, and using our voices and actions to make a difference.

Empathy isn't just nice to have; it's essential for creating meaningful relationships, supporting each other's wellbeing, and building a kinder, more inclusive world. It's about seeing the humanity in each other and responding with compassion and understanding. By nurturing empathy, we open our hearts and minds to the richness of human experience, paving the way for deeper connections, stronger communities, and positive change. Let's embrace empathy as a guiding principle in our interactions, one conversation, and one act of understanding at a time.

∼

ELEVATING SOCIAL AWARENESS: KEY STRATEGIES FOR DEEPER CONNECTIONS

BOOSTING social awareness isn't just about improving at small talk; it's about genuinely connecting with others, understanding them better, and building relationships that are both meaningful and rewarding. Here are hands-on strategies to enhance your social awareness:

- **Active Listening**: Dive into conversations with your full attention. Turn off your mental autopilot and listen—this means no planning what you'll say next while the other person is talking. Show you're engaged with nods, rephrase what they've said for clarity, and ask questions that show you're genuinely interested.
- **Reading Non-Verbal Signals**: A lot of communication is non-verbal. Keep an eye out for body language, facial expressions, and other subtle cues. They can tell you how someone is feeling, sometimes even more than their words. Remember, your own non-verbal cues are speaking for you too, so be mindful of what you're silently saying.
- **Walking in Their Shoes**: Try to see the world from others' perspectives. This isn't about agreeing with them but

understanding where they're coming from. It's a powerful way to build empathy and can change the way you interact with people.

- **Staying Present**: Sharpen your focus on the here and now. Mindfulness practices can help quiet the noise in your mind, making it easier to pick up on the subtleties of social interactions and be there with others.
- **Being Culturally Attuned**: Every culture has its own set of unwritten rules. Paying attention to these can help you navigate social interactions more smoothly and show respect for others' backgrounds. Embrace diversity and let it enrich your social awareness.
- **Asking Insightful Questions**: Encourage others to open up by asking questions that make them think and share more about their feelings and experiences. It's a great way to deepen conversations and connections.
- **Welcoming Feedback**: Ask people you trust for their opinions about your social skills. It can be eye-opening to learn how you come across to others and where there's room for improvement.
- **Boosting Emotional Intelligence**: Work on understanding and managing your own emotions. This self-awareness will help you better relate to others' feelings, leading to more empathetic and sensitive interactions.
- **Practicing Empathy**: Go beyond imagining how others feel; show them you get it. Confirm their feelings with supportive comments, letting them know they're not alone and that their feelings are understood.
- **Committing to Continuous Learning**: Social awareness is a lifelong journey. Keep exploring, learning, and growing. Books, workshops, and open discussions can all contribute to your understanding of the complex tapestry of human interactions.

By weaving these strategies into your daily life, you'll not only enrich your own experiences but also bring more depth and understanding to your interactions with others. Social awareness is a skill that benefits everyone involved, opening doors to richer, more connected relationships.

~

MASTERING INTERPERSONAL DYNAMICS: THE KEYS TO EFFECTIVE COMMUNICATION, RESOLVING CONFLICTS, AND NURTURING RELATIONSHIPS

NAVIGATING the intricate world of human interaction hinges on three core skills: effective communication, adept conflict resolution, and the art of forging strong connections. These skills aren't just nice-to-haves; they're essential tools that shape our personal and professional lives, turning everyday interactions into opportunities for growth and connection.

Unlocking Effective Communication: At the heart of every meaningful interaction lies effective communication. It's more than just swapping information; it's about ensuring your message lands as intended, with empathy and clarity steering the conversation. By honing your listening skills, ensuring your messages are clear, and approaching exchanges with empathy, you set the stage for mutual understanding. Whether it's sharing your deepest thoughts with a loved one or collaborating with colleagues, mastering communication lays the groundwork for trust and respect.

Navigating Conflict with Grace: Let's face it, conflict is a given in any relationship, but resolution counts. Skills like listening actively, embracing empathy, and seeking win-win solutions transform potential fallouts into moments of understanding and growth. These moments aren't just about finding peace; they're about valuing diverse viewpoints and forging deeper bonds. By tackling conflicts head-on with a cool head and a warm heart, you're not just putting out fires; you're building bridges.

Cultivating Strong Bonds: The relationships we nurture are the backbone of both personal fulfillment and professional success. Built on the pillars of trust, respect, and, you guessed it, effective communication, these bonds offer a support system through life's highs and lows. In our personal lives, these connections bring joy, support, and a sense of belonging. Professionally, they pave the way for teamwork, collaboration, and a positive work culture. Investing in these relationships means investing in a network that inspires, supports, and grows with you.

Mastering the art of communication, navigating conflicts with understanding, and nurturing strong relationships are more than interpersonal skills—they're life skills. They enrich our interactions, deepen our connections, and enhance our overall quality of life. As we journey through the complexities of human relationships, let's embrace these skills not just as strategies for success, but as pathways to a more connected, empathetic, and fulfilling life.

~

NURTURING STRONG BONDS: TECHNIQUES FOR EFFECTIVE RELATIONSHIP MANAGEMENT

FOSTERING SOLID RELATIONSHIPS, whether in the workplace or personal life, is an art that revolves around thoughtful communication and genuine appreciation. Here's how you can polish your relationship management skills with a few straightforward strategies:

Embrace Assertive Communication: Speaking up for yourself while respecting others is key. Assertive communication is about being clear and direct with your needs and thoughts, without stepping on anyone's toes. Use "I" statements to express yourself, listen actively to understand others, and approach conversations with an open mind. This ensures everyone's on the same page and misunderstandings are kept at bay.

Show Genuine Appreciation: A little thank-you goes a long way. Recognize the efforts and achievements of those around you — a heartfelt compliment, a written note, or even a small gesture can make people feel valued. Regularly acknowledging the contributions of others not only strengthens bonds but also creates a positive ripple effect in your environment.

Cultivate a Positive Atmosphere: The vibe you foster around you matters. Aim to build a collaborative and respectful space where trust and support are the norms. Celebrate successes together, promote a healthy work-life balance, and ensure everyone feels included and valued. A positive environment is fertile ground for strong relationships.

Practice Active Listening: Really hearing someone is a powerful way to connect. Give your full attention, maintain eye contact, and resist the urge to interrupt. Encouraging open communication and showing you value others' input can deepen trust and understanding in any relationship.

Leverage Emotional Intelligence: Being in tune with your own emotions and sensitive to others' can transform your interactions. Work on recognizing and managing your feelings to navigate social situations more adeptly. Empathy and emotional savvy can help you tailor your responses and actions to suit the moment, smoothing out potential wrinkles before they become issues.

Resolve Conflicts with Care: Disagreements are natural but resolving them effectively can actually strengthen your connections. Approach conflicts with a mindset geared toward finding solutions that work for everyone involved. Listen to understand, not to counter-argue, and aim for outcomes that respect everyone's needs and perspectives.

Engage in Regular Check-ins: Making time for one-on-one conversations shows you care. Use these opportunities to touch base, share feedback, and discuss any concerns. This not only helps keep relationships strong but also signals your investment in their growth and wellbeing.

Mastering the art of relationship management isn't an overnight feat — it requires patience, effort, and a genuine desire to connect with others. By integrating these strategies into your daily routine, you'll be well on your way to building more meaningful and enduring relationships.

UNLOCKING SELF-INSIGHT: THE TRANSFORMATIVE POWER OF JOURNALING

JOURNALING IS MORE than just a method to document your day—it's a transformative practice that opens doors to deeper self-understanding, emotional mastery, and richer relationships. Let's dive into how keeping a journal can be a game-changer in these areas:

Enhancing Self-Awareness: Diving into a journal lets you traverse the depths of your thoughts and emotions. It's like conversing with yourself, where you start to notice patterns, uncover underlying beliefs, and clarify what motivates you. This journey of self-discovery sharpens your ability to navigate life's choices with greater confidence and understanding.

Boosting Self-Management: Journaling is your personal lab for experimenting with ways to handle life's curveballs. It offers you a playground to reflect on what sets off certain emotions and brainstorm strategies for a more composed response. It's also a haven for goal setting, helping you carve out your path with intention and discipline.

Elevating Relationship Management: Your journal can act as a mirror reflecting your interaction styles and emotional responses in relationships. By examining your entries, you can identify any recurring themes that may affect your connections and work on refining your approach. Plus, it aids in untangling your thoughts and feelings, paving the way for clearer and more empathetic communication with those around you.

Providing Emotional Release and Stress Relief: Pouring your heart out on paper can be cathartic. It's a judgment-free zone where you can let go of all your burdens, worries, and fears, leading to significant stress relief and a more balanced emotional state.

Enhancing Problem-Solving and Decision-Making: Journaling lays out a canvas for you to sketch out problems, ponder over them, and explore various solutions. It helps you break down complex decisions into manageable bits, weigh your options with clarity, and align your choices with your core values.

Journaling is an invaluable practice that enriches your understanding of yourself, fine-tunes your emotional responses, and deepens your connections with others. By committing to this reflective exercise, you start a path of continuous growth, emotional resilience, and enhanced interpersonal dynamics. So, why not grab a journal and start this insightful journey today?

$$\sim$$

HARNESSING JOURNALING FOR EMOTIONAL GROWTH

JOURNALING ISN'T JUST about documenting your day; it's a voyage into the heart of your emotional world. It offers a reflective sanctuary to dissect your feelings, understand your interactions, and refine your emotional intelligence (EI). Here's how to wield this powerful tool to foster your EI:

Kickstart With Introspection:

- Dive into how you navigate your emotional landscape. Notice any recurring patterns?
- Pinpoint your EI strengths and spotlight areas ripe for growth.
- Think back on recent emotionally charged moments. How did you react? Is there room for improvement?

Deep Dive Into Your Feelings:

- Zone in on what you're feeling right here, right now. How do these emotions manifest physically and mentally?
- Trace the origins of your emotions. Are they tied to a specific event or a deeper history?

- Tackle the tough-to-name feelings. Can you describe them through metaphors or imagery?

Empathy & Perspective-Shifting Exercises:

- Recall a memorable emotional exchange. Step into their shoes —how might they have felt?
- Envision being in another's predicament, especially in tough scenarios. Jot down your hypothetical emotional response. This flexes your empathy muscles.

Confront Cognitive Distortions & Flip Negative Narratives:

- Identify any repetitive, harsh self-criticisms. Are they accurate? Challenge their validity.
- Transform negative self-talk into positive affirmations. What alternative, more positive angles can you explore?

Cultivate Gratitude & Celebrate Positivity:

- Reflect on the aspects and people in your life that spark gratitude. How do these gratitude moments influence your emotional state?
- Celebrate your personal strengths and the strides you've made in EI. Recognizing your progress fuels further growth.

By integrating these exercises into your journaling routine, you're not just writing; you're starting a journey of emotional enlightenment. Through introspection, empathy, and positive reflection, journaling becomes a cornerstone for developing a strong emotional intelligence that enriches both your personal and professional life. So, grab that journal and let the exploration begin!

~

CRAFTING YOUR EMOTIONAL INTELLIGENCE JOURNEY:

FOCUSING on honing particular parts of emotional intelligence (EI) can lead to profound personal and professional growth. Whether it's enhancing your self-awareness, boosting your empathy, mastering self-regulation, or polishing your social skills, here's how you can set actionable steps toward meeting these goals:

For Self-Awareness:

- **Mindfulness Moments**: Carve out time daily for mindfulness. Sit quietly, letting your thoughts and feelings flow without judgment, anchoring yourself in the present.
- **Journal Your Journey**: Make it a habit to jot down your daily experiences, emotions, and reflections. This practice deepens your self-understanding.
- **Feedback Loop**: Reach out to friends or coworkers you trust for candid feedback on your interactions and behaviors.

For Empathy:

- **Master Active Listening**: Practice giving your full attention in conversations, showing genuine interest, and asking questions to understand better.

- **Empathetic Imagining**: Before reacting, consider the other person's perspective and feelings. This helps in crafting a more empathetic response.
- **Community Engagement**: Participate in volunteer work or community service to expose yourself to diverse perspectives and nurture your empathy.

For Self-Regulation:

- **Emotion Tracking**: Stay alert to your emotional states and learn to accurately identify them. Recognizing negative emotions is the first step to managing them thoughtfully.
- **Stress-Busting Activities**: Incorporate stress-reducing practices like physical workouts, meditation, or breathing exercises into your daily routine.
- **Boundary Setting**: Clearly define your limits in both personal and work life to avoid emotional overdrive and plan for handling tough situations.

For Social Skills:

- **Enhanced Communication**: Work on expressing yourself clearly and with confidence while also engaging in active listening during conversations.
- **Conflict Management**: Arm yourself with strategies for constructive conflict resolution, focusing on mutual respect and finding solutions that everyone can agree on.
- **Expand Your Circle**: Take advantage of opportunities to meet new people and build networks, whether through professional events, group activities, or community service.

Emotional intelligence is not something you master overnight. It's a continuous process filled with learning and growth. Celebrate your progress, no matter how small, and stay committed to your journey.

ENHANCING EMPATHY AND SOCIAL CONSCIOUSNESS THROUGH INTERACTIVE ACTIVITIES

EMPATHY and social awareness are key to fostering understanding, compassion, and positive relationships in our diverse world. Here's how various activities and exercises can help nurture these essential qualities:

Role-Playing for Perspective: Dive into role-playing activities where you step into the shoes of someone from a different walk of life. This could be through acting out scenarios in pairs or groups, taking on roles that challenge your views or experiences. It's a hands-on way to grasp the complexities of others' lives and broaden your empathy.

The Power of Personal Stories: Organize or participate where people share their unique stories and experiences. Whether it's a community circle, workshop, or casual group chat, listening to others opens up new worlds of understanding and connection.

Cultural Deep Dive: Immerse yourself in cultures different from your own. This could mean visiting cultural museums, attending diverse cultural events, or simply engaging with communities different from yours. It's about appreciating the rich tapestry of human life and understanding the varied experiences that shape us.

Giving Back Through Community Service: Volunteering not only makes a real difference but also puts you in direct contact with diverse individuals and their stories. It's a practical way to build empathy and a deeper sense of community.

Walking in Others' Shoes: Engage in exercises designed to encourage perspective-taking. This could be as simple as journaling from another's viewpoint or participating in simulations that highlight different life experiences. Such activities challenge you to think beyond your own life and consider the wider human experience.

Diversity and Inclusion Education: Attend or organize workshops that dig into topics like unconscious bias, privilege, and social inequalities. Understanding these complex issues is the first step toward becoming more socially aware and active in fostering inclusivity.

Mastering Active Listening: Practice listening to others, not just hearing them. Through exercises focused on deep listening, you learn to absorb what others are saying, reflecting on their words, and responding with thoughtfulness and care.

By incorporating these practices into your life or community, you're not just learning about empathy and social awareness; you're living it. These activities encourage a lifelong journey of growth, understanding, and connection, helping build a more empathetic and socially conscious world.

∽

INTEGRATING MINDFULNESS INTO EVERYDAY LIFE: A GUIDE

MINDFULNESS ACTIVITIES CAN BE A GAME-CHANGER, not just for your personal wellbeing but also in the professional realm. They're like a Swiss Army knife for the mind, offering a wide range of benefits: think stress relief, sharper focus, better mood, stronger relationships, and a healthier body and mind. Let's dive into some of these transformative activities and break down how you can weave them into your day-to-day life.

1. The Art of Breathing Exercises

- **What's in It for You**: These exercises aren't just a breather from the hustle and bustle; they're your ticket to relaxation central. They help simmer down stress, tune up your emotion regulation, and sharpen your focus.
- **How to Do It**:
- Scout out a quiet spot where you can sit back or lie down without distractions.
- Let your eyes fall shut gently, and take a couple of casual breaths to ease into the moment.
- Inhale slowly through your nose, feeling your belly rise, and fill those lungs up with good old air.

- Exhale with ease through your mouth, staying mindful of the sensation of the breath waving goodbye.
- Keep this up for 5-10 minutes, guiding your focus back to your breathing if your mind goes on a wanderlust adventure.

2. Mindful Walking: Taking Steps with Awareness

- **What's in It for You**: Beyond the physical perks, mindful walking dials down stress and might just spark your next big idea.
- **How to Do It**:
- Pick a peaceful spot outdoors or a quiet room indoors.
- Start your walk, tuning into your body's symphony of movements.
- Feel the rhythm of your feet kissing the ground, and let the sensations of movement and the environment envelop you.
- Embrace the present, letting thoughts float by like clouds without latching onto them.

3. Gratitude Journaling: Counting Your Blessings

- **What's in It for You**: A daily dose of gratitude can boost your spirits and contribute to a healthier you.
- **How to Do It**:
- Carve out a moment each day for this practice, maybe during your morning coffee or as a bedtime ritual.
- Settle into a comfy, quiet corner.
- Jot down three things that spark gratitude in your heart— anything from a kind gesture from a friend to a personal achievement or a simple pleasure.
- Dig into why these things matter to you and the positive vibes they bring into your life.
- Aim to make this a daily habit, taking those few precious minutes to reflect and appreciate.

Wrapping It Up: Breathing exercises, mindful walking, and gratitude journaling are the tip of the mindfulness iceberg, but they're a solid start. They promise a bounty of benefits, from calming the storms of stress to enhancing your overall quality of life. By incorporating these practices into your routine, you're setting the stage for a more focused, content, and mindful existence.

~

MINDFULNESS: THE SECRET INGREDIENT IN EFFECTIVE GOAL SETTING

MINDFULNESS, often visualized as the art of being immersed in the present moment, is more than just a meditation buzzword; it's a powerful ally in the realm of goal setting. Traditionally linked to spiritual practices, mindfulness has woven its way into various facets of daily life, shining bright in the sphere of setting and achieving goals.

Goal setting is our roadmap for personal and professional advancement, a way to pinpoint our ambitions, chart a course, and steadily trek toward our targets. Yet, the path isn't always clear—distractions, doubts, and a scattered focus can cloud our journey. This is where mindfulness steps in, offering clarity and a laser-sharp focus that can transform the goal setting process. Here's how mindfulness can be a game-changer in setting and meeting your goals:

A Deep Dive into Self-Awareness: Mindfulness invites us to become observers of our own minds, to notice our thoughts, feelings, and actions without judgment. This introspective practice uncovers our core—our strengths, vulnerabilities, values, and true desires. It lets us set goals that genuinely resonate with us, sidestepping the noise of societal expectations. It shines a light on potential roadblocks specific to our journey, enabling us to strategize effectively around them.

Sharpening Your Focus: In today's whirlwind of distractions, keeping our eyes on the prize is tougher than ever. Mindfulness hones our ability to concentrate on the here and now, reducing the pull of external distractions and internal monologues. This improved focus channels our energy into actions that directly contribute to our goals, reducing procrastination and detours.

Mastering Emotional Regulation: The road to goal achievement is rarely without bumps. Mindfulness equips us with the tools for emotional steadiness, letting us acknowledge and navigate our feelings without getting swamped. This emotional agility fosters resilience and a can-do attitude in the face of setbacks, keeping discouragement at bay.

The Power of Mindful Action: Mindfulness extends beyond self-reflection to infuse presence into our actions. This means each step we take toward our goal is deliberate and aligned with our overarching aim. It ensures our efforts are purposeful and enriches the journey with a sense of fulfillment that isn't only tied to the destination.

Wrapping It Up: Pairing mindfulness with goal setting is like setting sail with a compass in hand. It nurtures self-awareness, fine-tunes our focus, steadies our emotional keel, and guides our actions with intention. By embedding mindfulness into the goal setting equation, we not only pave the way for more significant achievements but also enrich the journey with deeper satisfaction and authenticity. Embrace mindfulness in your goal setting endeavors for a journey that's as rewarding as the destination itself.

~

ALIGNING GOALS WITH CORE VALUES: A PATH TO FULFILLMENT

IN THE HUSTLE of today's achievement-driven world, it's all too easy to chase after goals that don't quite match up with what matters to us personally. We often sprint after what society considers important or what seems momentarily appealing, only to wind up feeling like we're running on empty, missing a sense of real achievement and motivation. This highlights the critical importance of ensuring our goals not just sparkle on the surface but resonate with our deepest values.

Think of your personal values as your life's compass—they're what guide your choices, actions, and your overarching sense of purpose. Ignoring these values can lead us down a path that feels unanchored and meaningless, while honoring them in our gcals taps into a deep well of intrinsic motivation, driving us toward true fulfillment and joy.

So, how do you start aligning your goals with your values? First, carve out some time for self-reflection. What principles hold deep meaning for you? It could be anything from integrity, compassion, and bravery to creativity. Dive deep and select values that genuinely reflect who you are at your core.

After pinpointing your values, ponder on how these can shape your goals. If creativity is a core value, maybe you aim to pick up a new artistic hobby or kickstart a creative venture. Goals rooted in your values aren't just checkboxes on a to-do list—they're milestones on a journey that brings real joy and satisfaction.

Having your goals in sync with your values makes decision-making more authentic. You'll have a clear standard to measure options against, ensuring your choices reflect your true self, bringing a sense of integrity and consistency to your life.

This alignment also offers a clearer sense of purpose. Knowing your goals mirror your deeply held beliefs gives you the resilience to push through obstacles, fueled by the knowledge that your efforts are meaningful and aligned with your life's direction.

As you set out to chart your goals, keep the power of aligning them with your personal values front and center. Reflect on what matters to you and weave these values into your aspirations. Let your core values be the compass that guides you not just to success but to a life rich in meaning and fulfillment.

~

TURNING MINDFUL GOALS INTO ACTIONABLE SUCCESS

Converting your mindful goals into tangible results hinges on crafting solid action plans. While it's fantastic to have high aspirations and a clear vision, the magic happens when you outline specific, achievable steps. This method not only adds structure to your aspirations but significantly boosts your shot of success.

Here's how to pivot from dreaming to doing:

Be Specific and Measurable: Rather than vague goals like "get healthier," dial it down to actionable goals like "exercise for 30 minutes daily" or "eat five servings of fruits and veggies each day." This specificity lets you track your progress and keeps you accountable.

Stay Grounded in Reality: It's important to align your goals with what's realistically achievable for you right now. Overly ambitious goals can lead to frustration and the temptation to throw in the towel. Balance pushing your limits and recognizing what's possible.

Anticipate Hurdles: Life's full of surprises, and not all of them are pleasant. By identifying potential roadblocks ahead of time, you can strategize ways to navigate them. If a jam-packed schedule makes daily workouts seem impossible, consider waking up earlier or identifying times during your day when you can sneak in some exercise.

Break It Down: Large goals can be daunting. By dividing them into smaller, more digestible tasks, you prevent burnout and keep the momentum going. Want to write a book? Start with an outline, carve out regular writing slots, and set weekly page targets. Celebrating these mini victories keeps you motivated.

Track Your Journey: Regular check-ins are important. They help you see how much ground you've covered and whether your plan needs tweaking. This ongoing reflection ensures you're always moving in the right direction.

Lean on Your Support System: Share your goals and action plan with friends, family, or a mentor. Having someone to cheer you on, offer advice, and keep you honest about your commitments can make all the difference.

Turning your mindful goals into reality is all about breaking them down into clear, attainable actions. By setting specific, realistic goals, preparing for potential setbacks, and celebrating your progress along the way, you're setting yourself up for success. And with a solid support network cheering you on, you're not just dreaming big—you're making big things happen.

～

MINDFULNESS: YOUR SECRET WEAPON IN ACHIEVING GOALS

NAVIGATING the path to your goals can often feel like steering through a storm. Distractions, wavering focus, and emotional turbulence are all par for the course. Yet, mindfulness emerges as a beacon of calm, offering strategies to stay the course with unwavering focus and emotional steadiness. Let's dive into how mindfulness can be your ally in the pursuit of your goals, providing practical ways to stay engaged and overcome hurdles along the way.

Laying the Groundwork with Clarity: Before you dive into action, take a beat. Find a quiet spot and meditate to clear your mind. It's about setting intentions with a clear head, ensuring you're firmly anchored in your purpose and direction.

The Power of Now: Mindfulness roots you in the present. It's about immersing yourself in the task at hand, not getting sidetracked by what's next on the agenda or fretting over past hiccups. This approach sharpens your focus and boosts your efficiency, allowing for a richer understanding and appreciation of the journey.

Dodging Distractions: Distractions are the nemeses of focus but recognizing and understanding them through mindfulness reduces their power. Identify what usually pulls you away from your work, observe these distractions without critique, and learn to gently guide your focus back to where it needs to be.

Embracing Mindful Productivity: Blend mindfulness into your daily grind. Whether it's sipping your morning coffee or drafting an email, do it with full attention. This not only enhances your productivity but also infuses your daily tasks with a sense of fulfillment.

Steadying the Ship Through Storms: When the going gets tough, mindfulness helps you navigate challenges with resilience. Acknowledge your feelings, allow yourself to feel them, and use mindfulness exercises like deep breathing to find your equilibrium again. It's about facing these challenges head-on, with a clear mind and a balanced heart.

Kindness Begins with You: Facing setbacks? Be gentle with yourself. Understand that hiccups are part of the journey. Offering yourself compassion rather than criticism paves the way for growth and learning, enabling you to bounce back with more vigor.

Incorporating mindfulness into your goal setting journey transforms it from a mere to-do list into a fulfilling expedition. It not only heightens your chances of success but enriches the entire experience, promoting a healthier, more balanced approach to personal and professional achievements. So, let mindfulness be your guide, illuminating the path to your goals with clarity, focus, and peace.

~

NAVIGATING YOUR PATH: THE ROLE OF MINDFULNESS IN GOAL EVOLUTION

EVALUATING our journey and fine-tuning our aspirations are important steps in the dance of personal evolution. This practice not only helps us gauge our strides and accomplishments but also encourages us to recalibrate our aims when necessary. Here, mindfulness emerges as a guiding light, enriching this process with its emphasis on self-awareness and acceptance.

Mindfulness teaches us to inhabit the present, casting a non-judgmental gaze on our thoughts, emotions, and actions. This heightened awareness becomes a mirror reflecting our journey's true picture, free from the distortions of self-critique or bias. It's like stepping back to see the broader landscape of our progress, providing a clearer view for introspection and evaluation.

Through mindful reflection, we uncover the growth we've achieved and pinpoint areas needing more attention or a different approach. It's about sifting through our mental and emotional patterns to identify what propels us forward or holds us back. This honest assessment lets us understand where our efforts should be concentrated or if we need outside support to overcome hurdles.

Mindfulness encourages us to honor our victories, big and small. In the rush toward the next milestone, we often overlook the importance of appreciating the ground covered. Mindfulness cultivates a sense of gratitude for our accomplishments, fueling our motivation and bolstering our confidence for the journey ahead.

Adjusting our sails is also part of the mindful journey toward our goals. As we move forward, our initial goals might not fit the person we've grown into or the new insights we've gained. Mindfulness aids us in letting go of rigid attachments to specific outcomes, letting us adapt our goals with flexibility and openness, informed by our experiences and growth.

Incorporating regular mindfulness practices into our daily lives enhances our self-awareness and emotional intelligence, essential tools for navigating the complexities of personal growth. By adopting a mindful approach, we're not just passively moving through life; we're engaging with our journey, making conscious choices that reflect our true selves and aspirations.

The path of personal development is ongoing, with mindfulness serving as a compass guiding us through self-reflection, celebration of achievements, and the thoughtful evolution of our goals. It's about embracing the journey with awareness, resilience, and a willingness to grow, making sure each step forward is aligned with our deepest values and visions for ourselves.

$\sim$

MINDFULNESS: THE KEY TO UNLOCKING YOUR FULL POTENTIAL

WRAPPING THINGS UP, weaving mindfulness into the fabric of our goal setting and daily life can be a game-changer. It's like shining a light on our inner workings, guiding us to live with more intention and purpose. This practice doesn't just help us set more resonant goals; it amps up our motivation and keeps the pesky specters of stress and worry at bay.

Mindfulness isn't just about being present; it's a tool that sharpens our focus and helps us navigate life's decisions with our values as the compass. By stepping back to simply observe our thoughts and feelings, we sidestep the trap of self-doubt and the negative chatter that often leads us off track.

But the magic of mindfulness doesn't stop with goal setting. Regularly dipping into this mindful state can transform our lives, nurturing self-awareness, emotional smarts, and deeper connections with those around us. It equips us to handle life's curveballs with grace and builds our resilience, so we're better prepared for whatever comes our way.

Making mindfulness a staple in our daily routine, far beyond setting and chasing goals, opens the door to a richer, more compassionate relationship with ourselves. This shift in perspective can touch every corner of our lives, blooming into a profound sense of mental and emotional wellbeing.

So, here's my nudge to you: Let mindfulness be more than just a tool for goals. Carve out moments for meditation, take mindful breaths, or immerse yourself in activities that bring you into the now—like jotting down your thoughts or taking walks that let you connect with nature.

Remember, mindfulness is more about the journey than the destination. It's a path that requires dedication and patience, but the transformation it brings to both your goal achievements and life's overall quality is worthwhile. Let's embrace this mindful journey together, unlocking a life filled with intention, fulfillment, and an ever-deepening appreciation for the here and now.

～

PART TEN WRAP-UP:

- Emotional Intelligence (EI) is critical for both personal and professional success, encompassing self-awareness, self-regulation, empathy, and social skills.
- Self-awareness involves understanding your own emotions, strengths, weaknesses, and their impact on decisions and relationships.
- Self-regulation allows for effective management of emotions and impulses, leading to resilience and adaptability.
- Social awareness and empathy enable understanding and connecting with others' emotions, improving communication and relationships.
- Effective relationship management is important for building and maintaining strong, positive connections, involving clear communication and conflict resolution skills.
- Journaling enhances EI by fostering self-awareness, allowing for emotional expression, and serving as a tool for reflecting on personal growth and goals.

- Empathy-building activities and exercises, such as role-playing and storytelling, promote understanding and connection with others.
- Mindfulness in goal setting focuses on aligning goals with personal values, enhancing focus, and managing distractions and emotional upheavals.
- Regular assessment and change in goals are essential for continuous growth, with mindfulness practices aiding in reflection and adaptability.
- Ongoing mindfulness practice helps overall wellbeing, enhancing focus, emotional regulation, and resilience in pursuing personal and professional goals.

Action Items:

- **Cultivate Self-Awareness:**
- Engage in regular journaling to explore personal values, emotions, and behaviors.
- Practice mindfulness and meditation to enhance present-moment awareness and emotional understanding.
- **Develop Self-Regulation:**
- Identify emotional triggers and create strategies for managing responses.
- Incorporate relaxation techniques, such as deep breathing and mindfulness exercises, to maintain emotional balance.
- **Enhance Social Awareness:**
- Participate in empathy-building activities, like storytelling or cultural immersion, to understand diverse perspectives.
- Practice active listening in conversations to deepen connections with others.
- **Improve Relationship Management:**
- Use assertive communication techniques to express needs and feelings respectfully.

- Apply conflict resolution strategies to navigate disagreements constructively and maintain positive relationships.
- **Leverage Journaling for EI Development:**
- Use prompts to reflect on emotional experiences, challenges, and successes.
- Set aside time for regular journaling to track progress and adjust personal growth strategies.
- **Implement Mindfulness in Goal Pursuit:**
- Set goals that align with personal values and use mindfulness to stay focused on present actions.
- Regularly assess and adjust goals based on mindful reflection and self-awareness insights.
- **Commit to Ongoing Mindfulness Practice:**
- Incorporate daily mindfulness practices, such as mindful walking or breathing exercises, to enhance overall wellbeing.
- Use mindfulness to navigate setbacks and maintain motivation toward achieving personal and professional goals.

By following these action items, you can effectively apply the key points covered in this Part to foster emotional intelligence, improve interpersonal relationships, and achieve personal and professional growth through mindfulness and goal setting strategies.

In Our Next Part...

Up next, we're setting sail into the profound waters of resilience and self-compassion, two important companions on our voyage to not only confront the fear of failure but to harness it as a catalyst for achievement. We're about to unpack actionable strategies and inspiring stories of folks who've journeyed from the shadows of fear to the spotlight of victory. This is about rewriting our script on failure, recognizing it not as a blockade but as a gateway, a wise mentor ushering us to our greatest selves. We'll unravel the psychology of our fears and chart out a course to meet them with bravery and poise.

Brace yourselves for an arsenal of insights and attitudes to tackle life's hurdles head-on and bounce back with vigor. We're diving into the essence of mindfulness and emotional intelligence, offering you real steps to weave these practices into your daily fabric for a transformative impact. From honing your people skills, tuning into deep listening, to standing your ground with assurance, the forthcoming Part is your lighthouse in the storm, guiding those ready to tread life's peaks and valleys with unshakable courage. Together, let's journey toward becoming more resilient, kind-hearted, and bold versions of ourselves.

～

PART ELEVEN
RESILIENCE AND SELF-COMPASSION: NAVIGATING LIFE'S CHALLENGES

NURTURING RESILIENCE THROUGH MINDFULNESS: A PATH TO EMOTIONAL STABILITY AND WELLBEING

IN TODAY'S whirlwind of life, where challenges loom at every corner, resilience becomes our shield and strength. It's that incredible ability to weather storms and emerge unscathed, or even stronger. And at the heart of fostering this resilience? Mindfulness. This piece delves into how mindfulness fortifies emotional regulation, slashes stress, and uplifts overall wellbeing, paving the way for a resilient spirit.

Emotional Regulation: A Mindful Approach Mindfulness trains us to anchor ourselves in the now, offering a unique lens to view our emotions, thoughts, and sensations without criticism. This practice sharpens our emotional intelligence, enabling us to greet our feelings with awareness, pause before reacting, and choose our responses wisely. It's a game-changer for maintaining emotional balance during tough times, preventing us from being swept away by the tide of our feelings.

Stress Reduction: The Mindfulness Oasis Stress is an unwelcome companion in our journey, capable of wearing down even the strongest among us. But mindfulness introduces techniques like meditation and deep breathing, serving as life rafts in turbulent waters. By centering our attention on the present, we can step away from past regrets and future anxieties, significantly dialing down stress. This not only bolsters our wellbeing but also sharpens our resilience, equipping us to face life's hurdles with grace.

Boosting Overall Wellbeing The ripple effects of mindfulness on our wellbeing are profound. It nurtures self-awareness, helping us recognize our strengths and areas for growth. Mindfulness cultivates self-compassion too, teaching us to be kinder to ourselves in the face of setbacks. It helps our physical health—think better sleep, lower blood pressure, and a stronger immune system—all important contributors to a solid resilience foundation.

Clear Decision-Making in the Eye of the Storm Resilience is more than just surviving; it's about making wise choices amidst adversity. Mindfulness keeps us grounded and attentive, clearing the fog for more thoughtful decision-making. By observing our thoughts and emotions without judgment, we can sidestep biases and make decisions that reflect our true intentions. This clarity and focus empower us to navigate challenges with resilience and poise.

Wrapping Up Mindfulness isn't just a practice but a powerful ally in building resilience. It enhances emotional regulation, cuts down stress, uplifts our wellbeing, and clears the path for sound decision-making. Embracing mindfulness means cultivating a presence that arms us against life's adversities, enabling us to face them head-on and bounce back with renewed vigor and strength.

~

EMBRACING EMOTIONAL INTELLIGENCE: THE KEY TO STRENGTHENING RESILIENCE

EMOTIONAL INTELLIGENCE (EI) is like having an internal compass that helps navigate the stormy seas of our emotions. It's about recognizing, understanding, and managing not just our own emotions but also those of the people around us. It involves skills such as being in tune with our feelings (self-awareness), keeping our impulses in check (self-regulation), walking in someone else's shoes (empathy), and navigating social interactions with finesse (social skills). Resilience, or our knack for bouncing back from tough spots, thrives when fueled by emotional intelligence. Let's dive into how these parts of EI cast a lifeline, strengthening our resilience.

The Starting Point: Self-Awareness It all begins with self-awareness, the cornerstone of EI. This is about recognizing our emotions as they bubble up, especially in tough situations. Knowing what we're feeling lets us address our emotions head-on, rather than letting them overpower us. This awareness is our first step in effectively managing challenges and stressors, setting the stage for resilience.

Keeping Cool: Self-Regulation Self-regulation is our emotional thermostat—it keeps our responses in check. With high emotional intelligence, we can steer clear of knee-jerk reactions and choose how we respond to stress and adversity. This control is important in managing stress, overcoming obstacles, and moving forward after a setback.

Connecting with Empathy Empathy is about feeling with others. In challenging times, this ability to understand and share the feelings of others not only helps us provide support but also strengthens our own resilience. It's a two-way street: empathy builds bridges, fostering connections that can offer support when we're the ones in need.

The Art of Social Skills Effective communication, assertiveness, and knowing how to resolve conflicts are social skills that are part of the EI toolkit. These skills help us have healthy relationships, build supportive networks, and find help when we need it. A strong support system is like a safety net, important for bouncing back from life's setbacks.

The Impact of EI on Resilience Emotional intelligence is a powerhouse when fostering resilience. Being emotionally intelligent means we can face life's challenges with more grace and less stress. It equips us with the ability to recover from setbacks, adapt to change, and keep pushing forward, even when the going gets tough.

By honing our emotional intelligence, we're not just improving our ability to navigate the emotional parts of our lives; we're also bolstering our resilience. It's about transforming challenges into steppingstones and maintaining a positive outlook, no matter what life throws our way. Investing in our emotional intelligence is, without a doubt, investing in our capacity to thrive amidst adversity.

~

TURNING THE TIDE ON NEGATIVE THINKING: A PATH TO RESILIENCE

THE ABILITY TO flip the script on negative thoughts plays an important role in forging resilience. Imagine you're navigating a stormy sea of challenges, and your thoughts are the sails of your ship. Reframing negative thoughts means adjusting those sails, steering away from the storm, and setting a course toward positivity and growth. It's about swapping out those self-defeating thoughts with ones that empower and uplift you, helping you bounce back stronger from life's setbacks.

Spotlight on Self-Awareness: Identifying those pesky negative thoughts is step one, and it hinges on self-awareness. If you're not tuned into your own mental chatter, you might not even notice these unhelpful thoughts weighing you down. Practices like meditation and journaling aren't just for finding your zen—they're tools to sharpen your awareness, catching those negative thoughts in the act.

Strategies for a Mindset Makeover: Aware of the negativity? Great! Now, let's tackle it. Cognitive restructuring is like being a detective with your own thoughts, examining them for evidence. Is there real proof behind these negative beliefs, or are they just old habits of thinking? By challenging these thoughts and looking for more balanced viewpoints, you start to loosen their grip on your emotions.

Cheerleading Yourself with Positive Self-Talk: Replace the inner critic with your own personal cheerleader. Swap "I can't do this" with "I can tackle challenges." These positive affirmations aren't just feel-good phrases—they're tools to reshape your thinking and bolster your belief in yourself.

Cultivating Gratitude: Gratitude isn't just for Thanksgiving. Making it a daily practice to reflect on what you're thankful for shifts your focus from what's going wrong to what's going right. This shift can dramatically change your outlook, turning your attention to life's positives, even during tough times.

Persistence Pays Off: Reframing isn't a one-and-done deal; it's more like going to the gym for your brain. It takes consistent effort, and sometimes you might slip back into old patterns. That's okay. The more you practice, the stronger and more automatic your new, positive thinking patterns become.

Wrapping Up: Cognitive reframing isn't just a neat trick—it's a fundamental skill for resilience. By challenging and changing our negative thoughts to ones that are more positive and constructive, we can navigate through life's challenges with a healthier mindset and emotional wellbeing. It's about ongoing self-awareness, challenging our thought patterns, cheering ourselves on, and finding reasons to be grateful. Dive into these practices, and watch as they transform not just your thoughts, but your resilience and overall happiness.

$\sim$

HARNESSING SELF-COMPASSION FOR GREATER RESILIENCE

RESILIENCE IS our inner strength to recover from difficulties—it's what helps us bounce back stronger than before. But here's a thought: what if the key to unlocking this resilience lies in how kindly we treat ourselves? That's where self-compassion comes into play, a practice all about greeting ourselves with kindness, understanding, and acceptance, especially when we stumble.

Exploring Self-Compassion and Resilience Together:

- **What is self-compassion?** It's giving ourselves a break, recognizing that being imperfect is part of being human, and staying mindful of our feelings without letting them define us.
- **Why does it matter for resilience?** Embracing self-compassion can lead to better emotional health, lower stress levels, and a stronger mental state. There's plenty of research backing up how self-compassion can make us more resilient.

Navigating Through Tough Times:

- **Feeling all the feels:** It's okay to acknowledge and sit with our emotions, confirming them as a natural response to challenges.

257

- **Switching up the self-talk:** Catch yourself when you're being your own worst critic and try to flip the script to something kinder, something that uplifts you.
- **Learning from the bumps in the road:** Every setback has a lesson tucked inside it. Reflect on these moments and grow from them.
- **Keeping the glass half full:** Cultivate a habit of looking at the bright side and focusing on growth.

Cutting Down on Self-Blame:

- **Realistic expectations:** Remember, no one's perfect. Mistakes don't mean failure; they're just part of the journey.
- **Kind words for yourself:** Speak to yourself like you would to a dear friend—with warmth, understanding, and forgiveness.
- **Accepting yourself fully:** Your worth isn't measured by your stumbles. Embrace your quirks and all.

Building a Positive Outlook:

- **Counting your blessings:** Take time to appreciate the good in your life. Gratitude can shift your perspective in powerful ways.
- **Staying in the now:** Mindfulness practices can keep you grounded and help maintain a positive outlook.
- **Positive affirmations:** Keep a list of affirmations that remind you of your strength, worth, and ability to face challenges head-on.

Self-Compassion Practices to Try:

- **Loving-kindness meditation:** This practice helps spread love and compassion toward yourself and others.
- **Writing a self-compassion letter:** Pen a letter to yourself, offering the same compassion you would offer a friend.

- **Affirmations for self-love:** Repeat phrases that reinforce your self-worth and resilience.

Wrapping Up: Self-compassion is a powerful ally in building resilience. By treating ourselves with kindness, learning from our experiences, and maintaining a hopeful outlook, we pave the way for stronger, more resilient selves. Through meditation, self-reflection, and positive affirmations, we can practice self-compassion daily. This journey toward self-compassion not only enhances our resilience but enriches our overall life experience, teaching us that true strength lies in how gently we can hold ourselves during our most challenging times.

ELEVATING RESILIENCE THROUGH SELF-CARE

IN THE WHIRLWIND of life's ups and downs, resilience is that steadfast force that helps us stand back up after a fall, keeping us moving forward with a hopeful heart. But there's a secret ingredient to boosting this resilience that often slips under the radar—self-care. Yes, the way we nurture ourselves, body and soul, significantly fuels our resilience tank.

The Bedrock of Resilience: Physical Wellbeing The journey to resilience starts with looking after our physical health. Exercise isn't just about staying fit; it's a natural stress-reliever that lifts our spirits and clears our minds, thanks to those feel-good endorphins. Whether it's a morning jog, a yoga session, or simply a leisurely walk, moving our bodies is a resilience booster. Eating well and catching enough Z's are equally important. They recharge our batteries, sharpen our minds, and set the stage for resilience to thrive.

Mental Wellbeing: The Mindset of Resilience Cultivating a resilient mindset involves more than just wishful thinking. It's about fostering positive self-talk and embracing the belief that growth is always possible. Breaking free from the clutches of negative thoughts and viewing challenges through a lens of positivity and realism can significantly fortify our resilience. Techniques like mindfulness and meditation also come in handy, offering clarity, reducing stress, and helping us navigate our emotions with ease during tough times.

Embracing Emotions for Emotional Wellbeing Our emotional landscape is intricate, and understanding it is key to resilience. It's okay to feel and express a spectrum of emotions; bottling them up does more harm than good. Embracing activities that support our emotional health—be it journaling our thoughts, connecting with friends, or seeking professional advice—lays down the steppingstones to resilience.

Self-Care Techniques for Resilience Self-care is all about finding what lights up our spirits and indulges our senses. Hobbies, nature walks, or creative pursuits offer us a haven from the hustle and bustle, rejuvenating our souls. Healthy coping mechanisms like deep breathing, visualizing peaceful scenes, or tuning into soothing tunes can dramatically dial down stress, keeping our resilience strong.

Self-Care: The Non-Negotiable Pillar of Resilience Remember, self-care isn't a luxury; it's essential. Dedicating time to our physical, mental, and emotional wellbeing equips us with the strength to face life's hurdles head-on. It brings balance, renews our energy, and boosts our resilience, enabling us to navigate life's storms with grace and vitality. So, make self-care a priority, and watch as your resilience blossoms, empowering you to tackle life's challenges with unwavering strength and optimism.

～

ELEVATING EVERYDAY RESILIENCE THROUGH MINDFULNESS AND EMOTIONAL INTELLIGENCE

IN OUR MODERN, whirlwind world, weaving mindfulness and emotional intelligence into the fabric of our daily lives can be a game-changer for our mental health and resilience. These powerful practices teach us to stay grounded, self-aware, and empathetic, equipping us with the tools to gracefully dance through life's storms. Let's dive into how you can seamlessly blend mindfulness and emotional intelligence into your everyday routine, highlighting the perks of sticking with it and sharing practical steps to build your resilience muscle.

Getting to Know Mindfulness and Emotional Intelligence: First off, get cozy with the ideas of mindfulness and emotional intelligence. Mindfulness is all about being present in the now, observing our moment-to-moment experiences without judgment. Emotional intelligence, on the other hand, is our knack for recognizing, understanding, and managing our emotions and those of others. The good news? These are skills you can improve with elbow grease.

Why Keep At It: Staying the course with regular mindfulness and emotional intelligence practice can transform your emotional landscape. Here's what's in store for you:

262

- Better control and balance over your emotions.
- Sharper focus and clearer thinking.
- A deeper understanding of yourself and how you tick.
- Smoother communication and stronger relationships.
- A noticeable drop in stress and a boost in your overall happiness.

Blending Mindfulness and Emotional Intelligence into Your Day:

- **Start fresh:** Kick off your day with a mindful moment—think a short meditation or deep breathing—to anchor yourself and set a positive tone.
- **Check in with yourself:** Throughout the day, take brief pauses to tune into your feelings. Just observe, no judgments here.
- **Take mindful pauses:** Use breaks to do something mindful, like a mindful walk or gentle stretching. Pay attention to your body, the surrounding sounds, and the flow of your thoughts.
- **Listen with your heart:** In conversations, practice listening— engage and respond with genuine empathy, tuning into both what's said and the unspoken.
- **Evening wind-down:** Reflect on your day before bed. Think over any tough spots, how you handled them, and the wins you should celebrate.

Growing Your Resilience Gradually:

- **Map out your resilience journey:** Jot down the mindfulness and emotional intelligence habits you want to embrace. Break them into bite-sized, achievable actions.
- **Make self-reflection a habit:** Regularly assess how you're doing. How well are you weaving mindfulness and emotional intelligence into your day? Face any hurdles head-on and tweak your plan as needed.
- **Be your own cheerleader:** Cultivate self-compassion. Understand that building resilience is a marathon, not a sprint. View any slip-ups as chances to grow, not as failures.

- **Lean on your tribe:** Consider joining groups, attending workshops, or even chatting with a coach or therapist who can deepen your practice and offer new perspectives.

Wrapping Up: Infusing your day-to-day with mindfulness and emotional intelligence isn't just about coping with the now—it's about thriving in the long run. This journey promises a richer emotional life, sharper self-awareness, and more meaningful connections. By crafting a tailored resilience-building plan, engaging in thoughtful self-reflection, and embracing a kind-hearted approach to self-growth, you're setting the stage for a deeply fulfilling and resilient life. Begin this journey today and watch as the quality of your daily existence transforms, one mindful moment at a time.

~

NAVIGATING THE NUANCES OF INTERPERSONAL RELATIONSHIPS: BLENDING MINDFULNESS WITH EMOTIONAL INTELLIGENCE

IN THE HUSTLE and bustle of everyday life, mastering the art of mindfulness and emotional intelligence is becoming important for enhancing our interactions with others. Mindfulness teaches us to be present, soaking in our thoughts, emotions, and the world around us with an open heart. Emotional intelligence, meanwhile, is our toolkit for recognizing, understanding, and managing our emotions and those of others. Together, these skills are the secret sauce to boosting our interpersonal skills, paving the way for more effective communication, deeper empathy, and stronger relationships.

Elevating Communication: Mindfulness and emotional intelligence are your allies in communication. Mindfulness sharpens your self-awareness, helping you understand your thoughts and feelings. This awareness is key to communicating your ideas and emotions and considering how your words affect others. Emotional intelligence brings empathy to the table, enabling you to grasp different view-points and respond thoughtfully. These skills together can transform your conversations, fostering trust and deeper connections in both your personal and professional worlds.

Deepening Empathy: At the heart of great relationships lies empathy, and mindfulness and emotional intelligence are its nurturers. Mindfulness encourages a non-judgmental and open stance, making you more receptive to others' emotions and experiences. Emotional intelligence takes it a step further by enabling you to recognize and resonate with these emotions. This empathy not only shows you care but also strengthens bonds, encouraging trust and cooperation in all your relationships.

Strengthening Connections: The journey to better interpersonal skills leads to stronger, more meaningful relationships. Mindfulness keeps you engaged and present in your interactions, ensuring you're listening and understanding others' points of view. Emotional intelligence rounds this out by helping you navigate conversations with empathy, manage conflicts smoothly, and adapt your communication style as needed. This thoughtful approach to interactions nurtures a supportive and respectful environment, ideal for collaboration and mutual respect.

Techniques for Becoming an Active Listener: Active listening is a cornerstone of effective communication, showing respect, empathy, and genuine interest. Here's how to hone this skill:

- **Be fully in the moment:** Give your complete attention to the speaker. Put away distractions and focus on their words, showing you value their thoughts.
- **Eye contact matters:** It's a simple yet powerful way to connect. It shows you're engaged and interested.
- **Let them speak:** Avoid interrupting. Give them the floor to express themselves, showing you're there to listen, not just respond.
- **Reflect and clarify:** Echo back what you've heard to ensure you've got it right. It's a great way to show you're paying attention and to avoid any miscommunication.
- **Read between the lines:** Communication isn't just verbal. Pay attention to body language and facial expressions for a fuller understanding of the message.

Why Active Listening Works Wonders: Active listening doesn't just improve understanding; it deepens your connections. Being heard makes people feel valued and understood, laying the groundwork for trust and open communication. It also enriches your understanding of the conversation, catching not just the words, but the emotions and unspoken messages too.

In wrapping up, blending mindfulness and emotional intelligence into your daily interactions is transformative. It's about improving communication, fostering empathy, and building strong, resilient relationships. By practicing active listening and embracing these skills, you set the stage for more meaningful connections and a richer, more compassionate interaction with the world around you.

～

MASTERING THE ART OF ASSERTIVE COMMUNICATION

ASSERTIVE COMMUNICATION IS the golden key to expressing your thoughts, needs, and boundaries in a way that's straightforward yet respectful. It's about finding that sweet spot between aggression and passivity, ensuring your voice is heard without stepping on toes. This skill is essential across all walks of life, from navigating personal relationships to thriving in professional settings. By mastering assertive communication, you pave the way for clearer boundaries, stronger trust, and smoother conflict resolution.

Why Assertiveness Matters: Assertiveness lets you put your thoughts and feelings out there without crossing into aggression. It's about standing firm in your beliefs while respecting others, reducing the chance of misunderstandings by making your message crystal clear.

It also empowers you to make your needs known in a balanced way. Assertiveness means recognizing what you want and asking for it in a way that respects everyone's rights. This approach fosters healthier relationships and ensures your needs don't get brushed aside.

Setting and maintaining boundaries becomes easier with assertive communication. It's about clearly defining what's okay and what's not, creating a respectful environment for everyone involved. This way, you protect your space and values without shutting down open dialogue.

Building Your Assertiveness Toolkit:

- **"I" Statements:** Kickstart conversations with "I" statements to express your perspective without blaming others. For example, "I feel overwhelmed with too many tasks" is more effective and less accusatory than "You're overloading me with work."
- **Active Empathy:** Even in disagreement, try to see where the other person is coming from. Acknowledging their viewpoint can make the conversation more productive and less confrontational.
- **Clarity is Key:** Be direct and to the point. Ambiguity only leads to confusion, so say what you mean concisely.
- **Non-Verbal Assertiveness:** Your body speaks volumes. Maintain eye contact, stand tall, and use gestures that convey confidence and openness.
- **Active Listening:** Give your full attention to the speaker. Listen carefully and respond thoughtfully, showing you value their input.
- **Learning to Say "No":** It's okay to focus on your needs and say "no" when necessary. It's an important part of setting healthy boundaries and respecting your limits.
- **Seeking Support:** If assertiveness doesn't come naturally, don't hesitate to seek help from a mentor, friend, or therapist. They can offer valuable feedback and guidance as you hone your skills.

In Summary: Assertive communication is an invaluable skill that enhances how you express yourself and interact with others. By using strategies like "I" statements, practicing empathy, and maintaining clear, confident body language, you can strengthen your assertiveness. This not only improves your interactions but also contributes to a more respectful and understanding environment. Dive into the practice of assertive communication and watch as your relationships and self-confidence flourish.

NAVIGATING CONFLICTS: TURNING CHALLENGES INTO OPPORTUNITIES FOR GROWTH

CONFLICTS ARE a natural slice of life when dealing with others, whether it's with friends, family, partners, or colleagues. They pop up not because we're out to get each other but because we're all unique, with our own views and ways of seeing the world. Though conflicts might seem like a thorn in the side, they actually hold the potential for growth, deeper understanding, and even strengthening the bonds we share, provided we handle them wisely. Let's dive into how conflicts arise in our relationships and explore effective ways to smooth things over and find common ground.

The heat of conflict often stirs up a storm of emotions like anger, frustration, or hurt, making it tough to keep the lines of communication open and clear. These feelings can lead to misunderstandings and might even make the situation worse. Plus, the fear of opening up or being misinterpreted can put up walls that keep solutions at bay.

To tackle conflicts head-on, empathy is your best ally. Walking a mile in someone else's shoes helps us see where they're coming from, shining a light on their feelings and perspective. When we approach a situation with empathy, we're more likely to handle it with care and less likely to let things spiral out of control.

Clear and open communication is the backbone of resolving conflicts. It's all about laying your cards on the table—sharing your thoughts and feelings honestly—while giving the other person space to do the same. Active listening is key here; it means hearing them out, tuning into their verbal and non-verbal signals, and showing them you're engaged. This approach lays the groundwork for mutual respect and understanding.

Finding common ground can turn the tide in conflict resolution. It's about discovering shared values or goals that both parties can nod to. Focusing on what you agree on, rather than where you clash, paves the way to collaborative solutions where everyone wins a little.

Don't underestimate the power of compromise and negotiation. These strategies are about bending to find a happy medium where everyone's needs are met. This requires flexibility, openness, and a dash of creativity to explore various avenues that satisfy both sides.

Remember, agreeing to disagree can sometimes be the endpoint of conflict resolution. Not all disputes will end in unanimous agreement, and that's okay. Maintaining respect and understanding for differing viewpoints is a resolution.

Conflicts, while challenging, are not insurmountable. By leveraging empathy, fostering open communication, seeking common ground, and being open to compromise and negotiation, we can transform these moments of tension into opportunities for personal and collective growth. Through these strategies, conflicts become less about winning and more about understanding, connecting, and moving forward together.

~

THE MAGIC OF MEANINGFUL CONNECTIONS: UNVEILING THE PERKS

In our whirlwind digital era, carving out meaningful relationships is more important than ever. These deeper connections offer a treasure trove of benefits, from a strong support circle to enhanced wellbeing and mental health. By weaving empathy, active participation, and vulnerability into our interactions, we not only enrich our current relationships but also pave the way for new, enduring bonds.

A Network of Support: At the heart of deep connections lies the invaluable social support they usher in. These bonds provide a sense of belonging and a safety net, ensuring there's always someone in your corner, rain or shine. This network isn't just about having people to celebrate the highs with; it's about knowing you have a crew ready to weather the storms with you, offering a helping hand, advice, or a listening ear whenever you need it.

Boosting Wellbeing: Immersing yourself in meaningful connections does wonders for your overall sense of happiness and satisfaction. Feeling seen, heard, and valued in your relationships can turn the mundane into the extraordinary. Sharing your life's rollercoaster - the ups, downs, and in-betweens - not only makes the ride more enjoyable but also reduces the weight of solitude.

A Shield for Mental Health: The link between strong, meaningful connections and mental health is undeniable. These relationships act as a buffer against the tides of stress, anxiety, and depression. They're like a protective barrier, bolstering your emotional resilience and contributing to a healthier, more balanced mental state.

Empathy: The Glue of Connection: Empathy is the cornerstone of deepening relationships. Stepping into someone else's shoes, if only for a moment, allows us a glimpse into their world. Through active listening and showing a genuine interest in their stories, we nurture a deeper understanding and connection. It's the little gestures of kindness and understanding that can draw people closer, laying down the bricks for a foundation of lasting relationships.

The Power of Engagement and Vulnerability: Active involvement is key to nurturing deeper ties. It's about making time for those moments that matter, whether it's a heart-to-heart chat, a shared hobby, or simply being there for one another. Showing up for these interactions signals your commitment to the relationship, tightening the bonds of trust and understanding.

Letting your guard down and embracing vulnerability is transformative. Revealing your true self – your hopes, fears, and dreams – can seem daunting but it invites authenticity into the relationship. It opens the door to honest conversations and a mutual understanding that can weather any storm.

Wrapping Up: The journey toward deepening our connections is laden with unmatched benefits – a solid support system, a boost in wellbeing, and a fortified mental health. Through empathy, genuine engagement, and the courage to be vulnerable, we forge stronger, more meaningful relationships. These connections are the lifeblood of a fulfilling life, sprinkling joy, comfort, and a sense of belonging across our days. Let's cherish and nurture these bonds, for they are the true essence of a rich, vibrant life.

~

CULTIVATING YOUR CIRCLE: CRAFTING A NETWORK FOR GROWTH

IN BOTH OUR personal and professional journeys, the strength of our support system can be a defining factor in our success. Having a strong network around us can open doors to new opportunities, offer critical insights, and provide the encouragement we need to push through challenges. Here's how you can build and nurture a network that genuinely supports your growth.

Start with Self-Reflection: Before diving into network building, take a moment to ponder over what you're aiming for. What are your ambitions? What hurdles do you foresee? Understanding these parts will guide you in seeking people who align with your path and can offer the support you need.

Finding Your Tribe: Connect with people who share your passions, values, and goals. Whether it's through industry meetups, seminars, or online forums, immerse yourself in spaces where these individuals gather. Genuine connections stem from shared interests.

Authenticity is Key: Build your relationships on a foundation of trust and respect. Be genuinely interested in others, listen actively, and be there for them without ulterior motives. Authentic connections, cultivated with care, evolve into a dependable support system.

Embrace Diversity: While it's comforting to surround yourself with like-minded peers, don't shy away from inviting diverse perspectives into your circle. People from different walks of life can offer insights you might not have considered, enriching your worldview.

Seek Out Mentors: Mentors can be your guiding light. Contact those who have tread the path you aspire to walk. Their wisdom, feedback, and encouragement can helped to navigate your journey. Keep the lines of communication open and cherish their guidance.

Network Actively: Put yourself out there at networking events and gatherings. These are golden opportunities to meet a variety of professionals and expand your circle. Engage in meaningful conversations, exchange contacts, and remember to follow up.

Stay Connected: Nurturing a network demands continuous effort. Regularly touch base with your contacts, share your milestones, and lend a hand when they need it. Being an active participant in your network's growth fosters lasting connections.

Welcome Feedback: Constructive criticism is a catalyst for growth. Embrace the feedback from your circle with an open mind. It's an opportunity to reflect, learn, and evolve. Responding positively to feedback solidifies your commitment to personal development.

Express Gratitude: Never underestimate the power of a heartfelt 'thank you'. Acknowledge the support and guidance you receive. Gratitude not only strengthens your bonds but encourages a culture of mutual support within your network.

Crafting a supportive network is a journey, not a sprint. Approach it with patience, authenticity, and an open heart. As you invest in these relationships, you'll discover a network that's not just about professional leverage but a source of inspiration, strength, and mutual growth.

∽

NAVIGATING THE PATH TO BETTER INTERPERSONAL SKILLS

EVER FELT like you're just not clicking with people the way you wish you would? That perhaps your relationships could be deeper, more meaningful. If that resonates with you, then you're ready to take a journey toward beefing up those interpersonal skills. Let's dive into how self-awareness, a dash of persistence, and a whole lot of practice can transform your interactions and help you forge stronger, more authentic connections.

Kickstart with Self-Awareness: Understanding others begins with understanding yourself. It's like setting the stage for your interpersonal skills to flourish. Reflect on what makes you tick, your strengths, the areas you could improve, and what pushes your buttons. This self-reflection is the cornerstone of relating better to others and developing empathy.

Stick with It: Rome wasn't built in a day, and neither are stellar interpersonal skills. It's a marathon, not a sprint. Embrace the journey, knowing there'll be bumps along the way. Every conversation, every interaction is an opportunity to improve. Persistence is your friend here, helping you to keep pushing forward, even when it feels tough.

Practice, Practice, Practice: There's no substitute for real-world practice. Throw yourself into situations that nudge you out of your comfort zone. Join discussions, network like a pro, or just start conversations with people you don't know. It's all about getting those hours in, learning from each interaction, and gradually becoming more adept and comfortable in social settings.

Empathy and Listening Go Hand in Hand: Listening isn't just about hearing words; it's about understanding the message behind them. Empathetic listening bridges gaps, builds trust, and deepens connections. Focus on what's being said, offer your full attention, and reflect back to show you get it. Empathy lets you connect on a human level, acknowledging others' feelings and experiences.

Authenticity and Respect Are Key: Genuine interactions are the foundation of strong relationships. Approach every conversation with the respect you'd expect. Be real, share your thoughts and feelings, and appreciate the uniqueness of others' perspectives. Authenticity fosters trust and encourages others to open up, creating a space where meaningful relationships can grow.

Wrapping It Up: Embarking on improving your interpersonal skills is an exciting journey toward deeper, more meaningful connections. Through self-discovery, commitment, and plenty of practice, you can enhance your ability to communicate, empathize, and connect with those around you. This adventure not only enriches your personal life but paves the way for professional achievements and self-improvement. Start today and look forward to the rich relationships and enhanced interactions that await.

∾

HARNESSING MINDFULNESS AND EMOTIONAL INTELLIGENCE FOR EMOTIONAL WELLBEING

MINDFULNESS and emotional intelligence stand as pillars in the realm of personal development, each playing a pivotal role in enhancing our emotional landscape. They're like two sides of the same coin, working together to polish our ability to navigate the complex world of emotions and interpersonal relationships. Let's dig into how these powerful ideas intertwine to enrich our lives.

Mindfulness, a gem from ancient Buddhist practices now shining brightly in modern psychological arenas, invites us to immerse in the here and now. It's about tuning into our current experiences, thoughts, and feelings without passing judgment. This practice not only deepens our self-awareness but also teaches us to meet our emotions with acceptance, paving the way for thoughtful responses rather than knee-jerk reactions to life's curveballs.

Emotional intelligence is our emotional compass. It guides us in identifying, understanding, and managing our emotions and those of others. It's about recognizing what we feel, why we feel it, and how to express these emotions constructively. Emotional intelligence is also about empathy—stepping into someone else's shoes to understand their perspective, fostering deeper connections, and navigating social interactions with grace.

Together, mindfulness and emotional intelligence form a dynamic duo. Mindfulness grounds us in self-awareness, a critical foundation for emotional intelligence. It lets us observe our emotions from a place of calm and clarity. From this awareness, emotional intelligence enables us to manage these emotions effectively, not just within ourselves but in our interactions with others.

Integrating mindfulness and emotional intelligence into our daily lives equips us with a strong toolkit for emotional resilience and interpersonal harmony. Mindfulness brings us into the moment, offering a clear view of our emotional landscape, while emotional intelligence teaches us to navigate this terrain with skill and empathy. By embracing both, we open ourselves to richer, more meaningful relationships and a deeper understanding of our emotional selves.

～

THE TRANSFORMATIVE POWER OF MINDFULNESS: ELEVATING EMOTIONAL WISDOM AND WELLBEING

MINDFULNESS, with its deep roots in timeless traditions, has captured the modern imagination for its profound impact on enhancing our overall quality of life. It's more than just practice; it's a way of being that enriches our connection with the moment, ourselves, and the world. Let's dive into the myriad ways mindfulness can elevate our daily experience, from sharpening our mental focus to deepening our emotional insights.

Stress Melter: At its heart, mindfulness serves as a potent antidote to stress. Engaging in this practice, we learn to anchor our attention in the now, releasing the grip of past regrets and future anxieties. Techniques like mindful breathing and body awareness bring us back to a place of calm, significantly lowering stress levels and enhancing our sense of peace.

Concentration Booster: In our distraction-filled lives, maintaining concentration is a feat. Mindfulness hones our attention, much like a muscle that strengthens with use. This practice teaches us to observe our wandering thoughts with kindness and gently guide them back to the present, paving the way for improved focus, clearer thinking, and heightened productivity.

Emotional Intelligence Enhancer: Emotional intelligence—the art of understanding and managing our emotions and empathetically navigating those of others—flourishes under mindfulness. Through mindful observation, we gain insights into our emotional patterns and learn to approach our feelings with understanding and control. This emotional acuity equips us to handle life's ups and downs with grace and resilience.

Relationship Builder: Mindfulness casts a ripple effect on our interactions, fostering empathy, compassion, and genuine listening. Present-moment awareness lets us engage more deeply in conversations, fostering connections rooted in mutual understanding and respect. The result is more harmonious relationships filled with meaningful exchanges.

Wellbeing Enhancer: At its core, mindfulness is a celebration of the present that leads to a richer, more contented life. It nurtures an attitude of acceptance, encouraging us to embrace ourselves and our experiences without harsh judgment. This mindset, coupled with a heightened awareness of our physical selves, encourages healthier living choices, from the food we eat to the activities we pursue.

In Summary: The journey into mindfulness is transformative, offering a treasure trove of benefits that extend from the mind's focus to the heart's capacity for empathy. Integrating mindfulness into our routine invites a wealth of positive changes, fostering a life marked by reduced stress, enhanced understanding of our emotional landscape, and enriched relationships. As we continue to explore and practice mindfulness, we unlock the doors to a more attuned, balanced, and fulfilling existence.

ELEVATING PERSONAL GROWTH THROUGH EMOTIONAL INTELLIGENCE

EMOTIONAL INTELLIGENCE (EI) is a game-changer in the realm of personal development and wellbeing. It's about mastering the art of understanding and managing our own emotions, as well as recognizing and reacting to the emotions of others. Let's dive into how boosting your EI can transform your approach to life, enhance your relationships, and guide you in making savvy decisions.

Mastering Your Emotional Landscape: At the heart of emotional intelligence is the ability to tune into your feelings, pinpoint what sparks them, and manage them wisely. This inner clarity and control are essential for personal growth. It's like having a roadmap of your emotional world; you understand where your strengths lie, what trips you up, and what makes you tick. Armed with this knowledge, you can steer clear of knee-jerk reactions and maintain your cool, setting the stage for focused growth and progress toward your aspirations.

Cultivating Richer Relationships: Emotional intelligence is your secret weapon for nurturing deep and lasting relationships. It equips you with the empathy to get where others are coming from and the finesse to respond to their feelings in a way that resonates. This skill is invaluable in fostering open, trust-filled, and meaningful connections.

Being emotionally intelligent means you can gracefully navigate through rough patches and disagreements, laying the foundation for relationships that not only endure but thrive. These relationships become pillars of support and mirrors for reflection, pivotal for personal evolution.

Making Decisions with Wisdom: When you're emotionally intelligent, your decision-making process is enriched with a blend of emotional and rational insights. You're in tune with your feelings, yet you can also weigh the logical parts of your choices. This balanced perspective lets you make decisions in harmony with your deepest values and long-term goals. It's about seeing the bigger picture, understanding the ripple effects of your actions, and choosing paths that lead to genuine growth and fulfillment.

Wrapping It Up: In essence, emotional intelligence is a powerful ally in the journey of personal growth. It opens the door to understanding and managing your emotions, building meaningful relationships, and making choices that reflect your true self. As you cultivate your EI, you'll navigate life's ups and downs with greater ease, confidence, and clarity. The journey to elevate your emotional intelligence may require patience and practice, but the rewards—a richer, more connected, and purpose-driven life—are worthwhile.

~

HARMONIZING MINDFULNESS WITH EMOTIONAL INTELLIGENCE FOR PERSONAL GROWTH

MINDFULNESS and emotional intelligence might seem like two separate paths, but they actually walk hand in hand, enhancing each other in profound ways. Let's dive into how these two ideas intertwine and boost our personal and professional lives.

Mindfulness: The Foundation of Emotional Awareness At its core, mindfulness is about living in the now. It's tuning into your thoughts, feelings, and sensations without passing judgment. This practice is important for building the bedrock of emotional intelligence—self-awareness. Imagine being so in tune with yourself that you recognize your emotional reactions as they happen. That's the power of mindfulness at play, setting the stage for deeper emotional understanding.

Self-Regulation Through Mindful Moments Mindfulness does more than just highlight our emotions; it offers us the steering wheel to navigate them. By becoming observers of our own minds, we learn to pause before reacting, choosing responses that align with our values and goals. This skill is a cornerstone of emotional intelligence, helping us manage our emotions in constructive ways.

Building Blocks of Emotional Intelligence Mindfulness isn't just about looking inward; it also expands our capacity for empathy and compassion. By practicing mindfulness, we foster a gentle approach toward ourselves, recognizing our struggles and triumphs. This self-compassion naturally extends outward, enhancing our ability to connect with others on an emotional level.

Enhancing Relationships with Presence The practice of being present, a key aspect of mindfulness, enriches our interactions with others. Engaging in conversations, free from judgment, we become better listeners, more empathetic companions, and clearer communicators. These qualities are essential for nurturing strong, meaningful relationships—an important part of emotional intelligence.

The Synergy in Practice So, how do mindfulness and emotional intelligence feed into each other? Mindfulness acts as the soil from which the flowers of emotional intelligence grow. By cultivating a mindful approach to life, we enhance our self-awareness, learn to manage our emotions more effectively, and deepen our connections with others. These emotional intelligence skills enrich our mindfulness practice, creating a virtuous cycle of growth and understanding.

Conclusion: A Unified Path to Wellbeing Mindfulness and emotional intelligence are more than just buzzwords; they're tools that, when used together, can transform our lives. By integrating mindfulness practices into our daily routines, we can elevate our emotional intelligence, leading to improved wellbeing, stronger relationships, and a deeper sense of fulfillment. Start weaving these practices into your life and watch how they enrich your journey toward personal and professional growth.

~

CASE STUDIES AND EXAMPLES:

NAVIGATING FROM OVERWHELM TO EQUILIBRIUM: JOHN'S JOURNEY

JOHN, a high-achieving attorney, grappled with the all-too-common foes of stress and burnout. His career, while successful, demanded more than he felt he could sustainably give. In search of solace and a way back to himself, John turned to mindfulness and emotional intelligence as his guideposts.

He began carving out time each day for mindfulness meditation, dedicating moments to simply be. In these moments, he practiced observing his whirlwind of thoughts and feelings without casting judgment, a task easier said than done.

This practice of mindful reflection brought something important into the light: John discovered a habit of harsh self-criticism and persistent negative thoughts fueling his stress fire. Armed with this newfound self-awareness, John leaned into his emotional intelligence skills to navigate his emotional landscape more skillfully. Confronted with challenges, he now paused, identifying, and acknowledging his feelings, and choosing a response steeped in empathy and understanding, rather than knee-jerk reactions.

The shift didn't happen overnight, but the impact was undeniable. John found resilience he hadn't known before, learning to separate his sense of wellbeing from the pressures of work. He crafted new coping strategies, embracing breaks, setting clear boundaries, and elevating self-care on his list of priorities.

The ripple effects were profound. Not only did John's productivity at work see an uptick, but he also rediscovered joy and satisfaction in his life outside the office. This tale of transformation from burnout to balance underscores the power of integrating mindfulness and emotional intelligence into our daily lives, a testament to the journey of rediscovering one's equilibrium amidst life's tumult.

Case Study 2:

Trish's Path to Empowerment: Mindfulness and Emotional Intelligence as Catalysts for Change

Trish's story is one of transformation, a journey from battling anxiety and self-doubt to embracing confidence and inner peace. As a young professional, the challenges she faced weren't just hurdles in her career but obstacles that affected her sense of self and happiness. Determined to turn things around, Trish ventured into the realms of mindfulness and emotional intelligence.

Her journey began with the simple yet profound practice of mindfulness. Through deep breathing exercises and body scanning, Trish learned to quiet her mind's chaos and anchor herself in the now. This practice didn't just offer her moments of calm but also helped her recognize and meet her emotions with compassion rather than judgment or fear.

Emotional intelligence training opened new doors for Trish. She started to untangle the web of her inner critic and shift away from the negative self-talk that had long been her companion. Embracing self-compassion, Trish learned to celebrate her strengths and accept her weaknesses with grace.

The impact of these practices on Trish's life was nothing short of remarkable. She noticed a palpable decrease in her anxiety and found herself better equipped to handle life's ups and downs. This newfound resilience was mirrored in her growing confidence, not just in her personal life but in the professional arena as well. Trish evolved into a more effective communicator, a listener full of empathy, and a team member who thrived on collaboration.

Her journey underscores the transformative power of integrating mindfulness and emotional intelligence into one's life. Trish's story is a beacon of hope for anyone looking for their footing amidst the storm of anxiety and self-doubt, illustrating how personal growth can lead to success beyond one's imagination.

~

TRANSFORMATIVE JOURNEYS: THE IMPACT OF MINDFULNESS AND EMOTIONAL INTELLIGENCE

THE STORIES of John and Trish are powerful testimonials to the life-changing effects of mindfulness and emotional intelligence. Each facing their unique struggles—John with burnout in his high-pressure legal career, and Trish with anxiety and low self-esteem affecting her job performance—they found common ground in the solution: embracing mindfulness and emotional intelligence.

Their journeys, though distinct, highlight a universal truth: the profound influence of developing self-awareness, managing emotions effectively, and building resilience. By integrating mindfulness into their daily routines, both John and Trish learned to live in the moment, observe their thoughts and emotions without judgment, and confront challenges with a calm and clear mind.

Emotional intelligence was the key that unlocked their ability to understand and regulate their emotions, leading to significant personal growth. It taught them empathy, not just for others but for themselves, letting them navigate their inner landscapes with compassion and grace.

The outcomes of their journeys speak volumes. John balanced his demanding career with his personal wellbeing, leading to enhanced productivity and a renewed sense of fulfillment. Trish, on the other hand, conquered her anxiety, gained confidence, and saw her career flourish because of her improved communication and teamwork skills.

John and Trish's stories are a testament to the transformative power of mindfulness and emotional intelligence. They prove that no matter the challenge, focusing on personal growth, emotional wellbeing, and resilience can lead to greater success and happiness in all areas of life.

~

INTEGRATING MINDFULNESS AND EMOTIONAL INTELLIGENCE INTO EVERYDAY LIFE: A PRACTICAL GUIDE

DIVING INTO MINDFULNESS and emotional intelligence need not be daunting. It's all about starting small, being consistent, and finding ways to seamlessly incorporate these practices into your daily life. Here's a friendly guide to getting started and making these practices a natural part of your routine.

Start Simple and Stay Consistent: Kick off with a few minutes of mindfulness each day and gradually increase the time. Consistency beats quantity every time. Apply emotional intelligence in your daily interactions by practicing skills like active listening and thoughtful self-reflection regularly.

Remind Yourself: Leverage technology to your advantage. Set alarms on your phone or computer to nudge you toward taking mindful moments throughout your day. These reminders can be cues to focus on the present or to engage in emotional intelligence practices, such as making sure you're listening in conversations.

Integrate Mindfulness Into Routine Tasks: You don't always need a quiet room and a meditation cushion. Turn daily activities, like enjoying your meal or doing household chores, into mindfulness exercises. Relish the flavors of your food or focus on the sensation of the water as you wash dishes, to bring mindfulness into the mundane.

Journal Your Journey: Keeping a mindfulness journal can be insightful. It's a space to jot down thoughts, experiences, and any aha moments you encounter along the way. This can also be a tool for exploring your emotions and behavioral patterns, enhancing both your mindfulness and emotional intelligence.

Embrace Gratitude: Take a moment each day to acknowledge what you're thankful for. Identifying three things that brightened your day can shift your perspective to the positive, nurturing a grateful heart and enriching your emotional wellbeing.

Lean on Community and Resources: Don't go it alone. Join a group, take a class, or link up with a mentor experienced in mindfulness and emotional intelligence. Connecting with others on a similar path can offer encouragement, fresh perspectives, and invaluable tips. Dive into books or podcasts on the subject for more guidance and inspiration.

By incorporating these practical tips into your life, you're not just adopting new habits; you're starting a journey toward a more mindful, emotionally intelligent you. With patience, practice, and creativity, these practices will become second nature, enhancing your overall wellbeing and enriching your interactions with the world around you.

~

EMBRACING MINDFULNESS AND EMOTIONAL INTELLIGENCE: A ROADMAP TO WELLBEING

As WE WRAP up our exploration of mindfulness and emotional intelligence, it's clear these aren't just buzzwords—they're tools for deep, meaningful change in our lives. From personal development to enhanced resilience and success, the journey through these ideas is nothing short of transformative. Let's reflect on the profound impact that mindfulness and emotional intelligence can have on our overall wellbeing.

Mindfulness teaches us the power of now living in the present, attuned to our thoughts, feelings, and physical sensations without judgment. It's about noticing life as it happens, which sharpens our ability to navigate challenges with grace and make informed choices.

Emotional intelligence, meanwhile, equips us to handle our emotions and understand those around us better. It's about more than just getting along with others; it's a framework for living that enhances decision-making, communication, and relationship-building. It's how we turn empathy into action and conflicts into opportunities for growth.

The secret to reaping these benefits? Consistent practice. Think of it as a mental workout: the more you flex these muscles, the stronger and more resilient they become. Whether it's through meditation, journaling, or simply reflecting on your emotions, a little daily practice goes a long way.

This journey isn't always smooth. Challenges and setbacks are part of the process. It's in these moments, though, that our dedication to growth is tested. Remember, progress is a slow dance, not a sprint. Each step forward, no matter how small, is a victory worth celebrating.

As you start this path to improved wellbeing, patience and kindness toward yourself are key. Embrace the journey, knowing that every effort you make is a building block toward a happier, more fulfilled you. Surround yourself with people who uplift and support you, and don't hesitate to dive into resources that expand your understanding and skills.

Trust in the journey. The path to meaningful change may be challenging, but the rewards—enhanced wellbeing, deeper relationships, and a richer, more contented life—are immeasurable. As you weave mindfulness and emotional intelligence into the fabric of your daily life, watch as your world transforms, revealing a brighter, more resilient you.

So, take that first step with confidence. You're not just starting a path of personal growth; you're setting the stage for a life that's enriched in every possible way. Remember, you have within you the strength and wisdom to make this journey a remarkable one. Let's move forward, together, toward a future brimming with possibility.

~

OVERCOMING SPECIFIC OBSTACLES:

UNDERSTANDING THE FEAR OF FAILURE: A COMMON HURDLE

LET's talk about a feeling we've all faced: the fear of failure. That nagging sensation creeps up whenever we're on the brink of something new or challenging, making us second-guess our every move. This fear is more than just a personal stumbling block; it touches every part of our lives, from our dreams and careers to the relationships we cherish.

At its heart, this fear often comes from a place of worrying about rejection, not living up to expectations, or simply not being "enough." It shows up differently for everyone. Some might shy away from any risk, haunted by the thought of judgment, while others might hold their dreams at arm's length, paralyzed by the possibility of not making the cut.

Regarding relationships, fear of failure can make us build walls. We might hesitate to let our guard down, worried that being vulnerable could end in hurt or rejection. It's this fear that can keep us from diving into the deep end of connection, robbing us of the chance to form profound bonds.

In our careers, this fear often plays the role of a roadblock, influencing us to choose paths that feel safe but unfulfilling, rather than following our passions. The dread of disappointment or not hitting the mark can keep us from venturing into new territories or embracing challenges that could lead to growth.

This fear can also take a heavy toll on our self-esteem. Constant worry over failure can lead us to doubt our capabilities and worth, stalling our progress and dimming our light. It's a vicious cycle—fear leads to self-doubt, which feeds more fear, keeping us from taking those leaps that could bring us closer to our goals.

However, it's important to remember that failure isn't the end of the story but a part of the journey. Many of the most successful folks out there credit their setbacks with providing invaluable lessons that paved the way for their success. Learning to view failure as a stepping-stone rather than a stumbling block can change the entire game.

The fear of failure is a universal experience, touching on everything from our personal lives to our professional ambitions. But by acknowledging this fear and learning to see failure as an opportunity for growth, we can break free from its hold and step into our full potential.

∾

UNPACKING THE FEAR OF FAILURE: WHAT'S REALLY GOING ON?

EVER FEEL like you're being held back by a nagging sense of dread thinking about not making the cut? You're not alone. The fear of failure is a common guest in our lives, sneaking into our decisions and dreams, often without an invite. But to kick this uninvited guest to the curb, we need to dig deep and understand where it's coming from. Let's dive into the roots of this fear, including the drive for perfection, the ghosts of past setbacks, the weight of societal expectations, and the whispers of self-doubt.

The Pursuit of Perfection: A big piece of the fear-of-failure puzzle is perfectionism. If you're always aiming for a flawless performance, fearing any slip-up as a mark against your worth, then you're probably familiar with this fear. Perfectionists often see failure as the enemy, believing that anything short of perfect is not good enough, which can paralyze them from taking any risks.

Echoes of the Past: Our history plays a big role too. If you've stumbled before and the experience left you more bruised than enlightened, that memory might hold you back. These experiences can make failure feel like an old foe, lurking around the corner, ready to strike again.

Shifting perspective to see these moments as steppingstones rather than stumbling blocks is key to moving forward.

The Weight of the World: Let's not forget about societal pressure. It seems like from the get-go, we're told that success is the end-all-be-all. With society's spotlight on achievements and accclades, it's easy to feel like falling short is the ultimate no-no. Breaking free from this mindset requires us to redefine success on our own terms, celebrating personal growth over the applause of the crowd.

The Doubt Within: Lastly, there's the inner critic—self-doubt. When we're not sure of our own abilities, the fear of failure is amplified. Doubting ourselves sets the stage for a fear that convinces us we're destined to fail. To counter this, boosting our self-esteem and adopting a growth mindset are essential. It's about silencing the inner critic and replacing it with a voice that cheers us on.

Getting to the heart of the fear of failure by addressing these under-lying issues is an important step toward overcoming it. It's about acknowledging that yes, the fear is there, but it need not control us. Understanding that failure isn't the end but a part of the journey toward growth and success can transform our approach to challenges. Remember, every misstep is a chance to learn, grow, and eventually, thrive.

~

NAVIGATING THE EMOTIONAL MAZE OF FEAR OF FAILURE

THE FEAR of failure is like a shadow that follows us around, casting a pall on our dreams and ambitions. It's not just about avoiding a misstep; the emotional whirlwind comes with it—increased anxiety, dwindling self-confidence, and the nagging sense that we're missing out on. Understanding the depth of this fear's impact is the first step toward reclaiming our confidence and stepping boldly toward our goals.

The Anxiety Spiral: It starts with anxiety, a constant hum in the background of our minds. The thought of slipping up or not meeting expectations can send our hearts racing and our minds spinning. This isn't just nerves; it's a physical and mental blockade that makes even the thought of taking a risk feel insurmountable. Over time, this anxiety isn't just about specific events; it becomes a part of who we are, affecting our mental health and quality of life.

Confidence Takes a Hit: Then there's the hit to our self-confidence. When fear of failure becomes our default setting, self-doubt isn't far behind. It whispers that maybe we're not cut out for this, holding us back from even trying to reach for new heights. This lack of confidence keeps us in our comfort zone, far away from potential failure but also from potential growth.

The Road Not Taken: What's really on the line here are the opportunities for growth and success we let slip through our fingers. Fear of failure acts like a roadblock to personal development, keeping us from exploring, learning, and ultimately, flourishing. It's the what-ifs and might-have-beens that haunt us, the chances we didn't take because we were too afraid to fail.

Belief Barriers: At the heart of this fear are the self-limiting beliefs that tell us we're not good enough. These beliefs convince us to play it safe, to make excuses, and to shy away from challenges. They limit our potential, keeping us from discovering what we're capable of achieving.

Wellbeing on the Line: Lastly, the fear of failure doesn't just affect our ambitions; it takes a toll on our mental wellbeing. The stress and self-criticism can lead to deeper issues, such as depression and anxiety disorders, affecting not only our personal ambitions but also our relationships and overall happiness.

Wrapping Up: The fear of failure is a formidable adversary, but it's not invincible. By acknowledging its impact and working toward resilience and a positive mindset, we can break its hold on us. Building self-confidence, embracing opportunities for growth, and viewing failure as a steppingstone rather than a setback can open the door to a fulfilling and successful life. Let's not let fear dictate our paths. Instead, let's navigate this emotional maze with our heads held high, ready to embrace whatever comes our way.

～

BREAKING FREE FROM THE FEAR OF FAILURE

TACKLING the fear of failure might seem like climbing a mountain, but guess what? It's doable with the right approach and mindset. Here are solid strategies to help you face down that fear and stride confidently toward your goals.

Flip the Script on Negative Thoughts: That little voice inside your head that whispers, "You can't do this"? It's time for a reality check. Start challenging these negative notions with positive affirmations. Swap out "I'm bound to mess up" for "Every step I take is a chance to learn and grow."

Goal Setting with a Twist: Setting sky-high goals can sometimes backfire. Try breaking your aspirations down into bite-sized, achievable goals. Celebrating these smaller victories can boost your confidence and keep you motivated on your journey.

Learning from the Tumbles: Mistakes are not roadblocks; think of them as steppingstones. Each time you stumble, there's an invaluable lesson tucked away. Reflect on these moments, gather insights, and adjust your sails.

Build Your Support Squad: Don't go it alone. Lean on friends, family, or mentors who get what you're going through. Sharing your worries and wins with them can offer new perspectives and the emotional boost you need to keep pushing forward.

Divide and Conquer: Feeling swamped by a project? Break it down into smaller tasks to avoid feeling overwhelmed. Ticking off these mini tasks can give you a sense of progress and make the overall goal seem more attainable.

Kindness Begins with You: Be your own biggest cheerleader, not your toughest critic. Embrace self-compassion, especially when things don't go as planned. Remember, failure doesn't define your value—it's simply part of the human experience.

Picture Your Success: Instead of dwelling on potential pitfalls, imagine reaching your goals. Visualization can be a powerful tool for building self-assurance and keeping your eyes on the prize.

Remember, shaking off the fear of failure is a journey, not a sprint. Be patient with yourself, savor the small wins, and don't shy away from seeking help when you need it. Armed with these strategies, you're well on your way to overcoming those fears and unlocking your true potential. Let's turn those "what ifs" into "why nots" and make things happen!

∼

EMBRACING RESILIENCE AND KINDNESS TOWARD YOURSELF

NAVIGATING the rough waters of fear and failure isn't easy, but arm yourself with resilience and self-compassion, and you're much better equipped for the journey. The dread of failing can act like an anchor, dragging down your aspirations and risk-taking spirit. Yet, by fostering resilience and nurturing a kind approach toward oneself, you can cut loose from this anchor and sail toward success and personal fulfillment.

Resilience: Your Comeback Power

Think of resilience as your internal comeback power—it's about bouncing back stronger every time life knocks you down. It's seeing a setback not as a measure of your worth but as a steppingstone to greater things. Building resilience means keeping a positive outlook, trusting in your ability to overcome, and staying motivated amidst adversity.

Self-Compassion: Your Inner Support System

Self-compassion is like being your own cheerleader, especially when things don't go as planned. It's about extending the same kindness and understanding to yourself that you would to a dear friend. Recognizing that stumbling is part of the human condition helps diffuse the fear of failure and paves the way for a more forgiving and supportive self-dialogue.

How to Build Your Resilience and Self-Compassion Toolkit:

- **Positive Self-Talk:** Make a conscious effort to silence your inner critic. Swap harsh self-judgments with words of encouragement and reassurance. Remind yourself that every misstep is a chance to learn and grow.
- **Mindfulness:** Embrace the present with open arms. Mindfulness helps you become observant rather than a critic of your thoughts and emotions. This clarity and acceptance can significantly ease the journey through challenging times, letting you tackle obstacles with calm and poise.
- **Self-Care Rituals:** Don't underestimate the power of taking care of your holistic wellbeing. Whether it's through physical activity, nourishing your body with healthy foods, ensuring restful sleep, or diving into hobbies, these acts of self-care reinforce your emotional durability and readiness to face fears.
- **Lean on Your Tribe:** Opening up about your fears and failures to those you trust can lighten your load. Whether it's friends, family, or mentors, a support network can offer fresh perspectives, encouragement, and remind you that you're not alone on this journey.

Wrapping Up: Cultivating resilience and self-compassion is an important strategy against the fear of failure. It empowers you to face down challenges, learn from missteps, and chase after your dreams with a heart full of courage. Through practices like positive self-talk, mindfulness, self-care, and seeking support, you're not just preparing to tackle failure; you're setting the stage for significant personal growth and success. So, take a deep breath, and step forward with resilience and kindness. The path ahead is yours to shape.

∼

TURNING SETBACKS INTO SUCCESS: INSPIRATIONAL STORIES OF PERSEVERANCE

IN THE PURSUIT of our goals, we often dread failure, seeing it as a fall from grace, a mark of not being good enough. But, imagine if we shifted our perspective to see failure not as a stumbling block but as a pivotal part of our journey toward success. This Part brings to light stories of individuals who turned their defeats into victories, proving that adversity isn't the end but an important ingredient for achievement. These narratives showcase that the roadblocks we encounter can actually be the things that propel us to new heights.

Thomas Edison's Bright Idea:

The tale of Thomas Edison is a classic example of persistence in the face of failure. Edison's journey to invent the lightbulb was filled with thousands of unsuccessful attempts. Yet, he famously remarked, "I have not failed. I've just found 10,000 ways that won't work." Edison's relentless pursuit and his view of failure as a necessary step in the discovery process helped to create the incandescent light bulb, changing the course of history.

J.K. Rowling's Magical World:

J.K. Rowling's path to publishing the Harry Potter series was fraught with rejection. Despite being turned down by many publishers and being advised to stick to a day job, Rowling's belief in her story never wavered. Her determination eventually led to the publication of the series, which captivated readers worldwide, turning Rowling into one of the most beloved authors of our time.

Walt Disney's Dreamland:

Walt Disney faced his share of skepticism and financial hurdles in bringing Disneyland to fruition. Critics doubted his vision, and Disney even risked his own home for funding. Despite these challenges, Disney's refusal to give up transformed his dream into a reality, making Disneyland a symbol of joy and creativity for generations to come.

Oprah Winfrey's Journey of Resilience:

Oprah Winfrey's life story is one of overcoming adversity. From a challenging childhood to professional setbacks, including the struggles of her network, Oprah faced many obstacles. However, she used these experiences as steppingstones, rising to become a source of inspiration and empowerment for millions across the globe.

In Conclusion:

These stories illuminate the truth that setbacks are not the end but important chapters in our story of success. The resilience and determination of Edison, Rowling, Disney, and Winfrey teach us that failures are not a measure of our worth but opportunities for growth and learning. By embracing our setbacks with a resilient spirit and a forward-looking mindset, we can turn our failures into the foundation of our greatest achievements. Let's take inspiration from these tales, view our failures as lessons, and leap toward our dreams with renewed vigor.

~

STEPPING BEYOND FEAR: A GUIDE TO EMBRACING GROWTH

As we wrap up this part, I want to leave you with a thought that's both simple and profound: it's time to face your fears, especially the fear of failure, and stride confidently toward personal and professional enrichment. Fear is part of the human experience, a common feeling that can either freeze us in our tracks or motivate us to leap forward. By acknowledging and addressing this fear, you're not just moving past a hurdle; you're setting the stage for significant growth, achievement, and happiness.

Redefining Failure:

Start by shifting your perspective on failure. It's not a setback or a mark against your value but a golden chance to learn, adapt, and emerge stronger. Every challenge or "failure" is a lesson in disguise, offering insights and opportunities to refine our approach. Welcome failure as a natural step in your journey of evolution and self-discovery.

Believe in Your Power:

To conquer the fear of failure, it's essential to have faith in yourself and your capabilities. Understand that the path to greatness is paved with trials and errors. Trust in your skills, your knowledge, and your resilience. Remember, every great success story is also a tale of persistence through failure.

Action is Key:

Overcoming fear requires more than just a change in mindset; it demands action. Begin with setting small, achievable goals that nudge you out of your comfort zone. Break larger goals into manageable tasks and face them step by step. Celebrate every win, no matter the size, to build your confidence and momentum.

Lean on Your Support System:

Journeying through fear can be daunting, but you need not do it alone. Surround yourself with people who lift you up and push you forward. Also, please tap into resources that can guide you through this process, whether it's inspirational books, skill-building workshops, or therapeutic interventions.

Resources to Guide Your Journey:

- **Books to Inspire:**
- "Daring Greatly" by Brene Brown for embracing vulnerability.
- "Mindset: The New Psychology of Success" by Carol S. Dweck for understanding the power of mindset.
- "The Obstacle Is the Way" by Ryan Holiday for leveraging challenges to your advantage.
- **Workshops for Skill Building:**
- Toastmasters International for honing public speaking and leadership.
- Dale Carnegie Training for mastering human relations and communication.
- CreativeLive for exploring creativity and entrepreneurship through online classes.
- **Therapeutic Approaches:**
- Cognitive Behavioral Therapy (CBT) for reshaping negative thoughts and behaviors.
- Exposure Therapy for gradually reducing fear response.

- Acceptance and Commitment Therapy (ACT) for aligning actions with your values despite fear.

Facing down the fear of failure not only broadens your horizon but also deepens your sense of fulfillment and authenticity. Dare to fail, learn from each fall, and let these experiences propel you to heights you once thought unreachable. You have the strength to overcome, to grow, and to succeed. Let's move forward fearlessly, embracing every part of the journey, failures included.

~

PART ELEVEN WRAP-UP:

KEY POINTS:

- **Emotional Intelligence and Mindfulness:** Understanding and managing one's own emotions and those of others plays a significant role in personal and professional success. Mindfulness enhances emotional intelligence by promoting awareness of thoughts and feelings.
- **Developing Self-Awareness:** The cornerstone of emotional intelligence involves recognizing one's emotions and their impact on behavior. Techniques like journaling and mindfulness practices improve self-awareness.
- **Enhancing Self-Management:** Strategies for managing emotions and impulses include developing emotional awareness, practicing stress management techniques, and building a strong support system.
- **Building Social Awareness:** Empathy and understanding the emotions of others are important. Techniques for improving social awareness include active listening and observing non-verbal cues.

- **Improving Relationship Management:** Effective interaction with others involves self-awareness, empathy, and strong social skills. Techniques include assertive communication and fostering positive work environments.
- **Using Journaling for Emotional Intelligence Development:** Journaling can enhance self-awareness, emotional regulation, and relationship management. Prompts for reflection include exploring emotions, practicing empathy, and setting goals for emotional intelligence development.
- **Empathy-Building Activities:** Activities like role-playing, storytelling, and cultural immersion can enhance empathy and social awareness. Practical techniques include active listening and perspective-taking.
- **Mindfulness activities for goal pursuit:** Incorporating mindfulness into daily routines, like breathing exercises and gratitude journaling, enhances focus and emotional balance.
- **Assessing progress and adjusting goals:** Regular self-reflection and goal adjustment are key to personal growth. Practicing self-compassion and seeking feedback are important steps.
- **Enhancing interpersonal skills through mindfulness and emotional intelligence:** Improved communication, empathy, and relationships result from mindfulness and understanding emotions. Techniques include active listening and assertive communication.
- **Integrating mindfulness and emotional intelligence into daily life:** Regular practice of mindfulness and emotional intelligence techniques, such as morning mindfulness and emotional check-ins, builds resilience and enhances wellbeing.

Action Items:

- **Practice Daily Mindfulness:** Dedicate time each day for mindfulness meditation or deep breathing exercises to enhance emotional regulation and awareness.
- **Engage in Self-Reflection:** Use journaling or reflection exercises to explore personal emotions, strengths, weaknesses, and emotional triggers.
- **Set Achievable Goals:** Break down larger goals into manageable steps and celebrate small achievements to build self-confidence and motivation.
- **Cultivate Empathy:** Practice putting yourself in others' shoes and engage in empathy-building activities to improve social awareness and relationships.
- **Develop Assertive Communication:** Use "I" statements to express your feelings and needs assertively, improving your relationship management skills.
- **Implement Stress Management Techniques:** Identify personal stress triggers and apply stress reduction strategies, such as mindfulness exercises or physical activity.
- **Seek Feedback:** Ask for constructive feedback from peers, mentors, or coaches to gain insights into your emotional intelligence and interpersonal skills.
- **Embrace Learning Opportunities:** Participate in workshops, courses, or therapy sessions focused on developing mindfulness, emotional intelligence, and interpersonal skills.
- **Build a Supportive Network:** Cultivate relationships with individuals who support your personal growth and can provide guidance and encouragement.
- **Reflect and Adjust Regularly:** Regularly assess your progress toward goals, embrace self-compassion, and adjust your approach as needed to continue personal development.

In Our Next Part...

Let's dive into something we've all grappled with - procrastination. It's that all-too-familiar scenario where tasks pile up, not because we can't do them, but because we keep putting them off. From the daunting fear of failure, striving for unattainable perfection, to simply lacking the drive, the reasons we delay are many. But we're not here to dwell on the problem. Our focus? Offering you real, actionable ways out of the procrastination maze.

We will dissect procrastination, helping you understand and recognize why you might hit the pause button a little too often. This isn't about a one-size-fits-all solution; it's about tailoring strategies to fit your unique situation. We'll walk you through setting achievable goals, adopting time management techniques that aren't just buzzwords but practical tools for focusing on your workload effectively.

And there's more to it than managing tasks. We'll delve into the transformative power of maintaining a positive outlook, the significance of having people in your corner to keep you accountable, and why self-care isn't just a buzzword but a foundational element in managing stress and maintaining focus.

From the motivational boost of positive affirmations and visualization exercises to the grounding effects of exercise and meditation, we're pulling out all the stops to help you break free from procrastination. Get ready to face your to-do list head-on, armed with a fresh, motivated, and stress-free perspective on both your personal and professional life.

Procrastination need not be your default. Let's move forward, turning procrastination into productivity and transforming challenges into achievements. Welcome to your new chapter of efficiency and success.

∽

NAVIGATING BEYOND PROCRASTINATION: STRATEGIES FOR SUCCESS

DECODING PROCRASTINATION: WHY WE DELAY AND HOW TO OVERCOME IT

EVER POSTPONED tasks you know need attention, only to wonder why? Procrastination isn't just about being lazy; it's a complex dance of emotions and psychological triggers. Let's dive into the three big reasons behind procrastination—fear of failure, perfectionism, and lack of motivation—and unpack how these factors play out in our lives.

First up, fear of failure. It's a big one. The dread of not measuring up or tripping up can paralyze. Facing a challenging task? That fear can kick in, making us dodge the task to protect our pride. It's like our mind's way of saying, "If I don't try, I can't fail." But in reality, this avoidance just hands the reins over to fear, keeping us stuck in a loop of inaction.

Then there's perfectionism. This is all about setting the bar sky-high. For perfectionists, it's all or nothing. Falling short of those lofty goals can lead to procrastination. Why start if it will not be flawless, right? But this mindset traps us in a cycle of waiting for the 'perfect' moment, which, spoiler alert, never comes.

Lastly, lack of motivation can be a major procrastination driver. Sometimes, we just can't muster up the energy or interest to tackle a task. This could be because we're overwhelmed, burned out, or just not that into what we need to do. Without that spark to get going, tasks get pushed back, hoping for a burst of motivation that might never arrive.

Recognizing these triggers is the first step to breaking free from procrastination's grip. Strategies like tackling the fear of failure head-on, setting more realistic goals to counteract perfectionism, and finding ways to spark motivation can make a world of difference. Whether it's breaking tasks down into bite-sized pieces, seeking inspiration, or simply giving ourselves a break, there are ways to move past procrastination and toward productivity.

By understanding the root causes of why we delay, we're better equipped to face procrastination and take back control. So, let's get to it —step by step, we can overcome procrastination and embrace a more productive, less stressful approach to tackling our tasks.

∼

NAVIGATING THROUGH PROCRASTINATION: A GUIDE TO RECOGNIZING YOUR PATTERNS

WE'VE ALL BEEN THERE, staring down a task with every intention to tackle it... later. Procrastination isn't just about being lazy; it's a complex web of habits that can hinder our progress and dampen our potential. To break free, the first step is shining a light on our procrastination patterns. Here's how you can become a detective in your own life, uncovering clues to why you delay and strategizing your way out.

Reflect on Your Procrastination History: Look back at times you've put things off. Notice any trends? Maybe certain tasks always get the "I'll do it tomorrow" treatment, or perhaps there's a time of day you're most likely to sidestep work. Spotting these patterns can clue you into your unique procrastination profile.

Identify Your Triggers: What sets off your procrastination alarm? It could be fear of not doing things perfectly, the lure of social media, or indecision about where to start. Pinpointing these triggers can help you understand what's holding you back.

Tune Into Your Inner Monologue: Pay attention to the thoughts and feelings bubbling up when you're about to procrastinate. Do you feel overwhelmed or doubt your skills? Recognizing these emotional hurdles is important in learning to leap over them.

Keep a Procrastination Diary: Yes, it's homework, but trust me on this one. Jot down when and why you procrastinate, including the task, the trigger, and what you're feeling. Over time, you'll see patterns emerge, giving you a roadmap for change.

Test Out Productivity Tactics: Dive into different strategies to find what clicks for you. Maybe it's the Pomodoro Technique, breaking tasks into bite-sized pieces, or setting laser-focused goals. The key is to experiment and discover what nudges you into action.

Learning of your procrastination habits is like turning on a light in a dark room. Suddenly, you can navigate through the mess and find a path forward. With introspection and some strategic tweaks, you can transform procrastination from a stumbling block into a steppingstone toward meeting your goals. Let's get moving, one mindful step at a time.

~

CRAFTING A ROADMAP: THE ART OF GOAL SETTING AND TIMELINES

TACKLING big projects or long-term goals can feel like trying to eat an elephant—one bite at a time is the only way to do it. The key to digesting these massive undertakings? Setting realistic goals and mapping out a timeline. It's like plotting a journey, where you identify the destination, plan the route, and make pit stops along the way. Here's how to chart your course:

Pinpoint Your Destination: First off, nail down exactly what you're aiming for. A fuzzy destination leads to a meandering path. Make sure your goal is as clear as a sunny day and within the realm of possibility.

Divide and Conquer: With your end goal in sight, chop it up into mini goals. These should be SMART—specific, measurable, attainable, relevant, and time-sensitive. It's like turning a daunting mountain into manageable hills.

Set Your Priorities Straight: Look at your list of tasks and decide which ones are the VIPs. Which tasks are mission-critical? Tackle those head-on before anything else.

Time is of the Essence: Try to gauge how much time each piece of the puzzle will take. Be honest with yourself about what you can achieve given your resources and constraints.

Lay Out Your Timeline: With your time estimates in hand, draw up a timeline. Whether you're a fan of digital tools, a classic calendar, or a good ol' to-do list, use whatever helps you keep track of your deadlines.

Stay Nimble: Life loves to throw curveballs. While sticking to your timeline is important, be ready to bob and weave when necessary. Adjust your plan as needed but keep your eyes on the prize.

Check In Regularly: Periodically review your progress. If you're lagging, don't beat yourself up—figure out why and adjust your plan or timeline.

Celebrate Your Wins: Don't wait until you've reached your final goal to give yourself a pat on the back. Celebrating milestones along the way can recharge your batteries and keep your spirits high.

Remember, setting goals and creating a timeline isn't about boxing yourself into a corner. It's about giving yourself a clear path to follow and making the journey to your destination less overwhelming. By breaking down your goals into bite-sized pieces and plotting a course, it is easier to start, continue, and ultimately cross the finish line. So, let's get planning and make those goals a reality, one step at a time.

$\sim$

MASTERING YOUR TIME: STRATEGIES FOR PEAK EFFICIENCY

IN THE WHIRLWIND of our daily lives, mastering time management is more of an art form than a skill. It's about making the most of our hours, reducing stress, and ticking off those to-do lists with a flourish. Here's a playbook to help you navigate the choppy waters of time management with grace:

Sort Your Priorities: Kick things off by laying out everything on your plate. What's urgent? What matters most? Ranking your tasks helps you zero in on the critical stuff and keeps you from spinning your wheels on things that can wait.

Sketch Your Game Plan: Whether you're a planner addict or a digital calendar devotee, carve out time slots for various activities. Mix in work, personal time, and some fun—balance is key. Remember, being realistic is your best friend here; overpacking your day is a recipe for frustration.

Find Your Prime Time: We all have that golden hour (or hours) when we're firing on all cylinders. Pinpoint yours and schedule the heavy lifting for those times. The less demanding tasks can fill in the gaps when your energy dips.

Deadlines Are Your Allies: Setting deadlines is like drawing your finish line—it gives you something to race toward. Make them achievable, though; setting the bar too high can backfire, leaving you more frazzled than focused.

One Thing at a Time: Juggling tasks might feel productive, but it's often a productivity killer. Dive deep into one task at a time for quality output and a real sense of accomplishment.

Cut Out the Noise: Distractions are the archenemies of focus. Identify your main culprits (looking at you, phone notifications) and find ways to keep them at bay. Sometimes, all it takes is a quiet room or a focused mindset to stay on track.

Delegate Like a Boss: If you've got the option, pass on tasks that others can handle. It's not just about lightening your load—it's a chance to empower your team or family members by trusting them with responsibilities.

Tool Up: Embrace the digital age with apps and software designed to streamline your workflow. From to-do lists to comprehensive project management tools, there's something out there to keep you organized and on track.

Don't Skimp on Breaks: Paradoxically, stepping away from work can boost your productivity. Regular breaks keep your mind fresh and prevent burnout. So go ahead, take that coffee break without guilt.

Assess and Adapt: Take a step back every now and then to evaluate how you're doing. What's working? What's not? Fine-tuning your approach based on your reflections can turn good time management into great time management.

By weaving these strategies into the fabric of your daily routine, you'll not only get ahead of your tasks but also find a deeper sense of fulfillment in your day-to-day achievements. Remember, time management isn't about filling every minute—it's about ensuring those minutes count.

~

CULTIVATING A POSITIVE MINDSET TOWARD TASKS: OVERCOMING NEGATIVE THOUGHTS AND SELF-DOUBT

LEVERAGING SUPPORT AND ACCOUNTABILITY FOR SUCCESS

IN OUR JOURNEY toward personal and professional accomplishments, leveraging a network of support and accountability can be a game-changer. Whether it's hitting those ambitious targets or simply staying on track with daily tasks, having the right support system in place can significantly boost your motivation and focus. Here's a closer look at how tapping into accountability partners and support groups can be your secret weapon for success.

Choosing Your Accountability Partner: Finding the right account-ability partner is like selecting a teammate who's as invested in your success as their own. This could be a trusted colleague, a close friend, or even a mentor. The key here is to choose someone who understands your goals, challenges you constructively, and cheers you on. Regu-larly updating them on your progress not only keeps you accountable but also provides an opportunity for valuable feedback and support.

Diving into Support Groups: Support groups bring together individ-uals with shared goals or challenges, creating a community of mutual encouragement and understanding. Whether it's a professional networking group or a hobby-based community, the collective wisdom and experience of the group can offer fresh perspectives and innovative solutions to common obstacles. The camaraderie within these groups often fosters a sense of belonging and motivation, propelling members toward their goals.

Finding the Right Fit: Compatibility is important when selecting an accountability partner or support group. Look for individuals or groups that align with your values, work ethic, and aspirations. The right match can inspire you to reach new heights, while a mismatch might lead to frustration and stagnation.

Setting Clear Expectations: For these accountability structures to work effectively, it's essential to establish clear expectations and regular check-in routines. Whether it's a weekly catch-up call with your accountability partner or monthly meetings with your support group, having a set schedule helps maintain momentum and focus. Be open about your goals, challenges, and progress; honesty and transparency are the cornerstones of a productive accountability relationship.

The Power of Community: Beyond the practical parts of keeping you on track, accountability and support systems offer invaluable emotional and psychological benefits. Knowing you're not alone in your journey can alleviate the pressure and isolation often felt in pursuit of big goals. These relationships not only help you grow professionally but can also lead to lasting personal connections.

In wrapping up, embracing the idea of support and accountability can transform the way you approach your goals. Whether through one-on-one partnerships or community groups, building a network of support can elevate your journey from solitary struggle to a shared adventure. As you forge ahead, remember that success is not just about the destination but also about the allies you gather along the way. So, let's step into a world where accountability and support light the path to achieving our dreams.

HARNESSING THE POWER OF TEAMWORK: BOOSTING PRODUCTIVITY AND MOTIVATION

IN THE JOURNEY toward personal and professional achievements, embracing the support of accountability partners and joining forces with support groups can dramatically transform your productivity levels and keep your motivation sky-high. It's about creating a network of cheerleaders, advisors, and fellow travelers who are as invested in your success as their own.

Finding Your Accountability Partner: Imagine having a buddy who's in the trenches with you, someone to check in with regularly on your progress, goals, and the inevitable roadblocks. This could be anyone from a friend or colleague to a mentor who aligns with your aspirations. Sharing your journey with this person not only keeps you accountable but enriches your experience with invaluable feedback and encouragement.

Diving Into Support Groups: Support groups bring a unique dynamic to the table, uniting individuals with shared goals or challenges. It's a space where triumphs are celebrated, obstacles are dissected, and wisdom is shared freely. The collective energy of a support group can provide a surge of motivation and a sense of belonging that propels you forward.

Choosing the Right Circle: The key to a fruitful partnership or group experience lies in compatibility and commitment. Seek individuals or groups that resonate with your values and dedication level. A harmonious match can elevate your journey, while a mismatch might dampen your spirit.

Setting the Stage for Success: To maximize the benefits of your support system, clear communication and regular check-ins are essential. Schedule times to share updates, discuss goals, and brainstorm solutions to challenges. Open and honest dialogue strengthens the bonds of accountability and fosters an environment of mutual support.

Beyond Productivity: These support systems aren't just about crossing items off your to-do list; they're about personal growth and building meaningful connections. Immersing yourself in a community that champions growth and encouragement can open your eyes to new perspectives and deepen your relationships.

In Summary: Embarking on the path to your goals with an accountability partner or within a support group can significantly amplify your chances of success. These relationships encourage you to stretch beyond your perceived limits and navigate your journey with confidence. So, as you chart your course toward achieving your dreams, remember that the strength of your network can be your greatest asset. Let's embrace the power of teamwork and make those dreams a reality.

~

ELEVATING FOCUS THROUGH SELF-CARE AND STRESS RELIEF

TACKLING procrastination isn't just about pushing harder; it's about stepping back and taking care of yourself. Yep, you heard that right. Slowing down with some good old self-care and stress management can rev up your productivity. Let's dive into how activities like exercising, meditating, and chilling out with relaxation techniques can be your secret weapons against the procrastination beast.

Kickstart Your Energy with Exercise: Nothing blasts through stress like a good workout. Whether it's hitting the pavement, twisting into a yoga pose, or taking a leisurely stroll, moving your body releases those happy hormones, endorphins. This natural mood lifter doesn't just chase away the blues; it pumps up your energy levels, making it easier to dive into tasks with gusto. Regularly slotting exercise into your day can also give your daily routine more structure, leaving less room for procrastination to sneak in.

Meditation: Your Focus Supercharger: Meditation might seem like you're sitting there, but it's a powerhouse practice for decluttering your mind. Spending a few quiet moments each day focusing on your breath can calm the storm inside, helping you tackle tasks with a clear head. This mindfulness practice sharpens your ability to remain present, which is key to keeping procrastination at bay.

Relaxation Techniques to Melt Stress Away: Feeling wound up? Techniques like deep breathing or progressive muscle relaxation can turn the stress dial way down. Deep breaths can slow your heartbeat and usher in calm, while systematically tensing and relaxing muscle groups can dissolve tension like magic. Integrating these relaxation hacks into your day can smooth out stress levels, making it easier to focus and get things done.

Breaks and Boundaries: The Unsung Heroes: Non-stop grinding leads to burnout, not breakthroughs. It's important to pause and give yourself permission to recharge. Setting clear boundaries for work and rest can prevent burnout, keeping stress in check and procrastination at arm's length. Remember, taking a breather is not slacking; it's smart strategizing for peak performance.

Shifting Mindsets: Self-Care as a Priority: Embracing self-care requires a mindset makeover. It's not about indulgence; it's about respecting and focusing on your wellbeing. Acknowledging that self-care is an important part of maintaining your mental and physical health can transform your approach to tasks, energizing you to tackle them head-on without delay.

Wrapping Up: Self-care and stress management aren't just feel-good buzzwords; they're practical tools in your fight against procrastination. By making activities like exercise, meditation, and relaxation a staple in your life, you're setting the stage for enhanced focus, motivation, and productivity. Let's flip the script and see self-care as the foundation for success. Here's to healthier habits, sharper focus, and saying goodbye to procrastination for good.

~

PART TWELVE WRAP-UP:

- Procrastination is often driven by psychological and emotional factors like fear of failure, perfectionism, and lack of motivation.
- Recognizing one's own procrastination patterns is crucial for developing strategies to overcome it.
- Setting realistic goals and creating a timeline can help break down tasks into manageable steps, reducing the overwhelming feeling that leads to procrastination.
- Effective time management strategies, including focusing on tasks, creating schedules, and reducing distractions, are essential for improving productivity.
- Cultivating a positive mindset toward tasks involves overcoming negative thoughts and self-doubt through practices like positive affirmations, visualization, and reframing thoughts.
- Using accountability and support systems, such as accountability partners and support groups, can enhance motivation and commitment to tasks.

- Embracing self-care and stress management techniques, including exercise, meditation, and relaxation techniques, is important for reducing stress and combating procrastination.

Action Items:

- **Reflect on past instances** of procrastination to identify common patterns and triggers.
- **Create a procrastination journal** to log instances of procrastination, including tasks, emotions, and outcomes.
- **Break down large tasks** into smaller, actionable steps and focus on them based on urgency and importance.
- **Use productivity tools** like calendars and task management apps to organize tasks and deadlines.
- **Practice mindfulness** and meditation to improve focus and reduce stress levels.
- **Set specific, measurable, achievable, relevant, and time-bound (SMART) goals** to provide clear direction and motivation.
- **Find an accountability partner** or join a support group related to your goals to enhance commitment and receive encouragement.
- **Incorporate regular physical activity** into your routine to boost mood and energy levels.
- **Schedule regular breaks** and relaxation activities to prevent burnout and maintain mental wellbeing.
- **Challenge and reframe negative thoughts** about tasks to foster a more positive and productive mindset.

By addressing the underlying causes of procrastination and implementing these practical strategies, individuals can enhance their productivity, meet their goals, and improve their overall wellbeing.

· · ·

In Our Next Part...

In our upcoming exploration, we're venturing into the realm of mastering the delicate art of work-life harmony. It's about striking that perfect balance where our ambitions fuel our happiness, not reduce it. We're set to unveil strategies for setting boundaries that ensure our work commitments don't encroach on our personal time. This journey is all about identifying what matters to us, learning the power of saying "no," and crafting a life where our professional and personal aspirations thrive in harmony. It's time to redefine what success looks like, emphasizing a holistic approach that values our mental and physical health as much as our achievements.

Gear up to start a transformative path that promises to change how you navigate your day-to-day life. We're diving into effective ways to focus on that not only enhance how you allocate your time but also enrich your life. From embracing technology to streamline tasks to discovering time management hacks that free you up to pursue what sets your soul on fire, we've got you covered. By the end of this Part, you'll be equipped to tackle your daily tasks with newfound efficiency and grace, all while keeping your wellbeing in the spotlight. It's not just about ticking off tasks—it's about making every moment count, doing what's meaningful, and doing it well.

～

PART THIRTEEN
TIME MANAGEMENT ISSUES:

LET'S TALK TIME MANAGEMENT: MASTERING YOUR DAY FOR SUCCESS

IN THE HUSTLE and bustle of today's world, mastering time management is more than just a skill—it's a necessity for balancing life and achieving our dreams. This Part is all about shedding light on why managing our time wisely is important for both our personal growth and professional achievements.

Ever feel like the clock is always against you? You're not alone. Many of us are swamped with endless tasks, bouncing from one priority to the next, and we're left wondering where all the time went. This chaos often leads to missed deadlines, forgotten tasks, and, let's not forget, a ton of stress. Without a solid grasp on managing our time, it's easy to feel like we're always playing catch-up.

One big hurdle is figuring out what to tackle first. Without a clear game plan, it's tempting to spend hours on things that, in the grand scheme, aren't that important leaving the important tasks by the wayside. This not only zaps our productivity but can also stall our progress toward bigger personal and professional milestones.

Then there's the double trouble of distractions and procrastination. Thanks to the digital world, distractions are a click away, luring us away from our priorities. And procrastination? Often, it's not just laziness—it's being overwhelmed or scared of failing that makes us put off important tasks.

The ripple effects of not managing our time can touch everything from our relationships to our career paths, keeping us from tapping into our full potential. But flip the script to effective time management, and we're looking at a game-changer: skyrocketing productivity, laser-sharp focus, lower stress levels, and opening doors to opportunities we never thought possible.

As we dive deeper into this topic, we'll explore actionable strategies and insights to revolutionize your time management game. From crafting achievable goals and getting your priorities straight to conquering distractions and making every minute count, we're here to arm you with the tools you need to seize control of your time and unlock your true potential. So, are you ready to take this journey? Let's turn the page on time management and step into a world where success and balance go hand in hand.

~

SPOTTING AND STOPPING TIME-DRAINERS: MAKING EVERY MINUTE COUNT

TIME IS one thing we always wish we had more of. Yet, despite our best efforts, it often feels like it slips through our fingers, leaving us puzzled about where it all went and why we haven't ticked off more from our to-do list. A big part of the puzzle? Time-wasting habits that stealthily eat away at our productivity. Let's dive into some of the biggest time-drainers and share smart strategies to help you reclaim your hours.

Social Media: The Endless Scroll Ah, social media – it's the modern-day black hole for our time and attention. It's all too easy to dive into a quick check and emerge hours later, wondering where your day went. But fear not, there are ways to tame the beast:

- **Schedule your scroll:** Allocate specific times for social media and stick to them. This discipline helps keep the endless scrolling at bay.
- **Use tech to your advantage:** There are tons of apps out there designed to limit your time on these platforms. Try them.
- **Out of sight, out of mind:** Move social media apps away from your home screen. Making them less accessible can significantly cut down on your usage.

Procrastination: The Silent Progress Killer We've all been there – putting off tasks for later and then scrambling to complete them at the eleventh hour. Here's how to beat the procrastination bug:

- **Break it down:** Large tasks can seem daunting. Split them into smaller, more manageable chunks.
- **Deadline it:** Setting clear deadlines for yourself creates a sense of urgency and accountability.
- **Pomodoro your way through**: This technique involves focused work intervals followed by short breaks. It's a great way to keep your energy up and procrastination down.

Multitasking: The Illusion of Efficiency Multitasking might feel productive, but it's often a fast track to frustration and subpar work. Here's how to single-task your way to success:

- **Prioritize ruthlessly:** Focus on completing tasks one at a time, starting with the most critical ones.
- **Clear the clutter:** Make your workspace a distraction-free zone. Silence your phone and close any tabs or apps that aren't essential to your current task.
- **Be here now:** Practice mindfulness. By engaging with the task at hand, you'll find your focus sharpens and your efficiency skyrockets.

By pinpointing these common time-sinks and implementing these straightforward strategies, you can significantly enhance your productivity and make the most of every day. Remember, time is precious – let's not let it go to waste.

∼

MASTERING THE ART OF GOAL SETTING AND TASK PRIORITIZATION

Navigating through life's daily demands requires more than just a to-do list; it demands a strategic approach to setting goals and prioritizing tasks. It's about zeroing in on what matters, optimizing productivity, and carving out a path to achievement and satisfaction.

Let's talk strategy, starting with understanding the urgency and importance of your tasks. Think of urgency as a ticking clock and importance as the value or impact of a task. Balancing these two can shift how you tackle your day. Enter the Eisenhower Matrix, a simple yet game-changing tool that sorts your tasks into four categories:

1. **Urgent and Important (Do it now!):** These are your non-negotiables—the tasks demanding immediate attention. Missing these could mean trouble, so they're top of your list.
2. **Important but Not Urgent (Plan it out):** Here lie the tasks that contribute to long-term goals. They're important but need not be rushed. Schedule these to avoid last-minute chaos.
3. **Urgent but Not Important (Delegate if you can):** These tasks scream for attention but don't significantly affect your goals. Where possible, pass these off to free up space for what matters.

4. **Not Urgent and Not Important (Reduce these):** The least impactful tasks fall here. Reduce these time-stealers to make room for the tasks that contribute to your success.

The Eisenhower Matrix isn't just about categorization; it's about making intentional choices that align with your goals, helping to slash stress and boost productivity.

But we're not stopping there. Consider these additional strategies to elevate your time management game:

- **Goal Clarity:** Define what success looks like with SMART goals—Specific, Measurable, Attainable, Relevant, Time-bound. This clarity transforms vague aspirations into actionable steps.
- **Break It Down:** Tackle larger goals by dividing them into smaller, digestible tasks. This approach makes daunting goals feel more approachable and less intimidating.
- **Keep an Eye on the Clock:** Identify deadlines and milestones to keep things moving. A sense of urgency can propel you forward and keep procrastination at bay.
- **Play to Your Strengths:** Prioritize tasks that align with your strengths and preferences. You're more likely to excel and find joy in these activities.
- **Stay Adaptable:** Regularly reassess your priorities. Life is fluid, and your priorities should be too. Adjust as needed to stay aligned with your goals and circumstances.

Incorporating these strategies into your daily routine isn't just about managing time; it's about leading a more focused, fulfilling life. By prioritizing effectively and setting meaningful goals, you're not just crossing items off a list—you're building the foundation for long-term success and wellbeing. Let's embrace this mindful approach to time management and unlock our full potential.

∾

NAVIGATING PAST PROCRASTINATION: STRATEGIES FOR ENHANCED PRODUCTIVITY

LET'S TALK ABOUT PROCRASTINATION—a hurdle many of us face, often without even realizing it. It's that sneaky habit of putting off tasks, which not only delays our personal and professional goals but also adds unnecessary stress to our lives. The good news? There's a way out. This part of our journey is all about tackling procrastination head-on, armed with strategies that have been proven to work wonders.

One of the biggest revelations is that big, daunting tasks are procrastination's best friends. The key? Break them down into bite-sized pieces. It's about making those tasks feel less like mountains and more like manageable hills. This approach not only eases the stress but also brings a sense of accomplishment with each small victory, fueling your drive to keep pushing forward.

Deadlines are not just dates on a calendar; they're commitments to ourselves. Setting precise, achievable deadlines transforms a vague intention into a clear target, making it much harder to justify any delays. It's about turning "someday" into a specific "by this date," and this shift in perspective is important for overcoming procrastination.

Accountability plays a massive role here too. Teaming up with someone who shares your goals, or joining a group with similar goals, can significantly boost your motivation. It's the power of not wanting to let others down that can drive you to stick to your commitments. Plus, sharing your progress (and struggles) with someone who gets it can make all the difference.

Distractions are the silent progress killers, lurking around every corner, especially in this digital age. Crafting a distraction-free zone, setting focused work periods, and using apps to keep digital temptations at bay can dramatically improve your ability to stay on task. It's all about creating an environment that fosters concentration.

Time management techniques are your allies in the fight against procrastination. Whether it's the Pomodoro Technique, time blocking, or any other method, finding a system that works for you can help structure your day, boost your energy, and keep the motivation high.

And let's not forget about celebrating milestones. Recognizing and rewarding your progress not only feels good but also reinforces your motivation to keep going. It's a reminder that every step forward is worth acknowledging.

Lastly, adopting a growth mindset can transform the way you view challenges. Seeing mistakes as learning opportunities rather than failures encourages action and helps overcome the fear of not being perfect. It's about valuing progress over perfection.

Beating procrastination is about embracing a blend of tactics and mindset shifts. From breaking tasks down and setting clear deadlines to fostering accountability, reducing distractions, and celebrating every win, these strategies are about reclaiming control over your productivity. Remember, consistency is key. By applying these methods regularly, you'll find yourself not just dreaming about success but making it happen.

~

HARNESSING TECH TO TAME YOUR SCHEDULE: A GUIDE TO TIME MANAGEMENT TOOLS

IN THE WHIRLWIND of our daily lives, mastering time management isn't just useful—it's essential. Luckily, we're living in a golden age of technology where there are a lot of tools at our fingertips designed to streamline our schedules, enhance productivity, and free up those precious hours for what matters. Let's dive into some standout tools and technologies that could be game-changers for your time management strategy.

First up, productivity apps. Think of these as your personal digital assistants, ready to help you organize your day, set and smash your goals, create to-do lists, and keep track of all your tasks. Popular choices like Todoist, Trello, Asana, and Evernote offer a variety of features to focus on your tasks, nail down deadlines, and send you reminders to keep you on your toes. They're like the Swiss Army knives of time management—versatile, reliable, and handy.

For those of you juggling complex projects with multiple moving parts and collaborators, project management software could be your best bet. Platforms such as Monday.com, Jira, and Basecamp are tailor-made for organizing tasks, managing resources, keeping tabs on progress, and ensuring everyone's on the same page. They give you a bird's-eye view of your project's landscape, making it easier to steer your team toward the finish line efficiently.

Now, let's talk about time-tracking tools. Ever wondered where all your time goes? Tools like Toggl, RescueTime, and Harvest offer valuable insights into how you're spending your day. They can help you identify patterns, pinpoint time drains, and adjust your habits. It's all about getting smarter with your time and making sure you're focusing your energy where it counts.

In our always-connected world, distractions are a click away, making focus a rare commodity. Enter notification control tools—your guardians against the constant barrage of pings, dings, and buzzes. Apps like StayFocusd, Focus@Will, and Freedom can help you block out the noise and zero in on your work. By limiting access to distraction-heavy sites and apps, you can create pockets of focused, productive time, even in the busiest of environments.

Lastly, let's not overlook the power of task automation tools. Zapier, IFTTT, and Microsoft Power Automate are the workhorses of the tech world, automating those repetitive, time-consuming tasks that bog down your day. Whether it's scheduling posts or managing emails, setting up smart workflows can free you up to focus on tasks that require your unique human touch.

The right time management tools can transform how you navigate your day, turning chaos into order and freeing you to pursue your ambitions with gusto. By embracing these digital allies, you're not just managing your time; you're maximizing your life's potential. So why not explore what these tools can do for you? The key to unlocking your most productive self might be a few clicks away.

~

UNLOCKING PRODUCTIVITY WITH TIME BLOCKING

EVER FEEL like there's just not enough time in the day? Time blocking might be the game-changer you're looking for. This method isn't about stretching your day beyond its 24-hour limit; it's about maximizing what you've got. Let's dive into how time blocking can transform your day-to-day efficiency.

Time Blocking 101: Time blocking is like Tetris for your schedule—fitting each task into a specific time slot, ensuring every piece falls perfectly into place. Instead of a never-ending to-do list or a vague plan, time blocking assigns each task a home in your day. You could plot out work projects, gym time, or even downtime, each getting a dedicated slot in your calendar.

This method shines by letting you focus intensely on one task at a time. You're not juggling; you're diving deep into what matters, one block at a time. And it's not just about work; it's about making time for life, too.

The Perks of Time Blocking:

- **Sharper Focus and Boosted Productivity:** By dedicating time slots to specific tasks, you're all in, reducing distractions and upping your efficiency game.

- **Streamlined Time Management:** It gets easier to gauge how long tasks actually take, helping you plan more accurately and saying goodbye to overbooking yourself.
- **Stress Be Gone:** Knowing what you're doing and when to lift a huge weight off your shoulders. Plus, seeing time given for work and play keeps burnout at bay.

Making Time Blocking Work for You:

- **Prioritize:** Start by figuring out what needs your attention. What makes the cut gets a slot.
- **Be Realistic:** Don't pack your schedule too tight. Leave room for life's little surprises.
- **Embrace the Digital:** Leverage apps and tools to keep your time blocks organized and visible.
- **Flex Your Schedule:** It's not about rigid blocks of time. Shift and adjust as life happens.
- **Celebrate the Small Wins:** Knocked out a task in its allocated slot? Give yourself a high-five and take a moment to appreciate the progress.

Tackling Distractions Head-On: Distractions, the arch-nemesis of productivity, can sneak up in many forms—from the lure of social media to the buzz of your phone. Conquering them involves turning off notifications you don't need, setting clear boundaries with those around you, and perhaps most important, scheduling breaks to recharge and refresh.

Adjusting as You Go: The real beauty of time blocking lies in its flexibility. It's not set in stone. Evaluate how well your blocks are serving you. Too crunched for time? Stretch blocks out. Tasks taking less time than expected? Tweak your schedule for efficiency. The goal is to find a rhythm that works for you, allowing for both productivity and peace of mind.

In wrapping up, time blocking is more than a scheduling tactic; it's a holistic approach to managing your day. It respects the fact that you're human—not a productivity robot. By allocating time wisely, priori-tizing tasks, and reducing distractions, you're setting the stage for a more organized, less stressful, and ultimately more fulfilling life. Give it a go and watch your days transform.

~

FINDING YOUR EQUILIBRIUM: THE ART OF WORK-LIFE HARMONY

Navigating the hustle of modern life, it's all too easy to find ourselves wrapped up in the endless pursuit of career milestones, often at the cost of our personal wellbeing and cherished moments. Yet, it's important to remember that true achievement isn't just about professional wins; it's equally about nurturing our health, relationships, and peace of mind.

Crafting a harmonious work-life balance is key to a rich, fulfilling existence. It's about drawing clear lines between work and play and ensuring one doesn't overshadow the other. Here's how to strike that delicate balance:

- Reflect on what lights up your world. Is it family time, a hobby, or simply moments of solitude? Pin down these priorities to guide your daily choices and actions.
- Establish firm boundaries around work. Set specific work hours and stick to them. Make it clear to your team and yourself that after hours are sacred, meant for rest or family.
- Don't underestimate the power of self-care. Regular exercise, enough sleep, and proper nutrition are your pillars of strength.

Allow yourself pauses throughout the day to simply breathe and regroup.

- Sharing the load is key. Whether at home or work, delegate tasks. It's a win-win; you lighten your load, and others get to shine and grow.
- Reserve time for passions outside work. Be it reconnecting with friends, digging into a hobby, or exploring new places, ensure you're feeding your soul with activities that make you beam with joy.
- Technology has its place, but remember to occasionally disconnect. Designate tech-free times to be present with loved ones or to immerse yourself in solitude without digital interruptions.
- Aim for achievable targets. Ambition drives us, but realism keeps us grounded. Focus on impactful, attainable goals to avoid the stress of chasing the unattainable.

Success is multidimensional, encompassing not just what we achieve professionally but how well we live and love. Embracing work-life balance isn't just about juggling duties; it's about making sure every day holds moments of joy, rest, and fulfillment. Let's redefine success to include a life well-lived, where professional ambitions and personal happiness coalesce beautifully.

∼

PART THIRTEEN WRAP-UP:

KEY POINTS:

- **Introduction to Time Management:** Emphasizes the critical role of effective time management in achieving personal and professional success. Highlights common challenges such as feeling overwhelmed, poor prioritization, distractions, procrastination, and the negative impacts of poor time management.
- **Identifying Time-Wasting Activities:** Discusses common timewasters like excessive social media use, procrastination, and multitasking. Offers strategies for overcoming these obstacles to enhance productivity and regain control of time.
- **Prioritizing Tasks and Setting Goals:** Stresses the importance of assessing task urgency and importance, utilizing the Eisenhower matrix to categorize tasks, and implementing strategies like setting SMART goals and breaking down larger goals into actionable tasks.
- **Overcoming Procrastination:** Provides methods to combat procrastination, including breaking tasks into smaller parts, setting specific deadlines, creating accountability systems,

eliminating distractions, using time management techniques, celebrating milestones, and developing a growth mindset.

- **Time Management Tools and Technology:** Introduces various tools and technologies to aid time management, including productivity apps, project management software, time-tracking tools, notification control tools, and task automation tools.
- **Mastering Time Blocking:** Explores the idea of time blocking as a strategy to improve productivity and focus. Offers guidance on creating realistic schedules, eliminating distractions, maintaining focus, adapting time blocks, and achieving a balanced and fulfilling life.
- **Practicing Work-Life Balance:** Highlights the significance of maintaining a healthy work-life balance for overall wellbeing. Provides tips on defining priorities, setting boundaries, focusing on self-care, delegating tasks, making time for joy, unplugging from work, and setting realistic goals.

Action Items:

- **For Time Management:**
- Assess current time management practices and identify areas for improvement.
- Implement the Eisenhower matrix to focus on tasks based on urgency and importance.
- Set specific, measurable, achievable, relevant, and time-bound (SMART) goals.
- **For Overcoming Procrastination:**
- Break large tasks into smaller, manageable steps.
- Set and adhere to specific deadlines for tasks.
- Create an accountability system with peers or use apps to track progress.
- **For Utilizing Tools and Technology:**
- Explore and integrate productivity apps and project management software that fit individual or team needs.

- Use time-tracking tools to understand and optimize time usage.
- Implement task automation where possible to save time on repetitive tasks.
- **For Mastering Time Blocking:**
- Schedule time blocks for focused work, ensuring time for both professional and personal activities.
- Identify and reduce distractions to maintain focus during time blocks.
- Regularly review and adjust time blocks to improve efficiency and productivity.
- **For Practicing Work-Life Balance:**
- Define personal and professional priorities and set boundaries to protect personal time.
- Incorporate self-care activities into the daily routine.
- Make time for hobbies, interests, and relationships outside of work.
- Regularly unplug from technology to engage in personal life.

Implementing these key points and action items can lead to significant improvements in time management, productivity, and overall quality of life.

In Our Next Part...

Picture a realm where setting goals isn't merely listing wishes but starting a well-mapped expedition, guided by apps that transform hopes into real outcomes. Visualize project management tools as conductors orchestrating the complex symphonies of our work lives into harmonious melodies, while mindfulness apps offer a sanctuary of peace amidst our hectic schedules. The era we live in equips us with the tools to carve out our paths, expand our knowledge, and enhance our wellbeing, even as we tread carefully through the minefields of online privacy, cybersecurity, and the steep learning curves that go along with new tech.

As we gear up for this exploration, let's embrace the extraordinary possibilities that lie a few clicks away. Whether it's harnessing digital tools to meet our goals with laser precision, bringing order to the chaos of our daily tasks, or pursuing a passion for lifelong learning, the resources for a transformative journey are right at our fingertips. Yet, this incredible power also demands a mindful approach—we must navigate our digital presence with care, protect our online identities, and face new tech challenges with resilience and eagerness. Together, let's tap into the vast potential of technology to not only envision a brighter future but to actively construct it, one digital milestone at a time.

$$\sim$$

PART FOURTEEN
EXPLORING THE DIGITAL TOOLKIT: UNLOCKING GROWTH IN OUR PERSONAL AND PROFESSIONAL LIVES

UNLOCKING DIGITAL HORIZONS: NAVIGATING THE CORE OF OUR CONNECTED LIVES

Welcome to the digital age, where technology isn't just part of our lives; it's at the core of everything we do. It's reshaping the way we connect, learn, work, and express ourselves. Imagine a world where your smartphone is the key to a treasure trove of opportunities for learning and growth, where artificial intelligence isn't just sci-fi, but a practical tool that enhances our daily productivity and creativity.

The impact of technology today is undeniable. It's woven into the fabric of our everyday existence, transforming how we interact with the world. Social media keeps us linked with loved ones near and far, while online learning platforms open doors to knowledge and skills once out of reach. Technology has essentially turned the world into a global village, making information and connection more accessible than ever.

On a personal level, technology is like having a personal coach, health advisor, and creativity partner all rolled into one Fitness apps not only track our workouts but also cheer us on toward healthier habits. Meditation apps offer a sanctuary of calm in the palm of our hands. These digital tools empower us to take charge of our health and happiness, giving us insights and support right at our fingertips.

And let's talk about creativity. The digital world has democratized art and self-expression in ways we could only dream of before. Whether you're mixing beats, editing photos, or cutting videos, technology has broken down the barriers to artistic exploration, allowing anyone with a vision to create and share their talents with a global audience.

In the professional sphere, technology is not just changing the game; it's rewriting the rulebook. Automation and AI are revolutionizing industries, making processes smarter and jobs more dynamic. As these technologies become everyday tools, they're also shaping the future of work, making digital literacy not just an asset but a necessity. Those who can navigate these tools lead an evolving job market.

The rise of remote work is another testament to technology's transformative power. Tools for communication and collaboration have made working across continents as simple as a click, offering unprecedented flexibility and challenging the traditional limits of the office. This shift toward telecommuting is redefining what work looks like, blending productivity with personal freedom.

In wrapping up, technology's role in our lives is more than significant —it's foundational. It offers endless pathways for personal improvement, creative expression, and professional advancement. By embracing these digital tools and honing the skills to use them effectively, we're not just keeping up with the times; we're unlocking doors to a world brimming with possibilities. The digital age is ours to explore, and the journey toward personal and professional growth is exciting, filled with potential at every turn.

∼

HARNESSING DIGITAL TOOLS FOR SMASHING YOUR GOALS

IN THE WHIRLWIND of our digital era, technology has woven itself into the fabric of our daily routines, becoming a powerhouse for personal development and achievement. Imagine transforming your aspirations into reality with the help of savvy digital tools designed to streamline the goal setting journey, track your progress, and boost your success rates. Let's dive into the world of digital goal setting, project management marvels, and habit-tracking geniuses that stand ready to catapult your aspirations from the drawing board into the real world.

Digital Goal setting Companions: Think of goal setting apps as your personal cheerleaders, equipped with intuitive interfaces that guide you through listing, categorizing, and refining your ambitions into actionable plans. They're the masters of nudging you toward crafting SMART goals—those gems that are Specific, Measurable, Achievable, Relevant, and Time-bound. With apps like Todoist, Habitica, and Evernote at your fingertips, you're never far from setting deadlines, getting gentle reminders, and celebrating the milestones that mark your journey to success. For example, visualize your progress with Todoist's progress bars, offering a tangible sense of achievement and that delightful nudge to keep pushing forward.

Virtual Project Management Platforms: Not just for the boardroom, online project management tools like Trello, Asana, and Monday.com have proven their worth as invaluable allies in the quest for personal goal attainment. These platforms offer a bird's-eye view of your goals, broken down into digestible tasks, complete with deadlines, resource allocation, and even collaboration features for team endeavors. Picture Trello's Kanban boards, where tasks glide from "To-Do" to "Done," visually mapping out your progress and keeping the momentum alive.

Habit-Tracking Heroes: The unsung heroes of long-term success, habit trackers, are your go-to for instilling life-enhancing routines or bidding farewell to those pesky bad habits. Apps like Habitify, Streaks, and HabitHub don't just track your progress; they offer a mirror to your behavioral patterns, serving up visual feedback and streaks of success that feed your motivation. Habitify, for example, doesn't just track; it analyzes, offering insights and visual streaks that make maintaining positive habits not just a duty but a delight.

In wrapping up, the digital landscape is rich with tools that are more than ready to support your goal setting endeavors. From the clarity and direction from goal setting apps, the organizational prowess of project management tools, to the motivational boost from habit trackers, these digital aids are here to ensure your journey toward goal achievement is smooth and successful. Embrace these digital allies, and you'll find yourself not just dreaming of what could be but building the future you want, one digital step at a time.

∾

MAXIMIZING EFFICIENCY: THE TECH ADVANTAGE

In our always-on, always-connected world, mastering the art of productivity is more than a skill—it's a necessity. Thankfully, technology is on our side, offering a lot of tools and resources to streamline our work, sharpen our focus, and make the most of every minute. Let's delve into how technology, from savvy apps to smart automation, can be your secret weapon in the quest for peak productivity.

Smart Apps to Keep You on Track: The heart of tech's productivity boost lies in its apps. These digital powerhouses are tailor-made to organize your chaos, enhance your focus, and push your efficiency to new heights. Whether you're juggling personal projects or coordinating a team effort, there's an app designed to keep you zipping along. Task management tools like Trello, Asana, and Todoist stand out in the crowd. They're the digital equivalent of a personal assistant, helping you to outline tasks, set firm deadlines, and track your journey to completion. Plus, they're built for teamwork, ensuring everyone's efforts are perfectly in sync.

Automate to Elevate: If repetition is the thief of time, automation is the superhero that fights it. By automating the mundane—think email campaigns, data entry, and customer follow-ups—you free up your calendar to dive into deeper, more meaningful work. CRM software is a prime example, handling the heavy lifting so you can focus on strategy and innovation. Imagine redirecting hours spent on routine tasks to brainstorming your next big idea. That's the power of automation.

Digital Calendars: Your Time-Management Ally: The humble digital calendar has evolved into a powerhouse of planning and coordination. Platforms like Google Calendar and Microsoft Outlook go beyond mere scheduling; they're your central hub for all things time management. Plan your day, set those all-important reminders, and never miss a beat. Also, these calendars play well with others, syncing seamlessly with your email and task apps to create a unified command center for your busy life. Accessibility is a breeze, too, with everything you need a tap away on whichever device you prefer.

Technology isn't just changing the game; it's redefining it. From intuitive apps that keep our tasks neatly lined up to automation that liberates us from the grind, the digital age is a boon for productivity. And with digital calendars to keep us all in harmony, we're free to focus on what matters. Embracing these tech tools means not just doing more, but achieving more—with less stress and more satisfaction. So, let's harness the tech advantage and turn our productivity goals from aspirations into achievements.

Digital Organizers: Your Toolkit for a Streamlined Life

Navigating the complexities of modern life without missing a beat requires a sharp organizational strategy. Thankfully, the digital realm offers a treasure trove of tools designed to keep our lives on track, from juggling daily tasks to overseeing entire projects. Let's dive into some of the standout apps that promise to put order into our chaotic schedules and share tips on picking the right ones to match your lifestyle.

~

STREAMLINING TASKS AND PROJECTS:

- **Trello** shines for both solo and team task management with its visual kanban boards, making project tracking a breeze.
- **Todoist** stands out with its sleek to-do lists and reminder systems, ensuring nothing falls through the cracks.
- **Asana** steps up for more complex project planning, offering detailed task assignments, timelines, and progress reports.

MASTERING DAILY ROUTINES:

- **Habitica** turns daily tasks and habits into a fun RPG adventure, rewarding your real-life progress with virtual perks.
- **Habitify** offers a polished platform to build and track habits, complete with insightful analytics on your progress.
- **Google Calendar** is the go-to for scheduling your day with precision, and it plays nicely with other Google apps for an integrated experience.

Managing Finances with Ease:

- **Mint** helps you keep a close eye on your spending, budget smartly, and uncover financial insights.
- **Personal Capital** merges budgeting tools with investment insights, making it a solid pick for a comprehensive financial overview.
- **You Need a Budget (YNAB)** focuses on giving every dollar a job, encouraging mindful spending and realistic budgeting.

Organizing Personal Projects:

- **Evernote** serves as a digital catch-all for ideas, notes, and web clippings, keeping your brainstorms neatly organized.
- **Notion** is the Swiss Army knife of organization, blending documents, tasks, and databases into a collaborative workspace.
- **Microsoft OneNote** caters to diverse note-taking styles, allowing text, images, audio, and video to coexist.

Choosing Your Digital Allies:

- **Pinpoint Your Needs**: What areas of your life are craving organization? Identifying your primary organizational challenges is the first step toward selecting the right tools.
- **User Friendliness is Key**: Choose apps with intuitive designs that promise a smooth learning curve.
- **Integration Matters**: Aim for tools that sync with platforms you already use, ensuring a seamless organizational flow.
- **Learn from the Crowd**: User reviews can offer invaluable insights into an app's performance and reliability, helping you gauge what to expect.
- **Test the Waters**: Many apps offer free versions or trials. Use these to test drive the tools and ensure they mesh well with your daily routines before committing.

The quest for the perfect organizational tools is deeply personal, with the ideal choice varying from one individual to another. Dive into the digital toolbox, experiment with what's out there, and tailor your tech stack to pave the way for a more organized, stress-free existence. With the right digital organizers at your disposal, mastering the art of organization becomes not just feasible, but enjoyable.

Harnessing the Power of Tech to Fuel Lifelong Learning

The digital revolution has drastically changed the landscape of learning, making education more accessible and engaging for everyone. It's an exciting time for lifelong learners, with a lot of online platforms, learning management systems, and virtual classrooms at our fingertips. These resources have made it easy to dive into new subjects, pick up new skills, and feed our curiosity anywhere, at any time.

Online Learning Platforms: The World's Classroom Imagine having the world's top universities and industry experts a click away. That's what online learning platforms like Coursera, edX, Khan Academy, and Udemy offer. These platforms are game changers, providing flexibility to learn at your pace, fitting education seamlessly into even the busiest schedules. Whether you're looking to advance your career, supplement your education, or explore a passion, these platforms connect you with courses in everything from technology to art.

Virtual Classrooms: Breaking Down Geographical Barriers The concept of virtual classrooms has taken distance learning to new heights. Through video conferencing and online collaboration tools, learners can engage in real-time discussions, participate in group projects, and connect with peers and instructors globally. This not only makes learning more dynamic but also fosters a sense of global community, enriching the educational experience with diverse perspectives.

Educational Apps: Learning on the Go For those who want to learn on the move, there's an app for that. Educational apps have transformed smartphones into portable classrooms, offering lessons in languages, critical thinking, and more. Duolingo, Lumosity, and TED are a few examples of apps that make it possible to learn during your commute, your lunch break, or any spare moment you have, turning downtime into productive learning time.

Making Learning Fun with Gamification One of the coolest things about modern educational apps is how they use gamification to keep learners engaged. By incorporating elements of play, challenges, and rewards, apps like Duolingo make mastering a new language feel more like a game and less like a chore. This approach not only makes learning more enjoyable but also increases retention and motivates learners to keep pushing forward.

Briefly, technology has opened up a world of opportunities for those eager to learn and grow throughout their lives. With the wealth of online platforms, virtual classrooms, and educational apps available, lifelong learning is more accessible and engaging than ever before. Whether you're aiming to brush up on professional skills, explore new hobbies, or simply expand your knowledge, the digital world is rich with resources to help you meet your goals. Embracing technology in our learning journey invites continuous growth and adaptation, keeping us relevant and resilient in a rapidly changing world.

~

TECH'S ROLE IN NURTURING OUR HEALTH AND HAPPINESS

IN THE WHIRLWIND of our digital lives, technology stands out not just as a tool for productivity and entertainment but as a powerful ally in our quest for better health and wellbeing. It's fascinating how tech advancements have brought to our fingertips a world of applications and devices designed to boost our physical fitness, mental clarity, and overall happiness. Let's dive into how these tech marvels are reshaping our approach to health and wellness, making self-care more accessible and engaging than ever before.

Wearable Wellness Wonders The rise of health-tracking wearables has been nothing short of revolutionary. From the sleek smartwatch around your wrist to the fitness bands that have become as common-place as smartphones, these gadgets are doing more than just telling time or sending notifications. They're keeping an eye on our heart rates, counting steps, tracking sleep patterns, and even nudging us to stretch our legs after a long stint at the desk. This constant flow of personal health data at our fingertips motivates us to move more, sleep better, and embrace healthier habits day by day.

Mindfulness at a Click Then, there are the mindfulness apps – digital sanctuaries that invite us to pause, breathe, and center ourselves amid the chaos of daily life. Apps like Headspace and Calm have popularized meditation and mindfulness, offering a slice of tranquility with guided sessions that promise to lower stress, improve focus, and even help us find peace. Whether it's through soothing sleep stories, focused breathing exercises, or daily meditation challenges, these apps are making mindfulness an easily adoptable practice for millions.

Fitness Tracking: Your Personal Coach Fitness trackers have transformed personal fitness from a hit-or-miss affair into a well-monitored journey toward health. These nifty devices do more than just count steps; they're your cheerleaders and coaches, tracking every jog, swim, or yoga session. Coupled with their companion apps, fitness trackers summarize your physical activity, set achievable goals, and keep you engaged with challenges and community competitions. It's like having a personal trainer in your pocket, always ready to inspire your next workout.

Nutrition at Your Fingertips Navigating the complex world of nutrition has also been simplified thanks to a lot of apps. These digital dietitians help track your food intake, balance nutrients, and even plan your meals. Whether you're counting calories, tracking macros, or trying to eat healthier, nutrition apps can guide you through making informed food choices and developing eating habits that support your overall health goals.

Access to Health Resources: Anytime, Anywhere Beyond personal health management, technology has opened doors to a wealth of health information and professional advice. Telehealth services and online forums have democratized access to healthcare, allowing for remote consultations, support groups, and a treasure trove of health-related content. This ease of access to professional guidance and community support is a game-changer, especially in areas where healthcare resources are limited.

In wrapping up, it's clear that technology is playing a pivotal role in fostering a culture of health and wellbeing. From wearables that track our every move to apps that guide us through meditation and meal planning, tech tools are empowering us to take charge of our health in ways we never thought possible. As we continue to navigate the challenges of modern life, leveraging technology for health and happiness not only seems wise but essential for a balanced and fulfilling life. Let's embrace these digital aids and make our journey toward wellness a priority.

~

NAVIGATING TECH HURDLES: A ROADMAP TO GROWTH AND MASTERY

DIVING INTO THE DIGITAL AGE, we're surrounded by a world where technology reshapes every part of our lives, from how we work to how we stay connected. Yet, with this digital revolution comes a set of hurdles—privacy concerns, security risks, and the daunting task of keeping up with rapidly evolving tech. Let's chat about how to tackle these challenges head-on, transforming them from roadblocks into steppingstones for personal advancement and achievement.

Keeping Your Digital Life Confidential Privacy in the digital world is a hot topic, and rightly so. But don't let it hold you back from leveraging the tech tools at your disposal. Here's how to keep your personal info safe without missing out:

- **Knowledge is Power:** Get savvy about privacy laws and settings. Understanding the ins and outs of your digital tools' privacy options is your first line of defense.
- **Choose Wisely:** Think before you share. Only give out personal info when necessary and only to platforms you trust. Always skim through those privacy terms to know what you're signing up for.

- **Fortify Your Digital Fort:** Strong passwords, two-factor authentication, and encryption aren't just tech buzzwords—they're your arsenal against intruders. Keeping your software up-to-date and investing in reputable antivirus solutions can also shield you from unexpected guests.

Safeguarding Your Cyber World As our reliance on digital tools spikes, so does the lure for cyber mischief-makers. Here's how to stay a step ahead:

- **Stay Informed:** Cyber threats are ever-changing, so keep a pulse on the latest security trends. Knowing a phishing email from a genuine one can save you a world of trouble.
- **Backup, Backup, Backup:** Regularly backing up your precious data means you'll always have a plan B, no matter what digital curveballs come your way.
- **VPN for the Win:** Public Wi-Fi can be a hacker's playground. A VPN encrypts your online activity, making your digital footprint harder to trace.

Overcoming the Tech Learning Curve Each new gadget or app comes with its own set of rules—a challenge, yes, but also a fantastic opportunity for growth. Here are tips to make the learning curve less steep:

- **Adopt a Learner's Mindset:** View each new tech challenge as a chance to grow. Every hiccup is a learning opportunity waiting to be unraveled.
- **Lean on Others:** The internet is teeming with tutorials, forums, and online communities. And don't forget about your tech-savvy colleagues or friends who can offer hands-on advice.
- **Take Baby Steps:** Introduce new tech into your life one gadget at a time. Mastering them bit by bit can make the process less overwhelming and more rewarding.
- **Practice Makes Perfect:** There's no substitute for hands-on experience. Experiment, make mistakes, and learn. Remember, every expert was once a beginner.

In wrapping up, while the digital era poses its share of challenges, approaching them with the right mindset and strategies can open doors to endless possibilities for personal and professional growth. By safeguarding our digital presence, embracing continuous learning, and tapping into the wealth of resources available, we empower ourselves to navigate the tech landscape confidently and securely. Let's transform these hurdles into opportunities to thrive in the digital age, embracing the journey toward becoming more tech-savvy and meeting our goals.

~

PART FOURTEEN WRAP-UP:

- **Introduction to Technological Tools:** Technology has become essential in personal and professional development, offering tools for communication, learning, creativity, and efficiency.
- **Leveraging Technology for Goal Achievement:** Utilizing goal setting apps, online project management tools, and habit trackers can significantly enhance achieving goals.
- **Enhancing Productivity with Technology:** Productivity apps, task management tools, automation, and digital calendars are important for improving efficiency and time management.
- **Online Tools for Organization:** Various apps and platforms help in managing tasks, daily routines, finances, and personal projects, helping to keep life organized.
- **Using Technology for Lifelong Learning:** Online platforms, virtual classrooms, and educational apps have transformed learning, making it more accessible and flexible.
- **Promoting Health and Wellbeing Through Technology:** Health-tracking wearables, mindfulness apps, fitness trackers,

nutrition apps, and online health resources support physical and mental wellbeing.

- **Overcoming Technological Challenges:** Addressing privacy concerns, security issues, and the learning curve associated with technology is essential for harnessing its full potential for personal growth and success.

Action Items:

- **Explore and adopt technological tools** that align with your personal and professional development goals.
- **Implement goal setting apps** and project management tools to organize and track your progress toward achieving specific goals.
- **Use productivity apps** to streamline tasks, automate repetitive processes, and manage your time effectively.
- **Leverage online platforms** for lifelong learning, accessing a vast array of courses and resources to acquire new knowledge and skills.
- **Incorporate health and wellness apps** into your daily routine to track your physical activity, practice mindfulness, and manage your nutrition.
- **Stay informed about privacy and security best practices** to safeguard your personal information while using technology.
- **Embrace a growth mindset** and seek resources and support to navigate the learning curve associated with new technologies.
- **Gradually incorporate new tools** into your routine, practicing and experimenting to become proficient and overcome any initial challenges.

In Our Next Part...

As we venture further, let's zero in on the essence of true, lasting success—melding ambition with ethical principles. It's about hitting that sweet spot where your personal wins and your contributions to society walk side by side, crafting a journey that's as morally sound as it is fruitful. We're set to dive into actionable strategies and draw inspiration from those who've walked this path, ensuring your dreams don't just take flight but also sprinkle some good in the world. This journey transcends the mere achievement of goals; it's about building a road marked by trust, positive influence, and unshakable integrity.

Gear up to explore the core of ethical leadership and the remarkable impact of syncing your ambitions with the collective wellbeing. We'll arm you with the know-how and perspectives needed to weave ethical thinking seamlessly into your everyday choices, prompting you to ponder the wider impact of your decisions. Whether you're on the cusp of leadership, a professional with a vision, or simply someone navigating the waters of ambition and morality, this Part is designed to give you the insight to steer through the intricacies of desire and duty. By starting this path, you're not just chasing success; you're laying the groundwork for a fairer, more just, and thriving world. Let's start this journey to sculpt a rewarding and ethically rich route to the pinnacle of achievement.

~

PART FIFTEEN
CRAFTING SUCCESS WITH A CONSCIENCE: MERGING AMBITION WITH ETHICS

NAVIGATING SUCCESS WITH HONOR: THE PILLARS OF ETHICS AND INTEGRITY

NAVIGATING the path to success is about more than just the goals we achieve; it's profoundly shaped by the values we uphold. Ethics and integrity aren't just fancy buzzwords; they are the compass that guides us through our personal and professional journeys. Ethics, the moral principles we stand by, and integrity, our unwavering commitment to those principles, play pivotal roles in not just reaching success but ensuring it's deeply rooted and enduring.

At the core, ethics and integrity lay the foundation for trust and credibility. Imagine being known for your unwavering moral compass, being that person others can rely on, rain or shine. This reputation is invaluable, not just for enriching personal connections but as a cornerstone for professional advancement. Trust is like currency in the realm of relationships, opening doors to new ventures and collaborations built on solid ground.

Ethics and integrity also act as the backbone of a thriving workplace culture. Setting the bar high for ethical conduct encourages a ripple effect, inspiring others to follow. This creates an atmosphere where transparency, fairness, and mutual respect aren't just encouraged; they're lived. And let's not forget, a workplace that radiates these values is a magnet for top talent, keeping the engine of innovation and success running smoothly.

When making tough calls, a solid ethical foundation makes all the difference. Faced with the complexities of modern choices, those grounded in ethics find clarity and direction, ensuring decisions are not just beneficial in the short term but sustainable and honorable in the long run. Ethical decision-making is about looking beyond the immediate, weighing the impact on others, and choosing the path of honesty, fairness, and compassion.

But perhaps the most personal benefit of living by ethics and integrity is the profound sense of purpose and fulfillment it brings. Aligning actions with deeply held values offers a satisfaction far richer than any material achievement can provide. This sense of integrity fosters personal growth, resilience, and an ever-evolving journey toward not just succeeding but feeling successful.

Ethics and integrity aren't just the icing on the cake of success; they're its very ingredients. They build trust, shape cultures of excellence, guide our decisions, and fulfill our deepest sense of purpose. By weaving ethics and integrity into the fabric of our actions, we not only pave our way to success but ensure this success is meaningful, respected, and rewarding. Let's commit to this honorable journey, where success is not just about reaching the top but about how we climb and the legacy we leave behind.

~

HARMONIZING DRIVE AND CONSCIENCE: NAVIGATING AMBITION WITH ETHICS

STRIKING the perfect balance between pushing for your dreams and staying true to your moral values is like walking a tightrope. It's about chasing what you want without losing sight of what's right. Let's break down key strategies to help you navigate this journey with both ambition and ethics in hand.

- **Lay Down Your Moral Compass**: Kick things off by pinpointing your core values. What principles are non-negotiable for you? This moral foundation will be your guiding light, helping steer your decisions as you chase your ambitions.
- **Self-Reflection Is Key**: Make it a habit to look in the mirror—metaphorically speaking. Evaluate your choices regularly to ensure they're in sync with your ethical standards. It's all about understanding the ripple effect of your actions and thinking ahead about their impact.
- **Aim High, But Keep It Noble**: Remember, ambition gets a bad rap only when it treads over others. Dream big but ensure those dreams don't become nightmares for others. Think about how your success can lift others up, not just elevate yourself.

- **Find Ethical Trailblazers**: Surround yourself with mentors and role models who've navigated their own paths to success without compromising their ethics. Their journeys can offer invaluable insights and serve as a moral compass in tricky situations.
- **Transparency and Integrity for The Win**: Keep your cards on the table. Honesty not only builds trust but also cements your reputation as someone who does things the right way. Remember, shortcuts might get you there faster, but the journey's quality matters.
- **Every Decision Counts**: Before making a move, pause and ponder its effects. How will your decisions ripple through the lives of those around you? Make choices that respect everyone's dignity and contribute positively to the broader community.
- **Sharpen Your Ethical Wit**: Dive into ethical theories and scenarios to broaden your understanding and enhance your decision-making. The more you know, the better equipped you'll be to face ethical dilemmas head-on.
- **Feedback and Accountability Are Your Friends**: Engage in honest discussions with peers or mentors who can keep you in check. It's about having someone to call you out when you're at risk of veering off your ethical path.
- **Turn Challenges into Learning Opportunities**: Ethical hurdles are inevitable, but they're also growth opportunities. Reflect on these moments, learn from them, and let them refine your ethical compass.
- **Lead with Ethics**: As you climb higher, remember to lead by example. Be the ethical leader you wish to see, inspiring others through your actions and fostering an environment where doing the right thing is celebrated.

Balancing your ambitions with your ethics isn't a one-off task—it's a continuous commitment to doing right by yourself and others. By embracing these strategies, you're not just chasing success; you're redefining it, proving that true achievement is about reaching your goals while uplifting those around you.

～

NAVIGATING THE RIPPLE EFFECT: HOW OUR CHOICES SHAPE THE WORLD

THE WAY our choices touch the lives of others and ripple through society is a profound reminder of our interconnectedness and the responsibility we carry in our daily actions. It's fascinating, yet daunting, to realize that everything we do, big or small, intentional or accidental, can set off a chain of events affecting those around us and even society. Embracing responsible and ethical conduct is not just noble; it's essential for weaving the fabric of a community that's fair, harmonious, and just for all.

Consider the domino effect: a vivid illustration of how one action can spark outcomes, affecting many. This phenomenon is clear in all spheres of life, from a workplace decision affecting team dynamics to a family choice that influences a child's growth and future. The realization that our actions are catalysts for change underscores the importance of thoughtful decision-making.

Our collective choices as consumers, for example, wield power to mold industries and steer environmental stewardship. By supporting ethical businesses, we champion sustainable and fair practices, nudging the market toward responsibility. But overlooking the ethical implications of our purchases can inadvertently sustain harmful practices, from environmental harm to labor exploitation.

The impact extends to societal structures, particularly affecting marginalized communities. Acts of discrimination, however subtle, contribute to widening social divides and reinforcing inequalities. Recognizing the broader societal tapestry to which our actions contribute can motivate us to foster empathy, compassion, and a commitment to equity.

Mitigating unintended negative consequences begins with a commitment to responsible and ethical action. This means contemplating the potential effects of our decisions and choosing paths that consider others' welfare. Embodying responsibility and ethical principles help navigate the complex web of societal interactions with fairness, honesty, and respect.

Education and awareness are indispensable allies in this journey. Cultivating empathy and critical thinking can deepen our understanding of our actions' impacts, empowering us to make choices that reflect our role as catalysts for positive change. Through education, we gain the insight and integrity to act thoughtfully, acknowledging our part in shaping a collective future.

The influence of our decisions on others and the broader society is significant and far-reaching. Recognizing the power of our actions compels us to move through the world with mindfulness, responsibility, and an ethical compass. By doing so, we contribute to building a society that values justice, equity, and mutual respect, where every decision is a step toward a more compassionate and connected world.

~

EXPLORING PATHS TO MORAL CLARITY: ETHICAL FRAMEWORKS IN DECISION-MAKING

MAKING choices that are not just good for us but also right in the moral sense can be a complex challenge. Ethical decision-making frameworks are like compasses guiding us through the moral landscape, helping us align our decisions with our values and aspirations. Let's unpack three key frameworks that illuminate different paths to ethical choices: consequentialism, deontology, and virtue ethics.

Consequentialism zooms in on the outcome of our actions. It's all about looking ahead and weighing the pros and cons to decide which option brings the most happiness or the least harm to the most people. Picture Jeremy Bentham and John Stuart Mill brainstorming utilitarianism, a consequentialist approach aiming to max out happiness. When leaning into this perspective, you'd play a fortune-teller, predicting outcomes to pick the path promising the best collective wellbeing.

Deontology switches the focus from consequences to duties and principles. This approach, championed by thinkers like Immanuel Kant, argues that certain ethical rules should steer our decisions. It's about doing what's right because it's right, like treating people with respect and upholding justice, no matter the outcome. Adopting a deontological lens means sticking to these moral compass points, even when the seas get rough.

Virtue Ethics takes a different tack, spotlighting the character traits we embody. Instead of fixating on actions or rules, it's about nurturing qualities like honesty, compassion, and integrity. This framework suggests that making ethical choices is part of being a virtuous person. Here, the moral questions revolve around who we are and aspire to be, guiding our actions to reflect the best version of ourselves.

Navigating ethical decisions often involves blending elements from these frameworks, tailored to the situation at hand. Each offers a unique perspective, yet no single approach has all the answers. The right path might vary with the context, highlighting the importance of flexibility in ethical reasoning.

In wrapping up, these ethical frameworks are invaluable tools, offering structured ways to ponder the moral dimensions of our choices. Whether you're drawn to the outcome-focused approach of consequentialism, the principled stance of deontology, or the character-centered virtue ethics, these perspectives enrich our decision-making. They not only guide us toward choices that resonate with our personal and professional aims but also steer us toward contributing positively to the wider world.

~

CASE STUDIES AND REAL-WORLD EXAMPLES:

CASE STUDY 1: Navigating the Ethical Quagmire: Lessons from the Enron Debacle

The tale of Enron, marked by its staggering fall from grace, starkly illustrates the perils of sidelining ethics in the relentless pursuit of success. Once a titan in the energy sector, Enron's journey into infamy began when its leadership chose a path mired in deceit, using creative accounting to embellish its financial health.

In the twilight of the 1990s, under the leadership of CEO Jeffrey Skilling and others, Enron started a risky venture. They cleverly concocted off-book entities—special purpose entities (SPEs), to be precise—to give the illusion of strong profits and shroud the company's burgeoning debts. This strategy was designed to woo investors, projecting an image of financial stability and growth far from reality.

However, like a house of cards, Enron's elaborate facade crumbled in 2001, dragging the company into bankruptcy. This collapse didn't just evaporate billions in wealth; it shattered the lives of countless employees and investors, leaving a legacy of financial ruin and eroded trust.

The aftermath for those at the helm was swift and severe. Jeffrey Skilling and former CEO Kenneth Lay found themselves in the eye of a legal storm, facing charges that ranged from securities fraud to conspiracy. Their convictions carried heavy prison sentences, forever marring their legacies. Beyond the boardroom, the fallout extended to Enron's employees and investors, who faced the dual blow of significant financial losses and a profound sense of betrayal.

The Enron scandal, far more than a cautionary tale of corporate malfeasance, underscores the critical importance of ethical integrity in business. It serves as a stark reminder that pursuing success, devoid of ethical considerations, can lead to catastrophic consequences not just for individuals, but for entire communities.

∾

CASE STUDY 2: A CLOSER LOOK AT THE VW EMISSIONS FIASCO: ETHICAL PITFALLS AND PURSUITS

THE VOLKSWAGEN (VW) EMISSIONS SCANDAL, unearthed in 2015, stands as a stark reminder of how ethical shortcuts can backfire spectacularly. VW found itself in hot water after it came to light that the company had rigged some of its diesel vehicles with crafty software designed to outsmart emissions tests. This clever but deceptive software could sense test scenarios, temporarily dialing down emissions to pass with flying colors—a stark contrast to its real-world pollution levels.

Driven by a desire to uphold an eco-friendly facade and boost vehicle sales, VW ventured down a slippery ethical slope. The fallout from this scandal was both swift and brutal. VW's once-stellar reputation for trustworthiness and commitment to the environment took a nosedive, dragging its sales and market value down with it. The company was besieged by legal battles, shelling out billions in fines and settlements, and was forced to recall millions of vehicles worldwide.

The individuals at the helm during this debacle weren't spared either. Martin Winterkorn, the CEO at the time, saw no other exit but to resign as the scandal unfolded. The repercussions didn't stop there; he later faced criminal charges, along with several other top executives who also had to abandon ship. Their professional standing and personal integrity were deeply scarred by their association with such unethical practices.

This episode not only illuminates the perils of focusing on short-term gains over ethical standards but also serves as a cautionary tale about the long-lasting impact of such decisions on a company's legacy and the careers of those involved.

~

CASE STUDY 3: THE THERANOS DEBACLE: A TALE OF AMBITION CLASHING WITH ETHICS

THERANOS, once a beacon of innovation in the biomedical field thanks to its founder Elizabeth Holmes, stands out as a cautionary tale about the dark side of ambitious pursuits lacking ethical grounding. The company caused conflict with claims of a groundbreaking blood-testing technology, capturing the imagination and wallets of investors. Holmes, with her compelling vision, positioned Theranos as a revolutionary force set to transform healthcare.

The unraveling of Theranos began regarding light that the company had been playing fast and loose with the facts. Despite Holmes' assertive promotions, but the much-touted technology was more fiction than fact, often delivering unreliable and downright inaccurate test results. This revelation not only shocked the healthcare and investment communities but also had dire consequences for Holmes herself.

From being celebrated as a pioneering female billionaire, Holmes found herself in the eye of a legal storm, facing charges of massive fraud. The fallout was catastrophic: Theranos crumbled, its once-bright reputation tarnished beyond repair, leading to its eventual closure. Investors were left grappling with monumental losses, and patients, who had placed their trust in Theranos' flawed technology, faced potential health risks.

This entire saga underscores the critical importance of aligning ambition with ethical integrity. It's a sobering reminder that while pushing the boundaries of innovation is important, doing so responsibly and truthfully is non-negotiable.

∼

These case studies highlight the potential ramifications of unethical behavior on personal and professional reputations. The Enron scandal, Volkswagen emissions scandal, and Theranos fraud show how individuals pursuing their goals through unethical means ultimately face legal consequences, damaged reputations, and financial loss. These examples serve as a reminder that ethical behavior is important in maintaining personal integrity and long-term success in any endeavor.

∼

CULTIVATING A CULTURE OF ETHICS AND INTEGRITY

IN THE MAZE of today's fast-paced environment, embedding a deep-seated culture of ethics and integrity within our organizations and communities is more important than ever. It's all about sparking a collective commitment to ethical practices and responsible decision-making at every level. Here's a rundown on how we can light that spark and keep the flame burning bright:

Educational Initiatives: Kickstart the journey with comprehensive ethics education and training. Imagine diving into interactive case studies, engaging workshops, and thought-provoking discussions that challenge us to reflect deeply on the moral compass guiding our decisions.

Crafting a Code of Ethics: It's like setting the ground rules for the game. A well-defined code of ethics acts as a beacon, guiding us through the murky waters of tough decisions. Making this code a living, breathing part of daily life ensures ethical considerations are never an afterthought.

Frameworks for Ethical Decisions: Equip everyone with a toolkit for ethical dilemmas. Tools such as the "Four-Way Test" can be real game-changers, offering a clear lens through which to view our choices and their ripple effects.

Leading by Example: When leaders walk the talk, it's infectious. Ethical leadership isn't just about making the right call; it's about being a beacon of integrity, fairness, and transparency, inspiring everyone to follow.

Fostering Open Conversations: Cultivate a space where talking about ethics isn't taboo but encouraged. Sharing experiences and dilemmas enriches the collective understanding and supports a culture where ethical discussions are the norm, not the exception.

Applauding Ethical Behaviors: Let's not just expect ethical behavior but celebrate it. Recognizing those who embody these values reinforces their importance and motivates others to emulate such actions.

Support Networks: Sometimes, navigating ethical waters can be daunting. Creating a safe channel for guidance or to voice concerns can make all the difference, ensuring no one must navigate these challenges in silence.

Joining Forces: There's strength in numbers. Teaming up with like-minded groups broadens our ethical horizons, pooling knowledge, experiences, and resources toward a common goal of fostering integrity.

Ethical Check-ins: Regularly taking the ethical pulse of our organizations or communities helps us stay on course, ensuring our actions consistently reflect our values.

Integrating Ethics into the DNA: Weave ethical considerations into the fabric of policies and everyday processes. This integration makes sure ethical thinking isn't an add-on but a fundamental part of all decision-making.

Starting this path is not just about dodging pitfalls; it's about building a legacy of trust, respect, and integrity. It's a journey toward not just individual growth but fostering a community where ethics and ambition harmoniously coexist, propelling us toward a future where success is measured not just by what we achieve, but by how we achieve it.

~

HARMONIZING INDIVIDUAL DREAMS AND COMMUNITY WELLBEING

IN THE VAST web of our global community, balancing our own dreams and the collective wellbeing of society is more than just a noble pursuit —it's essential. This piece digs into how our personal ambitions and societal responsibilities can not only coexist but enrich each other, offering a roadmap to achieving personal fulfillment while uplifting the community around us.

The Synergy Between Personal and Societal Goals: The dance between individual desires and societal needs is intricate but deeply interconnected. The fabric of society offers the backdrop against which we chase our dreams, giving us the necessary tools, opportunities, and support. Meanwhile, when we direct our talents and energies toward societal upliftment, we contribute to a culture that is vibrant, sustainable, and nurturing for all. It's a win-win: society flourishes with each individual's success, and our personal journeys gain depth and meaning as they contribute to a larger cause.

Charting a Course for Impactful Living:

- **Lifelong Learning:** Stay curious and informed about the world's pressing issues. An understanding of the challenges our society faces is the first step toward meaningful action. Knowledge empowers us to make choices that reflect our commitment to the greater good.

- **Discovering Your Why:** Dig deep to find the interPart where your passions meet the world's needs. Whether you're a tech enthusiast aiming to solve environmental problems or an artist seeking to inspire change, aligning your skills with your values can magnify your impact.
- **Joining Forces:** The power of collaboration cannot be overstated. Seek others who share your vision for a better world. Together, you can amplify your impact, pooling resources, knowledge, and energy to tackle challenges more effectively than you could alone.
- **Ethics Above All:** Let integrity be your north star. In pursuing our goals, choosing paths that uphold ethical standards not only ensures our success is rightly earned but also models the values we wish to see in the world.

The Rewards of a Balanced Approach:

- **Deep Fulfillment:** There's an unmatched satisfaction in knowing your achievements have broader significance. Contributing to societal progress brings a sense of purpose and joy that surpasses personal success alone.
- **A Legacy of Sustainability:** By aligning our efforts with the goal of societal improvement, we contribute to a legacy of positive change, ensuring a brighter future for generations to come.
- **Unity and Empathy:** Active engagement in societal wellbeing fosters a sense of belonging and unity. It builds bridges, encourages understanding, and cultivates an environment where everyone is invested in each other's success.

Closing Thoughts: The intertwining of personal ambitions with societal wellbeing isn't just beneficial—it's a cornerstone of a thriving world. By navigating our journeys with an eye toward the collective good, we not only enrich our own lives but also contribute to a tapestry of human experience that is richer, more diverse, and profoundly interconnected. It's in this delicate balance we find the true essence of success: a journey that not only elevates us but elevates those around us, weaving a story of progress, empathy, and shared triumph.

~

PART FIFTEEN WRAP-UP:
KEY POINTS:

- **The Importance of Ethics and Integrity:** Ethics and integrity are foundational to building trust, credibility, and sustaining long-term success. They guide decision-making, nurture positive organizational cultures, and contribute to personal fulfillment.
- **Balancing Ambition with Ethical Considerations:** Achieving goals while upholding ethical standards involves defining personal values, conducting ethical self-assessments, and setting goals that are both ambitious and morally sound.
- **Impact of Actions on Others and Society:** Actions have a ripple effect, influencing not just immediate stakeholders but also broader societal outcomes. Responsible behavior reduces negative impacts and contributes to a harmonious society.
- **Ethical Decision-Making Frameworks:** Consequentialism, deontology, and virtue ethics provide different lenses through which ethical decisions can be evaluated, helping to navigate complex dilemmas.
- **Case Studies:** Examples like the Enron scandal, Volkswagen emissions scandal, and Theranos fraud illustrate the dire

consequences of unethical behavior on personal and professional reputations and highlight the importance of integrity.

- **Raising Awareness of Ethical Considerations:** Education, ethical leadership, open dialogue, and ethical audits are among the methods to foster a culture of integrity within organizations and communities.
- **Balancing Personal and Societal Goals:** Individuals are encouraged to align their personal ambitions with societal wellbeing, leveraging education, collaboration, and ethical decision-making to contribute positively to society.

ACTION ITEMS:

- **Define Your Ethical Boundaries:** Clearly identify your core ethical values and principles to serve as a guide in personal and professional endeavors.
- **Engage in Continuous Learning:** Stay informed about ethical practices, participate in training, and seek mentorship to strengthen your ethical judgment.
- **Set Ethical Goals:** Ensure your ambitions do not compromise your values or harm others. Aim for goals that benefit both yourself and the community.
- **Practice Transparency:** Maintain honesty and openness in your actions, fostering trust and integrity in all relationships.
- **Utilize Ethical Decision-Making Models:** Apply frameworks like consequentialism, deontology, or virtue ethics to evaluate decisions from multiple ethical perspectives.
- **Learn from Ethical Challenges:** Reflect on and learn from real-world case studies and personal experiences to understand the consequences of unethical actions.
- **Promote Ethical Awareness:** Participate in initiatives that raise ethical awareness within your organization or community, encouraging a culture of integrity.
- **Balance Personal Ambitions with Societal Contributions:** Seek ways to align your personal goals with efforts that

advance societal wellbeing, ensuring your achievements also contribute to the common good.

- **Implement Ethical Leadership:** Lead by example, showing ethical behavior in all parts of life, and inspire others to do the same.
- **Evaluate and Adjust Practices Regularly:** Conduct ethical self-assessments and seek feedback to ensure your actions consistently reflect your ethical standards.

By adhering to these key points and action items, individuals can navigate the complexities of pursuing goals within ethical boundaries, contributing to their personal growth, professional success, and societal wellbeing.

In Our Next Part...

Ready to start a transformative journey that harmonizes your physical and mental realms to catapult you toward your goals? Picture a lifestyle where your physical vitality and mental acuity are in perfect sync, guiding you with precision and energy toward your ambitions. In this upcoming Part, we will dive into practical strategies that merge physical fitness and mental wellness, turning daily routines into exhilarating quests for personal growth. We're talking about more than just hitting the gym; it's about crafting a lifestyle where the right nutrition, rest, and activities make every day a step toward your ultimate aspirations.

And there's more. This isn't just a solo adventure. We're taking a holistic view, understanding that genuine success stems from a blend of personal wellbeing, happiness, and a deep connection with the community. Discover how integrating mindfulness and stress management into your everyday can turn resilience and emotional equilibrium into your default setting. Embrace a comprehensive approach to living, where your personal goals not only fulfill you but also contribute to the wider world, enriching your life with purpose and meaning.

So, buckle up for an enlightening journey in our next part. We're about to reveal how to live a life that's successful not just in achievements but in richness and fulfillment. Get ready to unlock the secrets to a life rewarding in every possible way.

～

PART SIXTEEN
HARMONIZING BODY, MIND, AND PURPOSE FOR PEAK PERFORMANCE

UNLOCKING SUCCESS: THE POWER OF PHYSICAL HEALTH AND MENTAL WELLBEING

THE INTERTWINING OF PHYSICAL HEALTH, mental sharpness, and personal success is a subject that's gaining more attention than ever in our busy, high-stakes world. It's well-known that staying physically fit is key to overall wellbeing, but it's the profound impact on mental acuity, motivation, and success that's capturing interest. This connection is deep and mutual, underscoring the importance of a healthy body as a lever to boost mental strength, drive, and success across the board.

The Brain-Body Connection: The brain, our command center, thrives on proper care and nutrition. Regular physical activity not only keeps us in shape but sharpens our cognitive skills—think memory, focus, and problem-solving. Exercise pumps more blood and oxygen to the brain, spurring the growth of new brain cells and releasing endorphins, those feel-good chemicals that lift our spirits. Plus, a fit body leads to better sleep, essential for keeping our minds and emotions in balance.

Physical Fitness and Drive: A strong body fuels motivation. Regular workouts help shake off stress and anxiety, elevate mood, and boost self-esteem. This mental uplift significantly affects our drive, making goal setting and achieving more attainable. With our bodies in peak condition, we're more inclined to tackle challenges, push through setbacks, and stay laser-focused on our goals.

The Foundation of Success: Physical wellbeing lays the groundwork for success in life's many arenas. It empowers us to engage in work and personal pursuits, keeping us resilient and energetic, even when times get tough. Without the burden of health issues, we're free to invest our resources in chasing our dreams with persistence and vigor. Plus, the discipline from maintaining fitness and a balanced diet translates into self-control and positive habits, important ingredients for lasting success.

In Closing: The bond between physical health, mental wellbeing, and personal achievement is crystal clear. Keeping our bodies healthy is not just about physical fitness; it's a critical piece of the puzzle for enhancing our minds, staying motivated, and achieving our fullest potential. So, let's commit to regular exercise, quality sleep, and nutritious eating. By nurturing both body and mind, we're setting the stage for unparalleled success and satisfaction.

∾

THE VITAL LINK BETWEEN PHYSICAL ACTIVITY, NUTRITION, AND MENTAL SHARPNESS

THERE'S a fascinating interplay between our physical health and mental wellbeing, a relationship key to living a well-rounded, satisfying life. The magic duo—regular exercise and good nutrition—stands at the core of this dynamic, having the power to sharpen our minds, melt away stress, boost our energy, and dial up our productivity and focus.

Exercise: The Brain's Booster Let's talk about the brain boost we get from regular exercise. When we get moving, we pump more blood to the brain, encouraging the growth of new brain cells and strengthening the connections between them. This isn't just good for our muscles; it elevates memory, sharpens focus, and generally lifts our cognitive game. Plus, hitting the pavement or the gym releases endorphins, those feel-good neurotransmitters that cut through stress and anxiety like a hot knife through butter.

Nutrition: The Brain's Fuel On the flip side, our brains need top-notch fuel to run smoothly, and that's where nutrition comes into play. A balanced diet, rich in omega-3s, antioxidants, vitamins, and minerals, is like premium gas for the brain. It keeps our cognitive functions running smoothly and supports emotional wellbeing. So, loading up on fruits, veggies, whole grains, lean proteins, and healthy fats is not just about physical health—it's about keeping our mental engine humming.

Stress Busters and Energy Boosters Both exercise and a balanced diet are ace stress busters. Physical activity helps us sweat out tension and combats chronic stress by boosting endorphins. It also improves sleep quality, which is a big deal for managing stress. A diet filled with essential nutrients helps our bodies handle stress better and keeps the mental clouds at bay.

And as for energy, regular exercise and the right diet have our backs. Working out ramps up oxygen and nutrient delivery throughout our bodies, keeping us alert and energized. Good sleep and a diet rich in complex carbs, lean proteins, and healthy fats ensure we're not just running well but running on high all day.

Ramping Up Productivity and Focus The ripple effect of all this? A significant boost in productivity and the ability to stay laser-focused on whatever we're tackling. With our cognitive functions in top form, stress levels down, and energy up, we're primed to concentrate better, solve problems more effectively, and make sharper decisions.

Wrapping It Up In essence, keeping our bodies in tip-top shape through exercise and nutrition isn't just a matter of physical health—it's a cornerstone of mental wellbeing. These lifestyle choices significantly affect everything from brain function to stress management, energy levels, and our ability to stay focused and productive. By weaving physical activity and smart eating into our daily routine, we're not just investing in our bodies; we're sharpening our minds and setting ourselves up for a more productive, fulfilling life.

〜

THE POWERHOUSE ROLE OF PHYSICAL HEALTH IN ACHIEVING YOUR DREAMS

PHYSICAL HEALTH ISN'T JUST about hitting the gym or eating your greens; it's a game-changer in setting the stage for smashing your goals, whether they're career milestones, academic success, or thriving relationships. Let's dive into how a strong bill of health is the secret ingredient to turning aspirations into realities.

Supercharging Your Career with a Fit Body

- Think of your physical health as the fuel for your brainpower; it sharpens your memory, boosts your focus, and unleashes your creative juices.
- A stress-free mind, courtesy of a vigorous body, paves the way for clearer thinking and sky-high productivity.
- Goals seem clearer, and the path to reaching them becomes less daunting when your mind and body are in sync.
- Bouncing back from career hiccups? Your physical fitness has your back, equipping you with the resilience to face any professional challenge head-on.

Academic Goals: A Walk in the Park with Physical Wellness

- Lace-up those sneakers! Regular physical activity not only keeps you fit but also sends a fresh supply of oxygen to your brain, making learning and retention a breeze.
- Hit the books or the track? Why not both? Exercise is proven to amp up academic performance, leading to better grades and laser-sharp focus.
- Don't underestimate the power of a balanced diet and quality z's – they're your brain's best friends, ensuring you're always at the top of your game academically.

Navigating Relationship Success Through Fitness

- A healthy physique boosts more than just your metabolism; it lifts your self-esteem and confidence, making you a magnet in social settings.
- Those workout-induced endorphins? They're not just good for your heart; they make you happier and more content, key ingredients for successful relationships.
- High energy levels, a gift of regular exercise, mean you're more engaging and present in your interactions, enriching your relationships.
- And let's not forget, a sound body supports a sound mind, important for navigating the ups and downs of personal connections with grace.

Wrapping It Up The link between physical health and reaching for the stars, be it in your career, studies, or personal life, is undeniable. A fit and healthy body isn't just a temple; it's a launching pad for ambition, resilience, and success. Keeping yourself in top shape is not merely a commitment to your wellbeing but a cornerstone for building the life you envision. So, as you plot your course to the stars, remember: your health is the rocket fuel you need to get there.

~

FITTING FITNESS INTO THE HUSTLE AND BUSTLE: SMART STRATEGIES FOR THE BUSY BEE

JUGGLING a packed schedule and trying to stay fit can feel like trying to solve a Rubik's Cube blindfolded—it's tricky, but not impossible. Here's a cheat sheet to weaving workouts into your whirlwind life, proving you can hustle for your health too.

Make Fitness a Firm Date

- Think of fitness as that must-attend meeting with a VIP (very important physique). Slot it into your calendar as you would any critical appointment. Whether it's a morning yoga session, a noon power walk, or an evening dance class, ensure it's inked in your planner.
- Set your phone or calendar to nudge you with reminders. It's like having a personal cheerleader pushing you to move.

Tech to the Rescue

- Embrace the digital age with fitness apps and gadgets. These clever tools can guide you through a 15-minute HIIT session in your living room or help you keep tabs on your daily step count and heart rate. It's like having a personal trainer in your pocket.

- Fitness apps can be a game-changer, especially for squeezing in workouts between Zoom calls or while dinner's in the oven.

Sneak in Some Steps

- Look for stealthy ways to get moving. Choose stairs over elevators, take a brisk walk during your coffee break, or stretch out while binge-watching your favorite show.
- Transform your commute into a mini workout. Bike or walk part of the way if you can. Even parking a little further from your destination can add valuable steps.

Mix Pleasure with Your Planks

- Pick activities that make your heart happy. Love the outdoors? Hit the trails for a hike. Enjoy team vibes? Sign up for a local sports league. When exercise doesn't feel like a chore, you're more likely to stick with it.
- Short on time? Divide and conquer. Break your exercise into bite-sized sessions throughout the day. A 10-minute morning stretch, a quick lunchtime walk, and an evening dance-off in your living room can add up to significant fitness gains.

Get Your Squad Involved

- Turn fitness into friend time or family fun. Rally your crew for a weekend hike, a friendly game of soccer, or a group workout session. It's a win-win: you get your workout in and catch up with your favorite people.
- Use idle moments wisely. Swap scrolling through social media for a set of squats or lunges. Or catch up on audiobooks or podcasts while you jog or cycle.

Remember, the goal is to make movement a natural part of your day, not another stressor. Even small amounts of activity can add a significant boost to your health and happiness. With these strategies, you can make fitness fit into your life, no matter how hectic it gets.

～

FUELING YOUR BRAIN: THE ULTIMATE NUTRITIONAL PLAYBOOK FOR SHARP THINKING

EVER WONDER how to keep your brain in tip-top shape? Turns out, what you eat plays a starring role in boosting your brainpower, memory, and keeping you sharp as a tack. Let's dive into the essentials of brain-friendly eating that'll have you acing life with mental clarity and vigor.

Balancing Act: The Essentials of a Brain-Boosting Diet

- Imagine your plate as a colorful palette of nutrients: whole grains, lean proteins, vibrant fruits and veggies, and yes, those oh-so-important healthy fats. This mix ensures your brain gets the full spectrum of brain-boosting goodies it needs to thrive.

Nutrient Superstars for Your Gray Matter

- **Omega-3 Fatty Acids**: These are your brain's best friends. Found in abundance in fatty fish, and for the plant-lovers, in chia seeds and walnuts, they're like the VIP nutrients for brain development and sharp thinking.
- **Antioxidants**: Picture these as your brain's personal bodyguards, shielding it from damage. Load up on berries,

leafy greens, and other antioxidant-packed foods to keep your brain cells fighting fit.

- **B Vitamins**: Think of B vitamins as the brain's energy managers, important for keeping your memory on point and your thoughts clear. Leafy greens, whole grains, and lean meats are your go-tos here.
- **Vitamin E**: Another antioxidant hero, Vitamin E keeps your neurons happy and healthy. Nuts and spinach are great sources.
- **Iron**: Low iron equals low energy and foggy thinking. Keep your iron levels up with lean meats, fish, and spinach.
- **Magnesium**: This mineral is like brain food that supports memory and learning. Nuts, seeds, and those beloved dark leafy greens are rich in magnesium.

Smart Eating Habits for Peak Performance

- **Breakfast of Champions**: Kickstart your day with a power breakfast. Think oatmeal with a berry and nut topping or a veggie-packed omelet with a side of whole-grain toast.
- **Eat the Rainbow**: Incorporating a variety of fruits and veggies ensures a broad range of nutrients. The more colors on your plate, the better.
- **Lean and Mean Proteins**: Focus on fish, poultry, and plant-based proteins like beans and legumes for essential amino acids that boost brain health.
- **Whole Grains for Brain Gain**: Swap out white bread for whole grains to keep your brain fueled throughout the day.
- **Snack Smart**: Reach for nuts, seeds, or Greek yogurt when hunger strikes. These snacks pack a nutritional punch that your brain will thank you for.
- **Stay Quenched**: Don't let dehydration dull your sparkle. Drink plenty of water to keep your brain hydrated and ready to tackle any challenge.

Remember, these tips are a guide, not one-size-fits-all. Tailor your diet to suit your unique needs, and please consult a nutrition expert for personalized advice. Eating well isn't just good for your body; it's a game-changer for your brain too. Here's to feeding your mind and meeting your goals with clarity and energy!

~

UNLOCKING YOUR FULL POTENTIAL: THE POWER OF REST AND RECOVERY

WE'RE all caught up in the hustle of daily life, chasing deadlines and pushing ourselves to the limit. But here's the thing: we're often skipping the secret ingredient that could turbocharge our performance – good old-fashioned rest and recovery. Believe it or not, hitting the pause button and getting enough sleep is like hitting the refresh button for your brain and body. It's not just about preventing yawns; it's about sharpening your mind, managing stress, and keeping your body in tip-top shape. Let's dive into why winding down and catching those Zs might be the best thing you can do for yourself.

Brain Power Unleashed: Think of sleep as your brain's nightly spa treatment. It's during those quiet hours that your brain sorts memories, solves problems, and gets you ready to tackle the world with renewed focus and creativity. Aiming for 7-9 hours of sleep isn't just nice to have; it's essential for staying sharp and on top of your game.

The Antidote to Stress: Ever noticed how everything seems more overwhelming when you're running on empty? That's because sleep deprivation throws your stress hormones out of whack. Getting enough sleep helps keep your emotions balanced and stress levels in check, so you're better equipped to handle whatever comes your way.

A Boost for Your Body: Your body is a marvel, constantly working to repair itself, fight off bugs, and keep you energized. But to do all that, it needs downtime. Skimping on sleep weakens your immune system, making you more likely to catch that cold going around. Plus, well-rested equals well-mooded. More sleep equals more smiles.

Crafting the Perfect Sleep Sanctuary:

- **Set the Scene for Snooze:**
- Keep your bedroom dark, quiet, and cool – think cave-like conditions.
- Splurge a little on a comfy mattress and pillows that make you feel like you're sleeping on a cloud.
- Banish screens and blue lights to avoid tricking your brain into thinking it's go-time instead of slow-time.
- **Rituals for Rest:**
- Try to hit the sack and wake up at the same time every day – yes, even on weekends.
- Wind down with a book, a bath, or some deep breathing – whatever tells your brain it's time to power down.
- Steer clear of late-night workouts, heavy meals, and caffeine that can throw off your sleep game.
- **Lifestyle Tweaks:**
- Move your body daily, but not right before bed. Think of it as wearing yourself out for a good night's rest.
- Watch the late-night snacking and sipping – a full stomach or bladder can be a real sleep disruptor.

Wrapping It Up: Don't underestimate the power of catching those Zs. Good sleep is your ally in boosting mental sharpness, keeping stress at bay, and keeping your body feeling spry. By fostering healthy sleep habits and creating a snooze-friendly environment, you're not just sleeping; you're setting yourself up for success in every part of your life. So, here's to embracing rest and recovery, not just as a luxury, but as a non-negotiable part of reaching your full potential. Sweet dreams and brighter days ahead!

A BALANCED PATH TO SUCCESS: EMBRACING WELLBEING IN EVERY ASPECT

IN THE HUSTLE and bustle of our daily lives, we often chase after professional achievements and financial goals, forgetting that true success is much more than just nailing those external milestones. Real achievement is about thriving in every part of our life - from keeping our bodies healthy and our minds sharp to maintaining emotional stability and feeling spiritually fulfilled. This broader, more holistic view of success ensures we're not just successful in one area of life but are genuinely fulfilled across the board.

Understanding that everything in our lives is interconnected is the first step. Your physical health affects your mental and emotional state, which can influence your spiritual wellbeing. By caring for each area simultaneously, we can find a more profound sense of balance and harmony.

Let's talk about mindfulness. It's not just a buzzword; it's a powerful tool to help us stay grounded in the present moment. Regular mindfulness practice can ease stress and anxiety, sharpen our focus, and boost self-awareness. Why not start with something as simple as mindful breathing? Spending a few quiet moments each day focusing on your breath can make a big difference.

Stress management is another key piece of the puzzle. Stress comes with the territory of aiming high and pushing ourselves. But managing it through physical activities, creative outlets, or relaxation practices like yoga can keep stress from undermining our health and clarity.

Self-care is our next cornerstone. It's all about carving out time for things that refresh and recharge us. Whether it's focusing on sleep, choosing nutritious foods, or indulging in hobbies that make us happy, self-care strengthens our mental and emotional fortitude, helping us navigate life's ups and downs.

And don't overlook the role of spiritual practices. Connecting with something greater than ourselves, be it through religion, meditation, or nature, can bring a richer sense of purpose and peace. This spiritual connection can be a powerful source of strength and perspective.

As you pursue your goals, remember that success is not just about ticking boxes or achieving specific targets. It's about cultivating a life that feels rich and rewarding on all fronts. By weaving together practices that support your physical, mental, emotional, and spiritual well-being, you can not only enhance your life's quality but also set the stage for meaningful, sustained achievements.

Start small, incorporating one or two practices that feel right for you, and gradually build from there. This journey of holistic self-improvement and growth is about more than reaching an endpoint; it's about discovering and nurturing your full potential in every way possible. So, take the first step today toward a more balanced, fulfilling path to success.

~

PART SIXTEEN WRAP-UP:

KEY POINTS:

- The intrinsic connection between physical health, mental wellbeing, and personal achievement emphasizes the need for a balanced lifestyle for ideal performance and success.
- Regular exercise and a balanced diet not only improve physical health but also enhance cognitive functions, reduce stress, and boost motivation, directly affecting personal and professional goals.
- Adequate rest and recovery are important for cognitive abilities, managing stress levels, and rejuvenating the body, underscoring the importance of establishing consistent sleep habits.
- Integrating fitness into a busy lifestyle requires prioritization, using technology, and finding enjoyable physical activities that fit individual preferences and schedules.
- Nutritional guidelines for ideal cognitive performance highlight the importance of a diet rich in essential nutrients, such as omega-3 fatty acids, antioxidants, B vitamins, vitamin E, iron, and magnesium.

- Adopting a holistic approach to personal achievement involves nurturing all parts of wellbeing, including physical health, mental clarity, emotional balance, and spiritual connection, to lead a fulfilling life.

Action Items:

- **Prioritize Physical and Mental Health:** Schedule regular exercise and ensure a balanced diet to enhance physical and mental capabilities. Integrate physical activity into daily routines, even in small increments, to maintain a healthy lifestyle.
- **Optimize Rest and Recovery:** Aim for 7-9 hours of sleep each night, create a conducive sleeping environment, and establish a consistent sleep routine to improve overall wellbeing and productivity.
- **Incorporate Mindfulness and Stress Management:** Practice mindfulness daily and find healthy stress outlets to enhance mental and emotional wellbeing. Engage in activities that reduce stress and promote relaxation, such as yoga or meditation.
- **Embrace a Holistic Approach:** Integrate practices that nurture physical, mental, emotional, and spiritual wellbeing into your daily routine. Recognize the interconnectedness of these areas and strive for balance to achieve personal growth and fulfillment.
- **Implement Nutritional Guidelines:** Follow a diet rich in essential nutrients that support cognitive performance and overall health. Include a variety of nutrient-dense foods and stay hydrated to optimize brain function and energy levels.
- **Seek Continuous Improvement:** Regularly assess your lifestyle and adjust incorporate holistic practices that support your goals. Embrace the journey of personal growth and be open to new methods that enhance your quality of life.

By focusing on these key points and taking actionable steps, individuals can build a foundation for sustained personal achievement and a more balanced, fulfilling life.

In Our Next Part...

In the next chapter of our journey, we're peeling back the layers to reveal the essence of true success, taking cues from the trailblazers who've redefined industries and reshaped our world. Think Apple, Tesla, Airbnb, Dollar Shave Club, and Amazon - these aren't just brands, but testaments to the power of simplifying complex problems through sheer innovation. We're not just recounting their victories but diving deep into their paths: the setbacks, the experiments gone awry, and their relentless pursuit of excellence. It's a narrative that reinforces success' being meticulously crafted, not granted.

These tales are more than mere motivational fodder; they're a masterclass in bouncing back stronger, staying agile, and never losing sight of your vision. As we journey through these success sagas, we aim to distill practical wisdom for tackling both personal and professional hurdles with a fresh lens. Whether it's learning to view failure as a cornerstone for growth, the value of seeking guidance, or finding the equilibrium between drive and self-care, this Part is designed to arm you with the tactics to carve your own success story.

Let these narratives serve as a powerful reminder that with a blend of the right attitude, unwavering dedication, and a sprinkle of creativity, transforming daunting challenges into groundbreaking achievements is within your grasp.

~

FROM VISION TO REALITY: LESSONS IN INNOVATION AND RESILIENCE

TRAILBLAZERS OF SIMPLICITY: HOW SIMPLIFICATION LEADS TO BREAKTHROUGH SUCCESS

LET'S look closely at some standout stories of success, where complexity was cut through with the sharp knife of simplicity, reshaping entire industries.

- **Steve Jobs and the Apple Revolution**: Steve Jobs didn't just create products; he redefined entire categories. From the Macintosh that made computing personal, to the iPod that changed how we listen to music, and the iPhone that put a computer in our pocket, Jobs's knack for simplifying complex technology into sleek, intuitive devices catapulted Apple into a global tech titan.
- **Elon Musk's Visionary Ventures**: Elon Musk has a talent for tackling Herculean challenges with straightforward solutions. Through Tesla, he made electric cars desirable to the mainstream, turning the industry on its head. SpaceX, meanwhile, is making space travel more feasible with its groundbreaking reusable rockets. His ventures into solar energy and beyond continue to simplify and innovate, proving that no industry is beyond transformation.

- **Airbnb's Accommodation Revolution**: By creating a platform where anyone with a spare room could connect with those looking for a place to stay, Airbnb didn't just simplify booking accommodations; it reinvented it. This model not only offered a unique and personal alternative to hotels but also sparked a global shift in how we travel.
- **Dollar Shave Club's Shave Space Shake-up**: Remember when buying razors was an expensive and often frustrating experience? Dollar Shave Club changed all that with its direct-to-consumer model, offering quality shaving supplies at a fraction of the cost. Their simple but effective approach shook up the shaving industry and carved out a massive market share.
- **Amazon's Shopping Simplification**: Before Amazon, online shopping was anything but straightforward. By creating a user-friendly platform that offers everything from A to Z, complete with fast shipping, Amazon has not only become synonymous with online shopping but has also changed our buying habits.

These narratives aren't just about triumphs but journeys – the idea that by stripping back the unnecessary and focusing on simplicity, entire realms of possibility open up. Each leader saw beyond the complications of their time, focusing instead on clear, direct paths to solutions that ultimately redefined their sectors. Their stories underscore a powerful lesson: simplicity isn't just about making things easier to use; it's about unleashing potential and opening doors to success that once seemed locked tight.

~

UNLOCKING SUCCESS: KEY INSIGHTS FROM THE PATHS TRODDEN BEFORE US

Diving into the stories of those who've carved their names into the annals of success, we uncover timeless wisdom that can guide our own ambitions. Here's what their journeys teach us:

- **The Unyielding Power of Persistence**: If there's one golden thread weaving through the tapestry of success stories, it's persistence. The road to achievement is littered with hurdles, but it's the relentless march forward, despite the falls, that marks the true path to victory. These narratives encourage us not to buckle under challenges but to view them as the forge of our determination.
- **The Art of Rising from Failure**: Failure isn't just a pitstop; it's a teacher. The greats didn't just stumble and continue; they analyzed, learned, and evolved from every fall. This lesson is a beacon for us, illuminating failure not as defeat but as a catalyst for growth and innovation.
- **The Pillar of Self-Belief**: Behind every success is a steadfast belief in one's potential. Doubt and criticism are but background noise to those focused on their dreams. Their

conviction teaches us to trust ourselves and our vision, even when the odds seem stacked against us.

- **The Gift of Mentorship**: No one climbs to the top alone. The guidance of mentors – those who've navigated their own treacherous paths – can be our compass. Seeking those willing to share their wisdom is not just beneficial; it's essential for our growth and learning.
- **Embracing Change with Open Arms**: The only constant in life is change, and adaptability is our greatest tool. Success stories are rife with unexpected detours and course corrections. Learning to pivot and embrace new directions can unlock doors we never knew existed.
- **The Strength in Unity**: Rarely is success a solo journey. Collaboration, networking, and building a circle of mutual support can amplify our efforts. It's a reminder that together, we can achieve far more than we ever could alone.
- **The Vitality of Balance and Self-Care**: Lastly, amid the hustle for achievement, the importance of self-care and balance cannot be overstated. True success is sustainable only when we focus on our wellbeing, both mental and physical. It's a call to balance our drive with downtime, ensuring our health is never the price of our ambitions.

By drawing on these insights, we don't just chase success; we build a foundation for enduring achievement. Each lesson is a steppingstone, not just to reach our goals but to surpass them, armed with the wisdom of those who've journeyed before us.

〜

PART SEVENTEEN WRAP-UP:

- **Simplification Leads to Success**: Real-life success stories like those of Steve Jobs, Elon Musk, Airbnb, Dollar Shave Club, and Amazon show that simplifying complex processes or products can significantly affect and transform industries.
- **Persistence is important**: Successful individuals show despite obstacles and failures, persisting with determination is key to achieving goals.
- **Learning from Failure**: Embracing and learning from failures, rather than being discouraged by them, is a common trait among successful people.
- **Self-Belief**: A strong belief in one's abilities and dreams underpins the success of many individuals, highlighting the importance of confidence and self-trust.
- **The Role of Mentorship**: Successful people often attribute part of their success to guidance received from mentors, underscoring the value of seeking advice and support.

- **Adaptability**: The ability to adapt to changes and unexpected challenges is essential for success, showing flexibility and open-mindedness.
- **The Power of Collaboration**: Building strong networks and collaborating with others can propel individuals toward their goals more effectively.
- **Importance of Self-Care**: Successful individuals stress the importance of self-care and maintaining a healthy work-life balance for sustainable success.

Action Items

- **Embrace Simplification**: Look for ways to simplify complex processes or products in your own projects or business ventures.
- **Cultivate Persistence**: Develop resilience and persistence by setting clear goals and not giving up in the face of obstacles.
- **Learn from Failures**: View failures as learning opportunities, analyze what went wrong, and use these insights to improve.
- **Build Self-Confidence**: Work on building your self-confidence and trust in your abilities through positive affirmations and celebrating small wins.
- **Seek Mentorship**: Actively seek mentors who can give you guidance, insight, and support in your personal and professional development.
- **Develop Adaptability**: Practice being flexible and adaptable by planning for various outcomes and being open to changing paths as necessary.
- **Engage in Collaboration**: Network and collaborate with others in your field to share resources, knowledge, and support each other's goals.
- **Prioritize Self-Care**: Make self-care a priority by ensuring a healthy balance between work and personal life, and engaging in activities that promote wellbeing.

. . .

In Our Next Part...

Welcome to the next chapter of your success story, where the end of one journey marks the beginning of another. Here, we dig into what lies beyond the euphoria of meeting your current goals. It's not just about reveling in the triumphs of today but also paving the way for the triumphs of tomorrow. This Part will teach you how to leverage your recent success as a catapult for future aspirations, ensuring your drive and ambition remain undiminished.

So, you've climbed to the top of your mountain—what now? We're here to navigate you through setting new, loftier goals, sustaining the discipline that has been your ladder to success, and choosing companions who inspire you to reach even higher. It's a journey of perpetual growth, where each achievement is a steppingstone to greater challenges.

In this segment, we focus on the continuous cycle of achievement: celebrating your victories, learning from your journey, and then setting the stage for further conquests. Success isn't a final destination but a launchpad for your next adventure. We're committed to keeping your motivation alight, inspiring you to consistently set the bar higher, embrace change with enthusiasm, and stride into the future with unwavering confidence. Let's start this journey together, transforming your accomplishments into the foundation for a legacy of continuous success.

~

PART EIGHTEEN
BEYOND THE FINISH LINE: CHARTING THE COURSE FOR CONTINUED SUCCESS

KEEPING THE DRIVE ALIVE: WHAT'S NEXT AFTER GOAL ACHIEVEMENT

CROSSING the finish line of your goals is an exhilarating moment. It's a testament to your dedication, hard work, and resilience. But what happens after the applause fades? The key to continuous growth and success lies in keeping the momentum going. Here's how you can keep the drive alive and set the stage for even greater achievements:

- **Take Time to Celebrate**: First off, give yourself a huge round of applause. You've earned it! Celebrating your victories isn't just about throwing a party; it's about acknowledging the effort you've put in. This recognition fuels your drive to dive into new challenges.
- **Reflect on the Climb**: Every journey teaches us something. Reflect on yours. What worked? What didn't? Understanding your journey helps you refine your strategies for future endeavors and highlights areas for personal growth.
- **Dream Bigger**: Achieving a goal is like reaching a summit and seeing new peaks on the horizon. Now's the time to set new goals, ones that challenge you to climb higher. New goals keep your journey exciting and your ambitions alive.

- **Stay on Track**: The discipline and habits that propelled you to your current success are the same ones that will guide you to your next. Keep up those good habits, and don't let success make you complacent. Discipline is the bridge between goals and accomplishment.
- **Choose Your Crew Wisely**: Who you journey with matters. Surround yourself with people who inspire you, challenge you, and cheer you on. Being around other high achievers keeps your motivation high and your focus sharp.
- **Never Stop Learning**: There's always more to know. Stay curious and hungry for knowledge. Whether it's deepening your knowledge or exploring new fields, continuous learning keeps your skills sharp and your mind open to new possibilities.
- **Welcome New Challenges**: Success isn't the absence of challenges, but the ability to tackle them head-on. Embrace the obstacles that come your way as opportunities to grow stronger and smarter. Remember, comfort zones are where dreams go to die.

Maintaining momentum after meeting your goals is all about setting the stage for success. It's about celebrating how far you've come, yet always looking forward to where you're headed next. By staying disciplined, continuously setting new goals, and embracing lifelong learning, you make sure your journey of achievement is never-ending. Let's keep the drive alive and turn today's success into tomorrow's starting point.

CHARTING NEW HORIZONS: CRAFTING YOUR NEXT SET OF GOALS

AFTER REACHING A MILESTONE, it's important to line up the next set of challenges. It's this continuous cycle of goal setting that fuels our growth, keeps us engaged, and infuses our lives with purpose. Let's walk through a roadmap for setting these new targets and starting your next adventure:

- **Celebrate and Reflect**: Before sprinting into the future, pause and give yourself a well-deserved round of applause for what you've already achieved. Reflect on the journey — the skills honed, hurdles leaped, and strides taken. This reflection isn't just about giving yourself a pat on the back; it's about setting the stage for what's next with renewed confidence and insight.
- **Ignite Your Passions**: Dive into what gets your heart racing and your mind buzzing. Aligning your goals with your passions not only fuels your drive but also makes sure the journey ahead is both meaningful and enjoyable.
- **Balance Your Strengths and Areas for Growth**: A candid look at what you're good at and where you could improve can guide your goal setting process. Aim for goals that leverage

your strengths while gently nudging you out of your comfort zone.

- **Craft SMART Goals**: Specific, Measurable, Achievable, Relevant, and Time-bound goals turn vague wishes into actionable plans. For example, swap "I want to get healthier" with "I aim to jog 30 minutes daily and eat greens with every meal for the next three months."
- **Break It Down**: Big goals can feel daunting. Slice them into smaller, manageable pieces. Each small win builds momentum and keeps the journey exciting.
- **Map Out Your Path**: Lay down the steps you'll take toward your goals. This could mean daily habits, weekly check-ins, or monthly milestones. The key here is consistency.
- **Gather Your Support Squad**: Share your aspirations with people who'll cheer you on and keep you honest. Having a support network can be the difference between faltering and flourishing.
- **Stay Flexible**: Be ready to tweak your plans as you progress. Adaptability is your ally, making sure you stay aligned with your core goals even as circumstances change.
- **Keep the Fire Burning**: Maintain your focus and drive, especially through the tough patches. Visualize your success, remember your 'why,' and draw inspiration from others who've trodden similar paths.
- **Celebrate Every Step**: Don't wait until the finish line to celebrate. Each milestone achieved is a victory and deserves recognition. These celebrations fuel your journey forward.

Setting new goals is a dynamic, ongoing process that keeps our lives vibrant and forward-moving. By embracing these strategies, you're not just chasing success; you're building a fulfilling journey rich with learning, growth, and achievement. Here's to your next set of goals — may they bring you even closer to your dreams!

∾

HARMONIZING LIFE: THE CORE OF TRUE WELLBEING

Harmony between our physical, mental, and emotional states is not just a lofty ideal—it's the bedrock of a satisfying life. Striking the right balance and nurturing our wellbeing is about making mindful decisions and consistently caring for ourselves in a holistic way.

Why does this matter so much? Here's the lowdown:

- **Health and Vitality**: Regular self-care rituals, like staying active, eating well, and ensuring we get enough Zs, directly influence our physical health. They're the fuel that powers our engines, keeping us strong and ready to tackle life's demands.
- **Mental Clarity and Emotional Equilibrium**: A balanced mind is a sharp mind. It helps us process information, make decisions, and handle stress with grace. Emotional stability helps us ride the waves of our feelings, fostering relationships that are both meaningful and joyous. Together, they form the foundation for productivity and goal pursuit.
- **Stress Busting**: Let's face it, the modern world can be a stress buffet. Finding your zen through self-care isn't just nice—it's necessary. It helps us keep our cool, making sure peace of mind isn't a rare luxury but a daily norm.

- **Enriching Relationships**: When we're feeling good, we're giving good. Balance lets us pour into our relationships with energy, understanding, and support, strengthening our connections and nurturing a sense of belonging.
- **Fueling Personal Growth**: With a solid wellbeing foundation, we're positioned to chase our dreams, explore our passions, and grow. It's about living and tapping into our potential.

Wrapping it up, it's clear that striking a balance in life is about so much more than just avoiding burnout. It's the key to thriving, not just surviving. It ensures we're not just busy, but also rich in the moments that matter. So, here's to making self-care and balance non-negotiables in our journey toward a life that's not only productive but also deeply fulfilling.

Navigating the Hurdles to Lasting Achievement

Aiming for long-term success is a journey filled with highs and lows. It's not just about the destination but also about overcoming the bumps along the way. Understanding common hurdles and knowing how to leap over them can keep you on track toward your goals. Let's dive into some typical challenges and smart strategies to tackle them:

- **Finding Your Toolkit**: Often, the roadblock is not having enough—be it money, tech, or knowledge. The key? Scour your surroundings for tools and aids. Hunt down scholarships, grants, and other funding avenues. Tap into the wealth of knowledge available online, at libraries, or through networking. Being resourceful is your secret weapon.
- **Facing Down Fear of Failure**: Ah, the dreaded fear of falling short. Like a shadow can cool your heels. The trick is to change how you view failure—think of it as a tough teacher rather than a dead end. Break your journey into smaller, achievable milestones and celebrate each win, no matter how small. This builds momentum and confidence.
- **Building Your Support Squad**: Going solo can be tough, especially without a cheering Part. If you're feeling alone in

your endeavors, it's time to find your tribe. Connect with folks who get your vision—through online communities, networking meetups, or mentorship programs. A strong support network can be your backbone.

- **Dodging Burnout**: Chasing after your dreams is exhilarating but can also be exhausting. Burnout is real and can sneak up on you. To stay in the race, self-care is non-negotiable. Draw clear lines between work and play, indulge in activities that recharge your batteries, and don't skimp on relaxation. A well-rested you is a more productive you.
- **Rolling with the Punches**: Rarely is the path to success a straight line. It zigs and zags, and sometimes, you've got to zig when you thought you'd zag. Embrace the uncertainty and see each twist as a chance to grow stronger and smarter. Cultivating a flexible mindset can turn obstacles into steppingstones.

Briefly, the road to success and sustainability is peppered with challenges, but they're not insurmountable. With the right approach—leveraging resources, reframing failure, building a support network, focusing on self-care, and staying adaptable—you can navigate through them. Stay focused, stay driven, and remember, every hurdle cleared is a step closer to your goals. Keep pushing, and you'll find that sustainable success is not just a dream, but an achievable reality.

∾

MASTERING CONTINUOUS GROWTH: THE CYCLE OF EVALUATION AND ADAPTATION

CONTINUOUS GROWTH ISN'T JUST a buzzword; it's a critical strategy for personal and organizational development. It's about constantly checking in on where you stand, figuring out where you can do better, and tweaking your approach to get there. This process of evaluation and adaptation is what keeps you learning from every step, and refining your path to success.

Let's break it down. Starting with clear goals is your first step. These are your lighthouses, guiding you through your journey. Without them, you're drifting. So, set those targets—make them sharp and measurable.

Next up, keep a close eye on your progress. This means diving into the nitty-gritty—tracking your performance, comparing actual results with what you aimed for, and using both numbers and feedback to get a full picture of how you're doing. This regular check-in is important for spotting both wins and areas where you're falling short.

Now, here's where it gets real: staying goal. It's easy to let your feelings color your perception, but this step demands a clear head. Stick to the facts and figures; they'll show you the true story of your progress, untainted by emotions or bias.

Identifying areas for improvement naturally follows. This is where you pinpoint what's not working—be it outdated methods, skills gaps, or strategies that aren't cutting it. Recognizing these gaps is your cue to act, whether that means learning new skills, tweaking your plans, or shaking up your resources.

Adjusting your course is the action phase. Armed with insights from your evaluation, it's time to make those changes aimed at boosting your performance. Stay flexible, ready to shift gears as needed. The goal is to keep evolving, responding to new challenges and opportunities as they come.

This cycle of evaluation and adaptation is what continuous improvement is all about. It's a balancing act—staying true to your core goals while being nimble enough to pivot when the situation calls for it. This approach keeps you learning, growing, and, ultimately, moving closer to your aspirations.

Continuous growth is about embracing the journey of evaluation and adaptation. By setting clear goals, tracking your progress, staying objective, pinpointing areas for improvement, and being ready to adjust your course, you're not just chasing success—you're living it, one thoughtful step at a time. Here's to embracing that cycle, keeping your growth journey dynamic, and unlocking new levels of achievement.

~

EMBRACING EACH STEP: THE ART OF CELEBRATING PROGRESS

SUCCESS ISN'T JUST about the big wins; it's about savoring the journey, each step, each hurdle crossed. Celebrating these moments isn't just rewarding—it's essential. It's about recognizing the hard work, the grit, and the perseverance that brought you to each new milestone. Here's how you can make the most of these celebrations and why they're so important:

- **Pause and Reflect**: Look back at where you started and the journey. Appreciate the distance covered, the challenges tackled, and the growth you've experienced. This reflection isn't just about patting yourself on the back—it's about understanding and valuing the effort it took to get here.
- **Celebrate the Small Wins**: Big goals can feel overwhelming but breaking them down into smaller achievements can turn the journey into victories. Each small win is a step forward, deserving of recognition and celebration. This approach not only keeps you motivated but also lights up the path to your larger goal.
- **Share Your Success**: Success is sweeter when shared. Bring in your cheerleaders—friends, family, mentors—who've been

there through thick and thin. Their support and encouragement amplify the joy of each achievement and remind you that you're not alone on this journey.

- **Reward Yourself**: Reached a milestone? Treat yourself! It could be a simple pleasure or a long-coveted reward. These moments of indulgence are not just treats; they're necessary breathers that rejuvenate you for the next leg of the journey.
- **Throw a Celebration**: Whether it's a quiet dinner with loved ones or a bigger bash, celebrating milestones with those who matter is a powerful way to acknowledge your progress. It's a shared joy, a collective pride in what you've accomplished together.
- **Visualize Your Achievements**: Create a real representation of your milestones—a journal, a vision board, or even a dedicated space on your wall. Seeing your progress visually not only keeps you motivated but also serves as a constant reminder of your journey and its many successes.
- **Say Thanks**: Never forget to express gratitude to those who've helped you along the way. A simple thank-you, a note, or a gesture of appreciation makes sure they know how much their support has meant to you.
- **Reflect on the Lessons**: Every milestone offers valuable lessons. Take the time to think about what each step taught you, the skills you honed, and the obstacles you overcame. This isn't just about celebrating success; it's about embracing the growth that comes with it.

Celebrating success, in all its forms, is important. It's not just about marking achievements but about appreciating the journey, acknowledging the support, and preparing for the next challenge. So, celebrate—each milestone is a testament to your journey, a step toward your dreams. Remember, the path to success is paved with these very celebrations.

Personal Case Study:

Charting New Courses: Simon's Journey Beyond the Finish Line

Meet Simon, a marathon enthusiast whose journey didn't end at the finish line of his first major marathon. Instead, it marked the beginning of a deeper dive into the world of long-distance running. Here's how Simon kept the fire of ambition burning bright after achieving his first dream.

The High After the Finish Line: Crossing that marathon finish line was a moment of pure elation for Simon. It was a dream he had nurtured and worked toward for over a year, and the victory was sweet. But soon after, Simon faced a new challenge: What comes next?

Avoiding the Post-Goal Blues: The thrill of meeting his goal left Simon with a sense of aimlessness. He was all too aware of the pitfall many fall into after reaching a significant milestone—complacency. Simon was determined not to let his success become a one-hit wonder.

Simon's Strategy for Sustained Success:

- **A Time for Celebration:** First off, Simon took the time to revel in his achievement, celebrating with those who supported him through his training. It was a moment to acknowledge the sweat, tears, and sheer grit it took to get here.
- **Reflecting with Purpose:** Simon then turned inward, reflecting on his journey. He looked at what strategies had propelled him forward and what obstacles had tested his resolve. This introspection was about learning, growing, and preparing for what's next.
- **Dreaming Bigger:** Buoyed by his accomplishment, Simon didn't rest on his laurels. Instead, he set his sights higher, dreaming of international marathons and better finish times. New goals meant new challenges and a renewed sense of purpose.
- **The Discipline Continues:** Understanding that discipline was the backbone of his success, Simon kept to his stringent training regimen. The routine that had brought him this far would be the one to take him even further.
- **A Community of Runners:** Recognizing the value of being surrounded by those who shared his passion, Simon joined a

running club. This community was not just about shared interests; it was about pushing each other toward greater heights.

The Road Ahead: Simon's story didn't end with one marathon. It was the beginning. With new goals in his sight and a community by his side, Simon conquered international marathons, improving with each race. His journey is a testament to the idea that true success is not just about reaching a goal but about setting new ones and facing them with the same zeal and discipline that got you to the first finish line.

Simon's story is more than just about running; it's about relentlessly pursuing passion, the importance of setting new challenges, and the power of a community. It's a reminder that every achievement is a starting point for the next adventure.

~

PROFESSIONAL CASE STUDY: BEYOND THE BREAKTHROUGH: BRENDA'S BLUEPRINT FOR ONGOING SUCCESS

LET'S TALK ABOUT BRENDA, an entrepreneur whose journey didn't stop at the launch of a groundbreaking product. Her story is a lesson in not just succeeding but nurturing it to flourish further.

The Launch and Beyond: Brenda hit a major milestone with her product launch, surpassing all market expectations. But for Brenda, this wasn't a finish line; it was a new beginning. She was all too aware that the real challenge wasn't just in reaching the peak but in staying there and climbing even higher.

Brenda's Game Plan for Growth:

- **A Moment of Celebration:** First off, Brenda took a moment to celebrate this achievement, not alone but with her team. It was their victory, a testament to their hard work and creativity.
- **Looking Back to Move Forward:** Brenda then dove into a reflective analysis, dissecting the launch strategy to understand what clicked and what could be better. This wasn't about basking in success but learning from it to pave the way for future triumphs.

- **New Horizons:** With the market ever-evolving, Brenda didn't rest on her laurels. She mapped out new goals, focusing on innovation and expansion to keep the momentum going.
- **The Discipline of Success:** Success didn't make Brenda complacent. She kept her team on their toes, focused on the big picture with a clear emphasis on continuous improvement and staying ahead of the curve.
- **Building Bridges:** Recognizing the power of collaboration, Brenda expanded her network, forging new partnerships that would open doors to fresh opportunities and pathways for growth.

The Outcome: Brenda's strategic and forward-thinking approach didn't just keep her company afloat; it propelled it to new heights. By embracing change and setting ambitious goals, she made sure her initial success was not just a one-time wonder but a launching pad for greater achievements.

The Lesson from Brenda's Journey: Success is not a destination but a journey that doesn't end with one accomplishment. It's about leveraging your achievements as a foundation for future goals. Brenda's story shows us the power of ambition, strategic planning, and the never-ending quest for improvement. Whether it's personal milestones or professional peaks, the journey continues, and with the right approach, the possibilities are limitless.

~

PART EIGHTEEN WRAP-UP:

- **Maintaining Momentum**: Achieving goals is the start; sustaining momentum is essential for ongoing success and growth.
- **Celebrating Success**: Acknowledging achievements is important for motivation and setting the stage for future endeavors.
- **Reflecting on the Journey**: Reflection helps identify successful strategies and areas for improvement.
- **Setting New Goals**: Continually setting new, challenging goals ensures ongoing engagement and growth.
- **Staying Disciplined**: Discipline and consistency are important to sustain momentum and further succeed.
- **Surrounding with Positive Influences**: A supportive network can motivate and inspire continued growth.
- **Continuous Learning and Growth**: Lifelong learning and embracing challenges are key to unlocking potential and achieving new heights.

- **Balance and Wellbeing**: Emphasizing physical, mental, and emotional wellbeing is crucial for a fulfilling and sustainable path to success.
- **Overcoming Challenges and Setbacks**: Addressing obstacles with resilience and adaptability is essential for long-term achievement.
- **Setting and Maintaining Boundaries**: Balancing work and personal life through clear boundaries is key to sustainable success.
- **Evaluating Progress and Adjusting Course**: Regular assessment and flexibility in approach allow for continuous improvement and adaptation.
- **Celebrating Milestones**: Recognizing and appreciating progress keeps motivation high and underscores the value of the journey.

Action Items:

- **Celebrate Achievements**: Take time to celebrate successes to boost motivation.
- **Engage in Reflection**: Regularly reflect on experiences to identify lessons learned and apply them to future endeavors.
- **Set and Pursue New Goals**: Always have new goals to maintain focus and direction.
- **Maintain Discipline and Routine**: Keep up with routines that have contributed to past successes.
- **Build a Supportive Network**: Surround yourself with individuals who inspire and support your growth.
- **Commit to Lifelong Learning**: Continuously seek opportunities for learning and personal development.
- **Prioritize Wellbeing**: Incorporate practices that support physical, mental, and emotional health.
- **Develop Resilience**: Cultivate a mindset that views challenges as opportunities for growth.

- **Communicate Boundaries**: Clearly define and communicate your work-life boundaries to those around you.
- **Assess and Adjust Strategies**: Regularly review your progress and be willing to adjust your strategies as needed.
- **Recognize Small Wins**: Celebrate small milestones along the path to larger goals.
- **Seek Mentorship and Guidance**: Look for mentors who can offer advice and perspective on your journey.

By following these key points and action items, individuals can sustain their success, overcome challenges, and continue to grow and achieve in all parts of their lives.

~

CONCLUSION: THE SIMPLICITY OF SUCCESS

As we wrap up our journey with "Simplifying Success: A No Nonsense Guide to Achieving Your Goals" let's take a moment to reflect on the essence of what we've uncovered together. Success isn't a one-size-fits-all destination; it's an individual path paved with purpose, dedication, and simplicity. It's about identifying what truly resonates with us, setting our sights on those aspirations, and navigating the challenges and triumphs with equal grace

At the heart of our exploration lies the principle of simplicity—paring down to what's truly important, focusing on those goals with intention, and embracing each step of the journey. We ve delved into how to articulate our visions, the importance of focus and consistency, the necessity of adaptability, the critical role of wellbeing, and the continuous cycle of personal growth. These aren't just strategies; they're cornerstones of a fulfilling approach to achieving our goals.

The path forward is yours to chart. With the insights and strategies we've shared, you're better equipped to face what lies ahead, turning obstacles into opportunities for growth. Remember, success is more about the journey than the destination. It's found in the lessons learned, the resilience built, and the moments of joy and satisfaction along the way.

So, as you step into the next chapter of your journey, carry with you the lessons of simplicity, focus, and resilience. Let your goals be guided by what truly matters to you, and let your actions be fueled by purpose and passion. And, most importantly, never forget that the journey to success is enriched by the moments of connection, growth, and fulfillment experienced along the way.

Thank you for joining me on this journey through "Simplifying Success." Here's to your continued exploration, growth, and achievement. May your path be illuminated by clarity, purpose, and the joy of the journey. The road ahead is bright, and with simplicity as your compass, there's no limit to what you can achieve. Onward and upward, with the courage to embrace the simplicity and the strength to make your dreams a reality.

Onward and upward, with simplicity as your guide.

Rae A. Stonehouse

Author

~

ABOUT THE AUTHOR

Rae A. Stonehouse is an author, speaker, and self-publishing consultant dedicated to helping others embrace constant improvement and overcome challenges. With over 40 years of experience as a Registered Nurse in psychiatry and mental health, Rae brings a wealth of knowledge and passion for self-development to his writing and presentations.

As a 30+ year member of Toastmasters International, Rae has systematically built his communication abilities and self-confidence to share his insights as an author and speaker. His self-help books and personal development presentations aim to have conversational one-on-one connections with readers and audiences.

Rae is known for his wry sense of humor and sage advice delivered in a relatable coaching style. After four decades as a nurse, Rae has *rewired* rather than retired, actively writing and pursuing public speaking. He strives to share lessons learned to help others achieve personal and professional growth.

To learn more about Rae and his approach to constant improvement, visit his website at https://raestonehouse.com or to learn more about his publications visit https://liveforexcellence.store

∼

ALSO, BY RAE A. STONEHOUSE

VISIT HTTPS://LIVEFOREXCELLENCE.STORE/ for a selection of personal/professional self-development books by Rae A. Stonehouse.

If you have found this book to be helpful, please leave us a warm review wherever you purchased it.

www.ingramcontent.com/pod-product-compliance
Lightning Source LLC
Chambersburg PA
CBHW071536210326
41597CB00019B/3019